WILL THE CIRCLE BE UNBROKEN?

Aboriginal Communities, Restorative Justice, and the Challenges of Conflict and Change

Embraced by a wide array of activists and policymakers, the restorative justice movement has promised not only to reduce the disproportionate rates of Aboriginal involvement in crime and the criminal justice system, but also to heal and rebuild entire communities. Such promises, made to what are often vulnerable and dependent communities, should be the focus of considerable analysis and evaluation, yet such scrutiny has been largely absent in the conceptualization, development, and implementation of the majority of Aboriginal community restorative justice projects. *Will the Circle Be Unbroken?* explores the potential pitfalls of restorative justice, offering a much-needed critical perspective.

Drawing on their shared experiences working with Aboriginal communities, as well as a comprehensive review of the research in the field, authors Jane Dickson-Gilmore and Carol La Prairie engage with the theory and reality of 'community' in an Aboriginal context, constructing a detailed portrait of contemporary Aboriginal communities, both rural and urban, along with their inherent patterns of daily life, agency, conflict, and disorder. The implications of these factors for the development, implementation, and sustainability of restorative justice projects are explored, with special attention to such prominent programs as conferencing, sentencing circles, and healing circles. Noting the lack of sound evaluation of such initiatives, the authors look to Aboriginal justice reforms in other countries, comparing and contrasting restorative efforts in New Zealand, Australia, and the United States with those in Canada. The authors conclude that without greater attention to the dynamics of communities and the realities of conflict patterns and social justice, restorative justice runs the risk of becoming another instalment in a long legacy of broken promises made to Aboriginal people in Canada.

JANE DICKSON-GILMORE is an associate professor in the Department of Law at Carleton University.

CAROL LA PRAIRIE is a consulting criminologist and a former senior researcher with the Departments of the Solicitor General and Justice of the Government of Canada.

WILL THE CIRCLE BE UNBROKEN?

Aboriginal Communities, Restorative Justice, and the Challenges of Conflict and Change

Jane Dickson-Gilmore and Carol La Prairie

UNIVERSITY OF TORONTO PRESS
Toronto Buffalo London

© University of Toronto Press Incorporated 2005
Toronto Buffalo London
Printed in Canada

Reprinted 2007

ISBN 0-8020-8922-4 (cloth)
ISBN 0-8020-8674-8 (paper)

Printed on acid-free paper

Library and Archives Canada Cataloguing in Publication

Dickson-Gilmore, E. J.
  Will the circle be unbroken? : aboriginal communities, restorative
justice, and the challenges of conflict and change / Jane Dickson-Gilmore
and Carol La Prairie.

  Includes bibliographical references and index.
  ISBN 0-8020-8922-4 (bound).   ISBN 0-8020-8674-8 (pbk.)

  1. Native peoples – Canada – Social life and customs.   2. Native
peoples – Canada – Religion.   3. Restorative justice – Canada.
4. Community-based corrections – Canada.   I. La Prairie, Carol   II. Title.

E78.C2D545 2005   364.6'8   C2005-900708-7

This book has been published with the help of a grant from the Canadian
Federation for the Humanities and Social Sciences, through the Aid to
Scholarly Publications Programme, using funds provided by the Social Sciences
and Humanities Research Council of Canada.

University of Toronto Press acknowledges the financial assistance to its publishing
program of the Canada Council for the Arts and the Ontario Arts Council.

University of Toronto Press acknowledges the financial support for its publishing
activities of the Government of Canada through the Book Publishing Industry
Development Program (BPIDP).

Contents

Introduction

For many First Nations, the circle has important and profound cultural significance. Symbolizing the interconnectedness of all things and directing consideration of the impact on all partners in that symbiosis when decisions are taken, the concept of the circle is synonymous with balance, openness, and a holistic approach to life. It is not surprising, then, that this concept, and the cultures which define it, have been closely linked with the restorative justice movement, which shares the values of the circle both philosophically and in much of its architecture. For many commentators, restorative justice is synonymous with historic forms of Aboriginal justice (Lee, 1996). It is a modern restatement of traditional values of balance between those in conflict and within their communities, and signifies an approach to crime and conflict that heals parties through embracing them and their place in the symbiosis while simultaneously rejecting the destructive act that sundered them.

As progenitors of the philosophical field currently occupied by restorative justice, First Nations find themselves in an ironic position. At the same time that influential others and outsiders have turned to traditional cultures to inform and legitimate much restorative justice programming (Hobsbawn, 1983), the communities which once lived within those cultures find themselves on the receiving end of much of that programming. This is not surprising, given the realities of life for a significant proportion of First Nations communities, which are charactertized by poverty and dysfunction, and by remarkable rates of crime and conflict that feed into gross rates of Aboriginal over-representation within Canadian prisons. That a history of repressive state policies and forced acculturation is responsible for much of that dysfunction, and for the erosion of traditional culture which is a significant part of it, is unquestioned. The irony is not lost, however, that those Aboriginal communities facing significant problems of conflict and disorder are deemed to be doing so owing to the loss of the very traditions which are not only held to account for much of their cultural dissonance with mainstream justice structures, but are now to save them through their embodiment in restorative justice programs.[1] Conflict and criminal justice, once the flashpoints of the troubled relationship between the state and First Nations, are now to provide an opportunity to return to traditional ways of resolving conflict and, in the process, restore entire communities to health and balance.[2] We seem to be asking the physician to 'heal thyself,' and to be making this request without due consideration of the tools and capacities at the physician's disposal.

At one level it is not terribly remarkable that those in the greatest need have come to the forefront of a movement that makes such promises. But at the same time that we applaud the movement for directing its attention to the greatest exigency, the very fact of that need may undermine the ability of restorative justice to keep its rather grand promises. Restorative justice is not about top-down efforts to revive communities; rather, it ideally embodies the opposite equation. Restorative justice projects are, or should be, grassroots initiatives which arise almost organically from a community's desire to improve its ability to deal with conflict among its membership. It is in this detail of the direction of reform that we encounter one of the devils in restorative justice projects in Aboriginal communities. These communities, which have embraced the promises of restorative justice, may be the least able to mobilize the agency necessary to make projects work – and yet they appear to be under increasing pressure from outside and above to do so. We are not the first to make this observation, but we would like to take the discussion further, arguing that not only is there some uncertainty about the direction of restorative programming in First Nations communities, but inadequate attention has been paid to both the idea and reality of such crucial elements as 'community' and culture in the Aboriginal restorative justice movement.

Even a cursory glance at the literature reveals the centrality of the concept of community in particular in restorative justice, however this may be defined. Within the oldest of restorative justice programs, the victim–offender mediation or reconciliation projects, community was defined as the dyad of the involved parties (Bazemore and Umbreit, 1999: 8). More recently, in the essentially pan-Indian sentencing and healing circles, community is more expansive and includes victim(s), offender(s), their 'communities of care,' and justice personnel such as judges, police officials, and, in some cases, legal counsel to those at the core of the conflict. Family and community conferences, to varying degrees, encompass the most inclusive view of community. Conferences may in some cases involve individuals who, in the general justice system, would be defined as unconnected with the case, but are perceived to have suffered some harm within the conflict. Other programs, such as reparative boards, victim and community impact statements, community service, and restitution (notwithstanding some controversy about the degree to which they qualify as 'truly' restorative, Presser and Gunnison, 1999), are seen to have 'community in focus' owing to the apparent devolution of power to 'do justice' from the system to the citizens central to a conflict. How a program chooses to define 'community' must be a critical factor in determining the nature and extent of citizen participation and ownership in the community justice project (Bazemore and Umbreit, 1999: 8).

We agree with this statement, but will take it further in this book. We believe that a critical weakness in much of the literature on Aboriginal community and restorative justice is an apparent reluctance to fully problematize the concept of 'community' across and within First Nations. This is not only a matter of considering the 'micro-communities' involved in particular restorative justice programs, it also requires a willingness to direct critical attention to the larger community experience. It is imperative that we overcome the apparent reluctance of many of those working and writing in this area to fully acknowledge and confront the considerable challenges facing many Aboriginal communities in Canada. To the degree that these challenges have a direct impact on levels of agency, and on the human and other resources necessary to mobilize, implement, and sustain community restorative justice projects, they demand critical attention. If restorative justice is to approach its goal of 'restoring communities,' those advocating it must be prepared to be realistic about those things which require restoration, and why they require it.

In addition, we need to engage the shifting understandings and realities that characterize the Aboriginal experience across Canada, most notably with regard to issues of culture and tradition. Cultural dissonance springing from very different traditions of conflict resolution are often central to explanations not only of why Aboriginal people clash more often with Canadian laws, but why the processes linked to those laws cannot, and will not, work for them. To the degree that restorative justice takes 'traditional justice' as both its blueprint and justification, the primacy of Aboriginal culture in community projects goes unquestioned. What, then, are we to make of statements by Aboriginal scholars that '[m]ost Aboriginal peoples in Canada have little or no knowledge of their own traditions' (Anderson, 1998: 316) – observations that are often sadly reinforced by time spent in Aboriginal communities? How compelling is cultural dissonance as a force supporting restorative initiatives when the mechanisms of that clash are no longer an issue? How 'traditional' can restorative structures be if they depend on knowledge or practices which are no longer in place, having fallen victim to historic state policies of 'civilization' and 'assimilation,' modern technology, and 'MTV'? Inadequate critical attention has been accorded to the dimension of traditional culture in restorative justice, and we hope to engage this issue more deeply in this text.

Beyond issues of culture and tradition, we must also understand the substantial variations across the community experience of Aboriginal people. It is important to explore the distinctions across and within the rural community existence experienced by the minority, as well as the complex urban lifestyles practised by almost 70 per cent of the modern Aboriginal population. In addition, there must be a recognition of the mutable nature of these communities and the interests of those who exist on their margins. This seems especially important given that the latter may well prove to comprise a substantial component of many restorative justice projects' caseloads, and that the reliance of much restorative justice programmings on a communal approach carries a risk of even further marginalization of those who reside on the fringes of communities (Anderson, 1998: 316).

Much of what follows is a critique of extant assumptions about the Aboriginal community in Canada, and an attempt to introduce greater complexity into debates about the imperative of community in restorative justice. As professionals involved in the development, implementation, and critique of justice policy, with first-hand experience of the impact of those policies in First Nation communities, we believe that a number of important questions concerning community justice have been lost in the enthusiasm generated by the promises of restorative justice. We believe in those promises; we believe in restorative justice and in restoring communities. Restoration, however, requires an acceptance of the complexity of the issues inhibiting it, and the location of the point of departure of the much larger social justice project. Community justice requires successful communities. We hope that this book can contribute positively to an understanding of the complexities of Aboriginal communities and thus to the design, implementation, and sustainability of successful and truly restorative justice projects.

The book is organized into three parts. The first, Defining the Challenge of Communities and Justice, is directed to establishing the larger context within which the Aboriginal community justice movement has developed and taken shape. Chapter 1 tackles the issue of community, both as a concept and locus of study, and attempts to provide a portrait of the variety of communities currently manifested among First Nations. Here we not only engage the theory of community generally, but compile a portrait of the diverse and often challenging communal contexts and social and cultural systems within which Aboriginal people in Canada live and experience conflict and its resolution (or persistence). We will look at demographic patterns and introduce some of the community variables and challenges that subsequently receive more detailed scrutiny for their impact upon community justice initiatives.

The second chapter focuses on the relationship of the community experience to the nature of conflict both within particular communities and between many Aboriginal people and the dominant criminal justice system. Here, we undertake a critical scrutiny of the phenomenon of over-representation, its costs and consequences for communities. We will explore and scrutinize the dominant themes in the literature directed to explaining this most intractable of challenges facing Aborginal communities and compelling the exploration of restorative alternatives. The third chapter consists of a critical review of past and present efforts to respond both to the disproportionate rates of conflict and disorder characterizing Aboriginal communities and the rise and appeal of the restorative justice movement.

The fourth chapter opens the second part of the book, entitled Restorative Justice: Theory and Practice in Aboriginal Contexts; it provides a 'primer' in restorative justice, both generally and more specifically in terms of the movement's substantial 'Aboriginal component.' We review the origins of the movement and introduce the primary program themes; we also look to the state of the research on the functioning and impact of extant programs and their evaluation. The fifth and sixth chapters provide a critical review of restorative justice programs in Aboriginal communities in Canada, from sentencing and healing circles through conferences and advisory panels.

The third and final section of the book, Completing the Circle and Advancing the Dialogue, pulls together and builds upon the challenges and issues made evident in the discussion to this point. Chapter 7 assesses the current state of evaluation research relevant to restorative justice programs in Aboriginal communities, and attempts to determine 'what works' and why. Chapter 8 then raises a range of issues we believe have been inadequately addressed or overlooked in the rush to 'restore' Aboriginal communities. We turn to the experiences of indigenous peoples in other countries for productive lessons that may ease the implementation and encourage the success of local efforts, and present what we feel are the crucial qualities and characteristics necessary to a successful restorative justice project in a First Nations context. We also outline what we perceive may prove to be the greatest challenges facing these programs. For example, critical scrutiny must be directed to the apparent reality that, while restorative justice was originally intended to provide alternative means for dealing with relatively minor and property crimes, this intention is not being realized in Aboriginal communities. Restorative projects have been employed to handle serious crimes against the person and to attempt to heal defendants with long and profound histories of conflict and disorder. It seems that in practice restorative justice is threatening to replicate the 'disparate justice' that too often results in the mainstream system, in which the 'justice' experienced and received by Aboriginal and non-Aboriginal participants is very different in form and consequence. If restorative justice cannot avoid the pitfalls into which mainstream justice structures appear repeatedly to fall, how can it possibly retain its credibility or realize the promises it has made to communities? Approaching our conclusion, chapter 9 focuses on the limited evaluation literature and embarks on a comparative discussion of findings concerning restorative programs in Canada, Australia, and New Zealand. Noting the limitations of much of this evaluation work, this chapter also raises such crucial issues as accountability and security in Aboriginal community justice. Chapter 10, the final chapter, offers a critical summary and some concluding thoughts on Aboriginal communities and restorative justice in Canada.

The restorative justice movement in First Nations communities is at least in part a consequence of the profound dissatisfaction among Aboriginal people with the dominant justice system. Ranging from perceptions that the system does little to encourage responsible citizenship in Aboriginal communities by diffusing accountability and taking the right to 'do justice' away from communities to more grand aspirations for 'traditional justice systems' as the jewel in the self-government crown, it is within concerns about 'legal cultural clash' and the reality of over-representation of Aboriginal people in the criminal justice system that the Aboriginal restorative justice movement finds its meaning and motivations. These are rooted in a profound frustration with a system that relies so heavily on imprisonments, with little positive impact for individuals or communities. Restorative justice has promised to ameliorate these evils, and to 'restore' and rebuild entire Aboriginal cultures and communities, yet those promises rarely seem informed by the circumstances which have fostered these evils or necessitated the rebuilding. This book is an effort to enchance an understanding of context and to encourage a more critical dialogue commensurate with the complexity and profound importance of the issues the movement claims it can address. Aboriginal people and communities have suffered too often in the past at the hands of 'policy experiments.' Insofar as restorative justice remains an 'ungrounded theory,' it behooves us to ensure that efforts to ground it do not come at the expense of those most in need of the realization of its promises.

Acknowledgments

I learned a great deal through this collaboration with Jane Dickson-Gilmore, a truly exceptional and insightful scholar. I fully expect great things from her in the years to come. I would like to thank Philip Stenning for taking the time to read a draft and for giving us valuable comments. My daughter Gillian's courage and strength are an inspiration. My dedication of this book is to her and her brothers, who constantly provide love and support.

Carol La Prairie

For my part, this book and the experiences which inform it would never have been possible without the support, wisdom, and sharing of some very important women. My most sincere thanks to Carol LaPrairie, a very wise mentor and an outstanding example to women academics everywhere, and to Christine Deom, who welcomed me into her home and community and has taught me so much. Christine, I dedicate this book to all our children, that they may together build a better future for our shared communities.

Jane Dickson-Gilmore

WILL THE CIRCLE BE UNBROKEN?

Aboriginal Communities, Restorative Justice, and the Challenges of Conflict and Change

PART ONE

Defining the Challenges of Communities and Justice

At the centre of the restorative justice movement is the community – an entity which is to be the driving force, the defining quality, and the primary focus of restorative justice projects. Communities, which in the simple act of moving to develop a community justice project acknowledge a certain measure of disarray and dysfunction among at least a portion of their membership, are at the same moment required to demonstrate the degree of agency and activism required to define, develop, and implement restorative justice projects. Yet despite its importance to the movement and the development and implementation of locally based justice projects, there has been remarkably little critical scrutiny of the concept or reality of 'community,' especially with regard to Aboriginal community restorative justice projects. Thus while commentators such as Clairmont (1996: 129) observe that 'the significance of the local community and the need for community development has been emphasized by all those writing about Aboriginal justice initiatives,' it does not seem unfair to remark that little of that emphasis has been either critical or willing to acknowledge the limitations and challenges facing communities. This may be due at least in part to the fact that community in restorative justice is almost certainly the proverbial straw that threatens to break the entire movement; it may also arise from a certain unwillingness to accept that a critical analysis of community may reveal not what may sustain and empower community projects, but rather what is no longer there. A search for the 'community' in restorative justice runs the risk of coming up empty, or at least short of our perhaps somewhat romanticized expectations.

The possibility that community may be a less than vital part of our lives is that much more threatening for many First Nations peoples, whose ancestors witnessed decades of efforts to usurp the traditional culture and institutions that once defined and maintained their communities. In the wake of attempts to 'Christianize, civilize, and assimilate' them, what little is left of many Aboriginal communities on modern reservations and in the north may be all that is left to them. And yet although aboriginal communities are in many cases impoverished, seriously factionalized, and struggling under a range of dysfunctions and disconnections with the outside world, they remain 'home' and occupy a crucially important place in the hearts of many First Nations peoples. Indeed, even in this historical moment, in which a majority of Aboriginal people have left their rural reservation communities to reside in urban centres, many return to their reserves as frequently as possible. The 'rez,' despite its problems, provides a measure of acceptance – and thus emotional, if not physical, security – which is often out of reach in the city, where many Aboriginal people are cut off, emotionally and psychologically, from the urban mainstream.

Community restorative justice projects present intriguing dilemmas for First Nations peoples. A successful project promises to reinvigorate and heal entire communities, radically reducing conflict and disorder and enabling a better, brighter future. A less than successful one – or worse, an outright failure – carries serious consequences. If the 'community' cannot make the project work, questions will focus on why the 'community failed,' and potential answers to those questions may well raise discomfiting queries about the health, agency, resources – indeed, the very existence – of 'community.' Insofar as community is the motor for which 'tradition' is the flywheel, a failed Aboriginal community restorative justice project may shatter not only any illusions about community, but about the endurance and resiliency of traditional culture as well. Aboriginal people are risking much through these projects, and they are spared none of that risk if we refuse to critically engage the issues that promise to impact directly and heavily upon their chances for success.

The chapters in this section are intended to explore the dynamic of community in First Nations, infusing debate with a more complex understanding not just of the larger Canadian Aboriginal experience, but of the individual communities throughout a range of geographical, political, and socio-economic locations within Canada. Patterns of conflict within these communities, and between their membership and the larger state criminal justice apparatus, will be defined and analysed in terms of their implications for the disproportionate involvement of Aboriginal people in Canadian courts and prisons, as well as for the form, content, and potentiality of community restorative justice projects and other attempts at reform.

CHAPTER 1

Deconstructing Community: The Theory and Reality of Communities in Aboriginal Restorative Justice

> The community has tools which the system does not have. The community has resources which the system does not have. The community has power which the system does not have. Criminal justice system activity needs to be built around a core of community activity – not the reverse.
>
> (Pranis, 1998: 1)

> Never was the word the word 'community' used more indiscriminately and emptily than in the decades when communities in the sociological sense became hard to find in real life.
>
> (Eric Hobsbawm and Terence Ranger, in Crawford, 1997: 148)

Bazemore and Umbreit have observed that 'the way community is defined and involved in restorative conferencing models is a critical factor affecting the nature and extent of citizen participation and ownership' (1999: 8). There can be little doubt of the veracity of this statement; how one chooses to define the core concept of a project will clearly impact significantly upon the shape which that project ultimately assumes. What seems to be less understood is that while definitions of 'community' may be imposed, whether from within or outside, and may thus exercise considerable influence on community projects, the community itself, however defined, will also exert a profound – and perhaps more important – influence on projects it undertakes. It is therefore imperative that we engage a greater problematization of community, both as theory and reality, and the implications these possess for successful restorative justice programs.

Notwithstanding romanticized notions of 'pan-Indianism' and the universality of traditional culture contained within much literature and research on Aboriginal peoples, it is necessary to explore dimensions of Aboriginal community as these exist at the level of the national 'macro-community,' as well as at the level of individual communities. And while it is impossible to offer individualized profiles of each of the approximately 609 bands as communities, we can focus on themes or trends within communities as these are relevant to, and informative of, the realities of community restorative justice projects, trends which may in turn be related to the larger context of Canadian Aboriginal peoples. While there are distinctions between the macro- and micro-communities as lived experiences, we initiate our discussion with a critical examination of the concept which is often used indiscriminately to refer to them both, namely, the concept of 'community.'

(i) Defining Community: Do We Know It When We See It?

Although debates about the nature of community have been a long-standing element of much social science research, the term seems nowhere near to a clear or widely accepted meaning. In part, this is probably due to the many masters the term must serve. 'Community' is simultaneously a geographic concept requiring clear boundaries and content and a 'lived experience' which, albeit highly individualistic, is at the time shared with others for whom that experience might be quite disparate. It is a term which requires operationalization, especially in the context of field work and social research, but it is highly resistant to the sort of precision preferred by researchers. In short, community is that most bedevilling of social constructs and while we can all claim to know it when we see it, defining it is quite another matter.

The impact of this ambiguity is evident in the literature on community. For example, Stoneall has observed that 'community as a concept has a definite center without a well-defined periphery' (1983: 5), and within that centre, the shared ground appears to be quite small. It is limited to a general concession on the part of a majority of sociologists that community is essentially a matter of sociality, time, and space. That is, there seems to be a basic agreement that 'community' exists wherever there are 'people in social interaction within a geographic area with one or more common ties' (Dasgupta, 1996: 7).[1] As a set of minimum requirements, however, these descriptions provide us with little direction for theorizing community, and even less insight supportive of a search for 'community' in the field. As usual, the devil resides in the details: how does one define 'social interaction'? What is meant by 'geographic area,' and what might constitute a 'common tie'? At one level, the answers are easy. For example, one might refer to a 'prison community' insofar as inmates maintain some degree of social interaction within the prison as a 'geographic area,' share the common tie of incarceration, and are labelled as 'inmates.' Prison walls provide a clear boundary around the core of the concept of community, but the edges blur when one heads beyond a 'total institution' context to less clearly circumscribed communities, where there are no walls to define community 'space' or overseers to direct and define 'sociality' or 'time.'

Indeed, if one limits the defining criteria to those articulated by Stoneall – sociality, time, and space – it becomes difficult to determine what might *not* qualify as a community. Social interaction can be as simple as the anonymous path-crossing of shared roadways, and roadways might easily traverse entire continents, suggesting a geography that would seem to challenge conventional assumptions of the intimate neighbourhoods we tend to envision when talk of communities arises. Yet is community primarily a matter of population size, implying that with increased size comes increased distance, and thereby the loss of familiarity and common ties? McCold suggests that 'community' would seem to deny popular assumptions that 'size matters.' He asserts that a 'local community' can be a social group of *any size*, provided its membership share such qualities as residence in a 'specific locality ... government, [and] a common cultural and historical heritage' (1995: 4). Here, it would appear that the nature of the ties is more important than the number of people they bind, and yet insofar as McCold has established as one parameter on his definition of community the notion of a common cultural and historical heritage, limitations on size may be implicit. Few communities within Canada – even those that may be termed 'local' – share the sort of homogeneity across their membership central to McCold's definition; indeed, most Canadian cities boast a rich and vibrant multiculturalism, a quality which, interestingly enough, would set them outside the definition even though many city-dwellers embrace diversity as a defining quality of both their communities and their country. That this embrace may be as imagined as the communities themselves does not render it any less compelling as one part of the means by which people understand and navigate their 'communities.'

Despite these blurred edges, within the literature as a whole 'community' emerges as a 'middle-sized' concept – 'larger than family or small groups ... smaller than regions or nation-states' (Stoneall, 1983: 19) – and hinges upon those concepts of shared space, time, and common ties. Beyond this, communities as individual objects of study seem to be defined largely by what they are not, leading to the uncertain boundaries on the concept noted above. Such imprecision, while rendering comparisons across communities difficult and generalizations of research findings problematic, has been suggested by some researchers as both 'an opportunity and a problem' (B.C. Resources 1998: 1). The problem resides in the challenge set by a concept which tends to resist operationalization and to defy the sort of predictable precision preferred by researchers. At the same time, however, in the absence of an agreed definition of 'community', the concept may become whatever the researcher chooses it to be. Thus one may craft an understanding of the term that is context-specific and may, in fact, improve the quality of methodologies, which can be tailored to correspond to the peculiar nature of the object of the study. Such an approach may foster the aforementioned problems with generalization, but these may be worth the potentially rich research findings facilitated by the ability to focus definitions unrestrained by externally imposed definitional conventions.

The value of a tailor-made definition of community will be determined primarily by its direction – is the definition top-down or bottom-up? Stated another way, where did the definition come from? Was it, for example, devised by the researcher and shaped primarily by considerations relevant to the research question rather than the lived experiences of those under study? Or perhaps the definition imposed was created by the state for purposes such as the determination of electoral boundaries. Such top-down definitions tend to have most relevance and practical value for those who create them, namely, those who reside at places outside and above the actual object of the definition. More useful for project development is a bottom-up definition 'which recognizes that communities are self-defined by people as a reflection of their local interactions and participation' (B.C. Resources 1998: 3).

In other words, communities are essentially more imagined than real, insofar as people will define them consistent with their own experiences. This would suggest that the most potentially fruitful definition of any community is one which draws upon the opinions of members to create a definition of what the term means for their purposes. Such a 'bottom-up approach is one which frees researchers from the challenge of definition by placing this task on the people who live there, who decide for themselves what constitutes "their" community' (B.C. Resources 1998: 2). This 'participatory' method is grounded in the belief that communities are 'self-defined by people as a reflection of their local interactions and participation. Certainly, communities can be a place – a locale in which one lives, conduct[s] business, and raises a family ('place-based' community). However, one's community also involves a set of relationships and personal ties (interest-based community). Following from this, people may belong to and interact with several distinct communities within any single locality. Layers of community ties and linkages bind people in different ways and to difference degrees, to places ...' (B.C. Resources 1998: 4). As community members are canvassed about those things which they view as definitive of their 'community', the researcher is able to compile a 'checklist' of the requisite ingredients of a 'community' for purposes of a given research project (B.C. Resources 1998: 4). This checklist can to some degree overcome the competition of disparate lived experiences, promoting a middle ground among the various definitions of community articulated by its members, drawing upon those elements which appear with most frequency across all the definitions.

There are, of course, challenges implicit in this approach. When one construes community as essentially a lived experience, the possibility is raised not only that persons living side by side, sharing time, space, and sociality, may have quite different lived experiences, but also that some community members may be better at communicating their particular experience. For example, while the 'checklist approach' can compensate for the possibility of as many definitions of community as there are members in a given community, retaining common or shared elements of that experience, it may be less sensitive to the internal dynamics of a community that may influence whose definitions of community are heard. If one chooses to extract these definitions through community consultations, there is the danger that the more influential or powerful members of the community may be more successful in communicating their definitions, leading to a partial picture of the collective 'lived experience.' Similarly, those powerful community actors may be motivated by very different interests in the consultative process than other members of the community risking a further skewing of the concept of 'community.' For example Aboriginal communities, in similar fashion to their non-Aboriginal counterparts, experience varying degrees of connection with, and representation by, their local governments, and researchers must be cautious about assuming that the visions of community articulated by elected officials are, in fact, those of all or even part of their electorate.[2] These are important issues in the consultative processes which frequently precede development of community-based justice projects in Aboriginal contexts especially, which often manifest what Andersen refers to as 'grotesque power centralizations,' which may render the process of securing a shared view of community that much more difficult (1998: 316). We will discuss this and related issues later in the chapter.

For purposes of the development of community restorative justice projects, the most important checklist may be the one that speaks directly to the community's needs in relation to justice or conflict resolution. While these may be broadly defined through community consultation, some researchers, such as McCold, appear to argue that the definition of community for purposes of conflict resolution is a much more narrow, mutable thing. Here we are told that 'community cannot be defined a priori, as it depends upon the nature of the conflict to which it is applied' (McCold, 1995: 4). Thus 'community,' for McCold, appears limited to the 'community of care' touched by a conflict and involved in its resolution. This 'community' may then be seen not as a single, persistent entity, but as a multiplicity of extant, nascent, and shifting smaller 'communities' defined by their respective conflicts, and populating a much larger grouping of people who share 'time, space, and sociality' in constituting the overarching community to be served by a justice project. These are the 'communities of interest' articulated by such researchers as Pranis, and they are found in the communities identified when a conflict has occurred and the question is asked, 'who has a stake in the outcome' of processes to resolve that conflict (Pranis, 1998: 2). Thus we see here an approach that is both idiosyncratic and individualized, and which requires the definition of community at two levels: that of the larger, geographic community – a definition which may be relatively enduring and consistent over time and which has been referred to as the 'community of place' (Pranis, 1998: 2) – and that of the myriad communities defined a priori by their interests in different conflicts and their resolution – these groups would appear to be both fleeting and enduring, depending upon the nature of the conflict and the approach to its resolution taken by the parties central to it. They may also be in competition for the often limited and strained human and monetary resources of the justice project, competition which may have further implications for the degree to which the larger community is a truly shared and common experience.

While the double-faceted approach to understanding community encountered in much restorative justice literature reflects an accurate impression of the complexity of the concept as it exists 'on the ground,' many approaches to community in restorative justice reflect a much more romanticized and often moralized view of community that may prove problematic in practice. For example, Pranis, in articulating the relationship between communities and crime, comments that the community is 'the source of moral authority or influence,' a 'center of action,' and, in the particular realm of crime control, the thing which 'exercises moral authority in denouncing crime and deciding requirements of offenders to make amends' (Pranis, 1998: 5). The assumption of a moral component is linked in with Pranis's apparent view of communities as revolving around a social contract, wherein 'crime represents a failure of responsibility,' the appropriate response to which resides within the community doing its 'moral work' (Pranis, 1998: 1). The difficulty encountered here, however, is that many of the communities served by a restorative justice project are quite a distance from 'healthy' – had these communities a 'healthy moral authority,' they would probably have little need for a restorative justice project. Indeed, as noted earlier, the greatest need for such projects arises in communities lacking both health and a functional, coherent morality shared – or at least known – by all members. In such contexts, dysfunctional power relations and structures of authority can easily be replicated in restorative justice programs – especially if those programs are developed and defined by those occupying key positions in the dysfunctional power structures. To the degree that 'community' is open to definition in restorative justice projects, and where those given the task of definition work within a less-than-salutary community setting, the 'community' in community restorative justice projects is clearly open to risk and dysfunction. This reality is one of the potential pitfalls encountered when those in most need are asked to provide the means by which their needs are to be met.

For researchers such as Pranis, 'community' has little articulation or existence outside the definitions imposed upon it by those who reside within it; those who would study 'communities' or work within them must 'simply' to tap into those definitions. This is clearly a convenient approach for researchers, as it relieves them of the often onerous task of operationalization prerequisite to most research undertakings. It is also, unfortunately, not without costs, as choices of 'key informants' based on self-identification by community members are replete with political, social, and methodological hazards, none of which can easily be overcome by arguments based on participatory research and the imperative of consultation. There is also the possibility that informants may have difficulty articulating the 'community' to which they belong, especially if they are queried within the context of a restorative practice within a reserve. In a geographically bounded area such as a reserve, an effort to animate the definition of a 'community of care' will likely lead to a multitude of such communities, some larger, some smaller, with almost all intersecting and, in a general fashion, replicating the extant local power relations. Thus unless the divisions that exist on reserves, and which are often generated by the same local power arrangements, are somehow healed to allow restorative processes to play out as theorists believe they should and could, it is entirely possible that the drive to define 'community' on a reserve may simply risk the imposition of yet another source of conflict. In this light, it is important to pause to consider whether restorative justice has the potential to increase and exacerbate existing social and power relations rather than creating the kind of harmony and transformation restorative justice advocates such as Stuart suggest. If, owing to the intimacy and transparency implicit in close quarters, restorative justice projects risk intensifying problems in small communities and reserves, is it possible that restorative justice, so long considered dependent on intimate communal ties, may hold greater promise and potential in larger or urban communities? Should the latter, where degrees of anonymity reduce the intensity of relations that often characterize smaller communities, form the central focus of restorative projects? While this focus would once again risk marginalizing the already marginalized rural reserve communities, there is little question that it would direct our efforts to the larger part of the Aboriginal population in Canada, given that 70 per cent of that population now resides in urban centres. And, as will be seen, insofar as the majority of Aboriginal offenders currently incarcerated in Canadian prisons are serving out warrants of committal for offences committed in urban contexts, a predominantly urban focus will take restorative efforts to the epicentre of Aboriginal conflict with the law. These issues seem to arise far more in the field than in the literature which would assist our work therein.

It seems, then, that the academic literature has little to offer in terms of a basic understanding of the concept of 'community' beyond a minimum requirement that a 'community' share a common land base as well as some degree of social connection or common ties – broad requirements that might easily be satisfied by the Aboriginal community at a range of levels. If we look first to the definition of the macro-community of the 'Canadian Indian,' it is possible to define this as both place-based and distinguished by a common tie and shared interest; that is, the macro-community shares a land base which is Canada, a common tie of Aboriginality and, to varying degrees, interests consistent with that common quality. Here we must grapple with the question of who is an Indian person in Canada, looking to national social, political, and economic demographics.

At the level of micro-communities, individual Aboriginal people share re-served territories, ethnicity, and membership (in the community, if not always legally in the band) as well as participation, in theory if not in fact, in shared political and social structures. Here, the key components of the definition are also place-based – community is a locale in which one lives, conducts business, and raises a family – and 'interest-based,' recognizing the networks of relation-ships and personal ties which are definitive elements of community (B.C. Resources 1998: 4). It is within the micro-community that we experience a further conceptualization of community, one which is unique to the processes and phenomenon of restorative justice. Here the concept is predominantly a strategic one, as it is both the location and mechanism through which restorative justice projects are received and function. We are speaking here of McCold's 'community of the conflict,' comprised of those persons who are parties to the conflict, as well as any individuals who feel connected to the conflict event either through a perception of harm or as a member of the 'communities of care' of the parties to the conflict.

Within these three constructions of community – national, local, and con-flict – size does matter, albeit to some degree by default. The macro-community, constituted by the totality of the Canadian Aboriginal population currently residing within Canadian borders and defined by broad, pan-Indian cultural characteristics and the shared interests that characterize the Aboriginal experi-ence writ large, is the biggest single category and largely a non-Aboriginal construction. The micro-communities are largely but not necessarily rural, contained within reservation boundaries and sharing therein a particular language and culture. These communities range in geographic size and population, and combined with those who reside in urban settings within 'urban Aboriginal enclaves' or as loose associations of individuals only vaguely connected with each other, comprise the larger macro-community. Finally, within the micro-communities active in the restorative justice movement, we encounter a range of much smaller communities constituted by the real and potential clientele of the justice project situated within a particular geographic community. This is that category of community which McCold observes will be defined largely by the 'nature of the conflict to which [they] are applied' (1996: 91). These categories of the concept of community are accretive; the macro-community is constituted by the micro-communities, significant aspects of which are comprised of the communities which are to be served by a restorative justice project. We will flesh out each of these 'communities' in turn, beginning with the pan-Indian macro-community.

(ii) Aboriginal People in Canadian Society: The 'Macro-Community'

Despite the fact that the term 'Aboriginal' is often used as if it applies to a large and homogeneous group of people, it is increasingly clear that there is considerable diversity not only in legislative status, tribal affiliations, and cultural artifacts, but in the broader Aboriginal experience in Canada as well. Indeed, what may be the most compelling characteristic of the macro-community is the degree to which it defies conventional notions of 'community,' embracing remarkable variation. Diversity across the national Aboriginal community is reflected in the ways people speak, in what they believe, the kind of work they do, their location on the social and economic ladder, how and where they live, and their involvement in state systems such as child welfare and criminal justice. In short, there may be no single, shared community or concept of community in which all Aboriginal people in Canada would assert membership exists. Given this reality, the characterization of Aboriginal people as a macro-community must be understood primarily as a heuristic tool to guide our exploration of the Aboriginal complex within Canada as a whole.

The richness of the diversity of Canada's Aboriginal population is reflected in the fifty languages and the fifty-two cultural groups, such as Haida, Cree, and Mohawk, found across the country. There are six major cultural regions in Canada – Woodland, Iroquoian, Plains, Plateau, Pacific Coast, and Mackenzie and Yukon River basins. This population is subject to a wealth of 'top-down,' externally derived and imposed definitions of who they are and what their Aboriginality means. While anthropologists have contributed to these categorizations, the impact of their 'categories' pales in comparison to the consequences of state definitions of and for Aboriginal people. Nowhere is this impact more compelling than in the context of the legal definitions of 'Indians' invented and imposed by the state. The latter find their origins in the 1850 *Act for Lower Canada* (13 & 14 Vict. 1850, c. 42), which defined 'Indians' without any input from Aboriginal people, and included anyone living among, 'intermarried,' or adopted into a 'tribe of Indians' (Dickason, 2002: 228–9). This definition would be subject to considerable narrowing and qualification over time, and after Confederation the quantum of 'Indian Blood' would become central to determining individual 'Indianness' (229). As increasing numbers of Aboriginal micro-communities assume control over the determination of membership in their communities, and thus over the definition of an 'Indian' for purposes of an individual band, the struggle to overcome externally derived criteria for belonging have resulted in significant social and political problems for many reserve communities. This issue will be touched upon briefly in the third part of this book.

While the definition of 'Indian' enlisted by the federal Department of Indian Affairs and Northern Development now eschews a focus on blood in favour of a tracing of lineage (an interesting splitting of hairs – or heirs – at best), the constitution recognizes three categories of Aboriginal people in Canada: Indians, Métis, and Inuit. The Inuit are an Aboriginal people in northern Canada who live above the tree line in the Northwest Territories and northern Quebec; the single largest Inuit population resides in the territory of Nunavut. Although the Inuit are explicitly omitted from the definition of Indian contained in the *Indian Act* (s. 4.1), following from the determination of the Supreme Court of Canada in *Reference re the Term 'Indians,'* Inuit people have been defined as 'Indians' for purposes of section 91(24) of the *Constitution Act, 1867*, and are therefore considered to fall within an exclusively federal legislative jurisdiction.

The Métis are people of mixed First Nation and European ancestry; they are distinct from other groups and tend to reside predominantly in cities and towns within western Canada. While this 'category' has long proven resistant to precise definition, the Métis National Council (MNC) has defined the Métis as 'an Aboriginal people distinct from Indian and Inuit; descendants of the historic Métis who evolved in what is now western Canada as a people with a common political will [and] descendants of those Aboriginal[s] who have been absorbed by the historic Metis' (Burrows and Rotman, 1998: 469). The breadth of this definition reflects the complexity of the Métis population without diluting their Aboriginal rights. In their decision in *Sparrow*, the Supreme Court of Canada stressed that the constitutional rights contained within section 35(1) fall to Métis people, as they do to Indian and Inuit (Burrows and Rotman, 1998: 471), a determination which was reinforced in the court's more recent decision in *Powley*.[3]

The term 'Indian' can be used in a general sense to describe all Aboriginal people in Canada who are not Inuit or Métis.[4] Four key terms are applied to describe Indians, in Canada: Registered (Status) Indians, band Indians, non-Status Indians and treaty Indians. The first three of these terms are derived from the federal *Indian Act*, first passed in 1876, which sets out certain federal obligations to Indians and regulates the management of Indian reserve lands (Department of Indian Affairs and Northern Development [DIAND], 2001). According to the *Indian Act*, a Status Indian is an individual who is 'registered as an Indian, or eligible to be registered as an Indian' (hence the terms Status or Registered Indian are used interchangeably), and who is thus entitled to live on reserves, which are lands set aside by the federal government for the use and occupancy of an Indian group or band. The overlap and, in some cases, confusion generated by these terms is considerable. For example, the term 'Status Indian' does not actually appear in the *Indian Act,* but is commonly understood to refer to a Registered Indian, that is, a person who is, or is entitled to be, registered as an Indian under the Act. The term 'treaty Indian' is used (not too often in recent times), to refer to a person who is a signatory – or a descendant of a signatory – to an Indian treaty. Such a person might or might not be a Status (Registered) Indian under the *Indian Act*. Although the *Indian Act* refers in section 72 to the payment of treaty money 'to Indians or Indian bands,' it provides no definition of a 'treaty Indian.' This raises a question as to how treaty descendants who lack status or band membership can receive treaty benefits. There is also ambiguity in the term 'treaty.' Since the term 'treaty' can refer to a modern land claims agreement, arguably a Nisga'a Final Agreement beneficiary is technically as much a treaty Indian as is a descendent of a signatory of one of the classic pre-1922 treaties.[5] The term 'band Indian' refers to those individuals who acquired band membership through Bill C-31, but who do not necessarily possess Registered Indian status;[6] the legal benefits flowing to band Indians are unique and follow directly from their recognition as a band member.

Status Indians may be contrasted with their non-Status counterparts, who, despite possessing the requisite blood quantum and at least theoretical entitlement to Status, are not listed on the federal Indian Register and thus are impeded in their access to many of the services and rights accruing to those with Status. The variations in fortune of Aboriginal persons with Status and those without it are interesting. Despite popular stereotypes of the economic benefits of state paternalism towards Indians, Status Indians, who tend to reside on reserves, emerge as consistently disadvantaged compared to their non-Status counterparts.

The Indian population group is 2.6 times larger than the Métis population, and 13 times larger than the Inuit population. Disbursement of the three Aboriginal groups across the country varies widely by group and by region. The largest Indian group is found in Ontario, followed by British Columbia; the largest Métis group is in Alberta, followed by Manitoba. However, in comparison to the total populations of provinces, the North American Indian and Métis populations of Saskatchewan comprise the largest part of any provincial population.

With the exception of the definition of Métis set out by the MNC, these categories of Aboriginal peoples are essentially externally derived, 'top-down' constructions of the macro-community of Aboriginal Canada. As such, they serve primarily the interests and purposes of their creators and may have little, if any, relevance to the true nature of the national Aboriginal community. Much better – or at least more relevant and informed – definitions of communities tend to emerge from the bottom up, shaped by the individual and collective lived experiences of community members participating in the construction of the definition. We recognize the limitations of top-down definitions, and enlist them simply as a point of departure for a descriptive analysis of the current lived experience of the macro-community in Aboriginal Canada.

Examination of the overall social and economic characteristics of the three groups reveals that the Inuit have the youngest population, the fewest seniors living alone, the fewest single mothers, the most who speak an Aboriginal language at home, the fewest fifteen–twenty-four-year-olds attending school, and the least education. By contrast, Métis have the oldest population, the fewest seniors with extended family, the highest incomes, the most education, and the highest employment levels of the three Aboriginal groups. While not approximating the social and economic characteristics of the general Canadian population, the Métis population comes closer to it than either the North American Indian or the Inuit population.

As of 1997, there were 609 bands in Canada – a band being a group of people for whom lands have been set apart and money is held by the Crown. While most Aboriginal people live outside reserves, less than half of the Status or Registered Indian population live off-reserve. Many reserve communities have fewer than five hundred residents, and only about 11 per cent have more than two thousand residents. Migration from reserves to urban centres, and the reinstatement of Status Indians under Bill C-31 (many of whom already lived in or migrated to urban areas), means that the Aboriginal population in Canada is increasingly urban. Fully 65 per cent, of the Métis population is urban, whereas 78 per cent of the Inuit population is rural/isolated (DIAND, 2001).

The consistent movement from reserves to urban areas has been noted by several commentators, including Newhouse and Peters, who recently observed that: 'In 1951 the Census of Canada showed that 6.7 percent of the Aboriginal population lived in cities. By 2001, that proportion had increased to 49 percent. Now 245,000 Aboriginal people, or 25% of the total Aboriginal population reporting Aboriginal identity, live in 10 of the nation's largest cities: Winnipeg, Edmonton, Vancouver, Calgary, Toronto, Saskatoon, Regina, Ottawa-Hull, Montreal and Victoria. Aboriginal people are now part of the urban landscape and will remain so, most likely in increasing numbers, over the decades to come' (2003: 5). While the increasing presence of Aboriginal communities in large cities is a dominant demographic trend across First Nations, Siggner argues that we must be cautious about assuming that all Aboriginal urbanization is of this dominant type: both large and small urban areas gained in their share of the total Aboriginal population between 1996 and 2001. For example, the percentage of Aboriginal identity people living in urban census metropolitan areas (CMAs) increased from 26.3 in 1996 to 27.8 per cent in five years, reaching about 280,000; whereas in smaller urban areas (those with populations under 100,000) it reached about 214,000, or 21.3 per cent, of all Aboriginal identity people (Siggner, 2003: 15–21).

As observed by La Prairie in her 1994 study of Aboriginal city-dwellers, 'people come to cities looking for a better life, or to escape a bad situation or to lose themselves in one' (37). Whatever their motivations, it is clear that, with the exception of the Inuit, the Aboriginal macro-community is increasingly a predominantly urban one. As we will demonstrate below, this trend, and the distinctive patterns of disbursement, settlement, and migration which accompany it, have profound implications for understanding the nature of the Aboriginal 'macro-community,' as well as for the continued existence of the classic rural, reserve-based micro-community.

Our understanding of the size of the Aboriginal macro-community in Canada has changed as census takers have expanded the way in which data are collected and Aboriginal people described. For example, in 1981, 491,465 people said they had Aboriginal origins, but by 1996, fully 1,101,960 made this 'origins' claim, while 799,010 made an Aboriginal 'identity' claim (Siggner, 2001). Since Statistics Canada did not include both 'Aboriginal Origin' and 'Aboriginal Identity' categories until 1991, it is unclear if those who responded in 1981 identified themselves as Aboriginal. Given that the highest proportion of people who claim both Aboriginal Origin and Identity live in the western provinces (primarily in Prairie urban areas) it is also unclear if this reflects a more intensive politicization of Aboriginal issues, higher concentrations of Aboriginal people, and/or a different sense of identity in those provinces where, in contrast to eastern provinces and cities, Aboriginal people comprise a significant proportion

Table 1.1
Aboriginal population by 'Origins' and 'Identity' definitions, 1981–2001

Origins			Identity		
Year*	Number	% Change	Year	Number	% Change
1981	491,465		1991	625,620	
1996	1,101,960	124.2	1996	799,010	27.7
2001	1,319,850	19.7	2001	976,305	22.2

*'Origins' and 'Identity' definitions are not both available for 1981 and 1991.

of the general population (the relation of Origins and Identity populations in Thunder Bay are similarly sized to those in the western cities). What is beyond dispute is that there is diversity across the country even in the way Aboriginal people identify their Aboriginality.

Diversity has a number of other regional and local aspects. As mentioned above, the 1996 census put the Aboriginal identity population at 799,010 – an increase of 173,390 or 27.7 per cent since the Identity category was first used in 1991[7] – or 2.8 per cent of the total Canadian population. The 2001 census shows an increase, with 1.3 million people, or 3.3 per cent of the Canadian population, reporting having some Aboriginal ancestry (see table 1.1).

Of the Aboriginal Identity group in 1996, 66 per cent were Indian, 25.5 per cent Métis, 5.03 per cent Inuit, and 3.2 per cent belonged to an 'other' Aboriginal category. The 2001 census data are difficult to compare because of definitional changes, but those reporting Métis identity increased by the largest amount. In terms of actual numbers, the largest Aboriginal populations reside in Ontario and British Columbia, but Manitoba and Saskatchewan have more than double the Aboriginal population of any of the provinces (11.7 and 11.4 per cent, respectively),[8] when compared to the non-Aboriginal population. As expected, the territories have the highest Aboriginal populations. The Aboriginal population of the Northwest Territories is 51 per cent of the general population; in Yukon it is 23 per cent and in Nunavut, 85 per cent (Statistics Canada [Statscan], 1999a).

Within these populations, the demographics of the Aboriginal macro-community are quite distinct from those of their non-Aboriginal counterpart. The Aboriginal population is predominantly female and a much younger group – 33 per cent of the Aboriginal population is under fifteen years of age as compared to 19 per cent of the non-Aboriginal population, and this is especially pronounced in the west. For example, in Saskatchewan in 1996, 41 per cent of the Aboriginal population was under fifteen (Kaufman and Associates, 2000: 5). The Registered Indian population is even younger (over 51 per cent is under twenty-five years of age) and growing at a rate almost twice that of the Canadian population as a whole. As a result, the Registered Indian population could exceed 790,000 by the year 2008. The Prairies are experiencing the largest growth, particularly Manitoba, followed by Alberta and Saskatchewan. By 2008, Manitoba may have the largest Registered Indian population in Canada after Ontario. The policy implications of these patterns of growth are interesting, particularly with regard to the Registered Indian population. The increasing urbanization of Aboriginal people presents political, economic, and social challenges for Aboriginal organizations and government alike. Hanselmann, for one, comments that the urban Aboriginal policy and programming gaps are noteworthy and suggests that, despite some promising initiatives, such as those reflected in the 2003 budget, more needs to be done particularly by federal, provincial, and municipal governments (2003: 167–71). As the Aboriginal population grows and moves into its labour force years, the pressures for employment, housing, and other services will grow both on- and off-reserve. At the same time, Kaufman and Associates note that the 'government and the business community [in Manitoba] are beginning to see the growing Aboriginal labour force, if properly trained and developed, as an important asset for the province' (2000: 50).[9] While attention to pressures for employment is important, it may be argued that much more compelling are the policy issues that arise from the nature of the social, political, and cultural pressures which will weigh upon a much larger, younger, and urban Aboriginal population and which, if left unattended, may greatly undermine the potential of Aboriginal workers to meet corporate need. Restorative justice appears to have stepped in to respond to many of those pressures, as evidenced in the statements of its proponents that their programs will 'rebuild communities.' It remains to be seen whether restorative justice can achieve greater social justice through its resolution of criminal justice conflicts.

As noted above, the Aboriginal macro-community is not only younger, it is also predominantly female. Fully 51 per cent of the Aboriginal population is female, but this varies by place of residence: more males live on-reserve and more females off-reserve. The male/female discrepancy in population is greatest in large cities. There are approximately 6.3 per cent more females than males in urban centres (Kaufman & Associates, 2000: 50), and this discrepancy is highest for females twenty-five years of age and over (Statscan, 1999a). The discrepancy assumes an additional dimension when it is recognized that in urban areas, in 1996, over twice (2.4 times) as many Aboriginal as non-Aboriginal children belonged to single-parent families; this situation is especially marked for children who live in Thunder Bay, Winnipeg, Regina, Saskatoon, or Edmonton (Siggner, 2001). The numbers suggest that the majority of those single-parent families were headed by women. At the same time that children in these centres are likely to live in female-headed single-parent families, Thunder Bay, Winnipeg, Regina, Saskatoon, and Edmonton also manifest high concentrations of unemployed people and single-parent families in their inner cores. To the degree that these categories overlap, a significant percentage of the next generation of Aboriginal adults face daunting challenges in childhood, despite their parent's search for a better life in the city. The research supports this observation; Sampson and Raudenbush (2001) argue that these two characteristics of inner core areas – single-parent families and high unemployment – reduce the socialization and other options available to parents, children, and youth in more demographically balanced and economically advantaged Aboriginal and non-Aboriginal areas. This situation, coupled with Aboriginal population growth, will create significant policy challenges.

Although Aboriginal people are found across the economic spectrum (Satzewich and Wotherspoon, 1993), data indicate that the urban Aboriginal population is generally more mobile, less well educated, less employed, and poorer than the non-Aboriginal one. At the same time, however, there appear to be distinct regional differences, with the most disadvantaged, at-risk groups found in the Prairie provinces. Winnipeg, Regina, Saskatoon, and Edmonton maintain the most pronounced employment and income gaps between the Aboriginal and non-Aboriginal populations across Canada (Statscan, 1999a). The one exception is the northern Ontario city of Thunder Bay, where the income and employment gaps are almost as large as in the Prairie cities (Siggner, 2001). A comparison of annual income for the Aboriginal Identity and the non-Aboriginal populations in eastern and western Canadian CMAs reveals surprisingly little difference between the two groups in Montreal and Toronto (less than $6,000 and slightly over $7,000, respectively), but a $10,000 or more difference in all the other CMAs (including Thunder Bay), except Vancouver, where it is somewhere between the two. This pattern is replicated for the Aboriginal Identify and non-Aboriginal populations below the Low-Income Cut-Off (LICO)[10] level in select CMAs. There are also *concentrations* of Aboriginal people in the inner cores of these cities with larger proportions of the lower income/LICO groups, but this is not the case in other CMAs.[11] In the cities where people are more likely to claim Aboriginal Origin but not Aboriginal Identity (Montreal, Toronto, Vancouver) the incomes of the Aboriginal Origin groups are higher (although still below those of the non-Aboriginal group) than those of the Aboriginal Identity groups (Siggner, 2001).

Interesting findings arise again when we turn to an examination of the kinds of communities in which Aboriginal people live. The urban Aboriginal population is more mobile than the reserve one, and certainly more mobile than the non-Aboriginal population; this is especially true in the Prairie cities (Winnipeg,

Regina, Edmonton, and Saskatoon) (Kaufman and Associates, 2000; DIAND 2001; Statscan, 1999a). La Prairie's analysis of data from nine CMAs found that the Prairie cities and Thunder Bay have the largest, the youngest, the least educated, the poorest, and the most mobile Aboriginal populations (La Prairie, 2002). By contrast, eastern cities have the best-educated and the most well-off Aboriginal populations. The Prairie cities of Regina, Saskatoon, and Winnipeg, and the northern Ontario city of Thunder Bay, are consistently on the negative side of the nine-city mean or average scores, whereas the eastern cities are consistently on the positive side. Vancouver, and to a lesser extent Edmonton, are closest to the average scores in almost all categories and, therefore, straddle the two more extreme groups of cities.

In exploring the 'degree of disparity' between the Aboriginal and non-Aboriginal populations in each of the nine cities, La Prairie (2002) found the most extreme disparity between the two populations in the Prairie cities, followed by Thunder Bay; the least amount of disparity is found in Halifax, followed by Montreal and Toronto. These findings would suggest that the Aboriginal populations that must feel the least amount of deprivation in relation to their non-Aboriginal neighbours are in the eastern cities. Data on Registered Indians supports this assumption. To the degree that perceptions of deprivation feed into feelings of hopelessness and despair, it may not be too great a reach to suggest that such perceptions may play some part in the greater degree of dysfunction characterizing many urban Aboriginal families in the Prairie cities.

There are also considerable distinctions with regard to issues of language and culture within the Aboriginal macro-community; as will be seen, these distinctions may affect the development of community restorative justice programs. Aboriginal people who live in Nunavut and Quebec are far more likely to speak an Aboriginal language than those living elsewhere in the country. The youngest Aboriginal populations are found Nunavut and Saskatchewan, followed by Manitoba and Alberta. Quebec, Ontario, Yukon, and British Columbia have the smallest population under twenty-four years of age, which means that these provinces generally have older populations. There is little difference across regions in the percentage of the population that lives in a family arrangement, but Yukon and Ontario have the fewest seniors living with extended families. Saskatchewan, followed by Manitoba, has the highest percentage of single female parents, Nunavut, Quebec, and the Atlantic provinces the lowest. Nunavut and Manitoba have the fewest fifteen to twenty-four-year-olds attending school and Ontario the most. Saskatchewan, Manitoba, and the Atlantic provinces have the lowest employment rates and the territories, Alberta, Ontario, and British Columbia, the highest. Not surprisingly, Saskatchewan and Manitoba populations are the most dependent on government transfers. More Aboriginal youth (fifteen to twenty-four) in Prince Edward Island, Ontario, Yukon, and Nova Scotia are attending school than elsewhere in the county (Statscan, 1999b). The largest percentages of Aboriginal youth who are neither attending school nor participating in the labour market are found in Manitoba and Saskatchewan (Drost, 2001).

In terms of within-group differences (i.e., Registered versus non-Registered Indian), La Prairie's nine major cities analysis revealed that discrepancy in socioeconomic indicators is greater across the country for the Registered Indian group than for the total Aboriginal group. In other words, on most variables the Registered Indian group is 'below' the total Aboriginal group mean scores, but there is considerable city-by-city variation. There is also considerable variation in the range differentials for labour participation rates, and the percentages of lone parents, population under twenty-four years of age, and post-secondary education completion. The differences are much greater within the Registered Indian city populations than within the general Aboriginal ones. Registered Indians in Halifax, Montreal, and Toronto are clearly much better off in terms of employment, income, and education than Registered Indians anywhere else in the country, and are even better off than their total Aboriginal counterparts in those three cities. In fact, Registered Indians in those cities look demographically more like the non-Aboriginal than the Aboriginal groups. It may be more than coincidence that Thunder Bay, Regina, and Saskatoon have the highest Registered Indian populations, and that Halifax, Toronto, Winnipeg, and Montreal have the lowest.

(a) The On-Reserve 'Community'

Over one-third (36.4 per cent) of all reserves in Canada are geographically in urban areas, while 44.4 per cent are in rural areas, 17.4 per cent in special access areas, and 1.7 per cent in remote areas. Only in Yukon and the Northwest Territories does a considerable percentage of this population live in remote or special access (fly-in) areas. The majority of on-reserve Registered Indians in Quebec and Alberta, and one-half in Ontario, live in urban areas; the majority in Saskatchewan, Manitoba, and the Atlantic provinces live in rural areas. On-reserve Registered Indians in the remaining provinces and territories are distributed across urban, rural, remote, and special access communities (DIAND 2001).

Those who live on-reserve are much more likely to speak an Aboriginal language than those living elsewhere, especially in urban areas. The youngest groups live on reserve, followed by 'Other urban areas,' that is, in cities other than those defined as CMAs. Census Metropolitan Areas have the highest percentage of single female parents and seniors living alone, but urban areas have the largest percentages of people aged fifteen to twenty-four attending school, the highest percentage of those with a university degree, and (related to education), the highest employment levels. Reserves have the most income from government transfers and the lowest income overall. Reserves and rural areas have the largest number of people with less than grade nine education. In real terms, reserves may have the lowest incomes, but they may not be worse off financially than off-reserve areas, largely because of social and housing benefits that may accrue with living on-reserve. As well, supports may exist on-reserve that are absent in more anonymous urban contexts. The reserve may be where family reside, and family members can assist with daycare in the event of a job opportunity arising for a parent, or provide living space for older children waiting for a home of their own. There may also be informal social control on the reserve, such that inappropriate behaviour is sanctioned and children protected. This is not always the case, but it is a reality for some reserves and some families. The same social forces which work for the good of the community, however, may also work to the detriment of some members, who may find the gossip, pressures, and 'inconsistent justice' implicit in such forces alienating and confining. We will deal with the social context of the micro-communities in detail when we turn our attention to community restorative justice project development, implementation, and sustainability.

Data about Aboriginal groups and the geographic location of reserves reveals considerable diversity among Aboriginal people and Aboriginal communities. While some may believe that diversity exists only in off-reserve areas, an examination of the reserve literature suggests otherwise. For example, in 1979, anthropologist Linda Gerber documented the degree to which variation existed among bands, and how bands with certain characteristics cluster together in different parts of the country (Gerber, 1979). To categorize these communities, Gerber adopted a conceptual framework that included, among others, measures of 'institutional completeness' and 'personal resource development.' Gerber viewed institutional completeness as the degree to which bands responded to modern management and organizational conditions and increased group resources (while still perhaps retaining cultural traits to a greater or lesser degree), and personal resource development as the degree to which bands emphasized personal resources such as education, job skills, and employment experience. Bands with high levels of personal resource development 'have potentially mobile members who are relatively well prepared to cope with the urban industrial world' (Gerber, 1979: 406).

Using these concepts, Gerber developed a typology of five-hundred reserve communities based upon the categories of 'inert,' 'pluralistic,' 'integrative,' and 'municipal.' Bands classified as inert were geographically isolated and manifested the least institutional and personal resource development; those deemed pluralistic were the most developed in institutional completeness. Integrative bands tended to neglect overall community development, but had many members actively involved in the mainstream, while municipal bands had balanced both institutional completeness and personal resource development, largely because of geographic proximity to urban areas. Gerber found the different types to vary significantly on a wide range of community characteristics and to cluster geographically, and that it was highly misleading to stereotype reserves. She discovered that bands with high personal resource development were more prevalent outside the Prairie provinces but that pluralistic bands were more numerous in them. The vast majority of bands in the Prairie provinces were organized communally, whereas those of the non-Prairie provinces were conceived in more individualistic terms.

Although more than twenty years have passed since Gerber's typology was published, and profound political, economic, and social changes have occurred in the Aboriginal landscape, particularly in the self-government movement and the creation of Nunavut, there is little reason to believe that a contemporary version of the same typology would not be relevant today. While off-reserve migration has increased dramatically, it is unclear how this has affected the propensity for institutional completeness and/or personal resource development on reserves. However, the geographic context, population size, and other factors that influenced bands towards institutional completeness and/or personal resource development in 1976 may be expected to influence contemporary First Nations communities in a similar fashion.

(b) The Off-Reserve 'Community'

Approximately 71 per cent of Aboriginal people in Canada live off-reserve. In 1951, 27 per cent of all Aboriginal people lived in large cities. By 2001, roughly half the total Aboriginal (identity) population lived in urban areas (as defined by Statistics Canada).[12] This dramatic increase draws its numbers not only from reserves but from smaller urban centres as well (Drost, 2001). Nearly 28 per cent of the Aboriginal population now lives in CMAs, 21.8 per cent in 'Other Urban Areas,' and 21.5 per cent in Rural areas (Statscan, 1999a). Registered Indians living on-reserve decreased from 71 to 58 per cent in the twenty-year period from 1978 to 1998.

The proportions of off-reserve populations in Canada are largest in Yukon, Ontario, and Saskatchewan, followed by British Columbia, and smallest in the Northwest Territories and Quebec. For the off-reserve population, of whom 50 per cent reside in urban centres, this translates into 69.5 per cent for British

Columbia 75.8 per cent for Alberta, 66 per cent for Saskatchewan, and 62 per cent for Manitoba. There are also increasingly large concentrations of Aboriginal people in cities and towns across the West. In the 2001 census, Winnipeg had the largest number (55,755) of Aboriginal people of all the major cities in Canada, and Registered Indians comprised half of the Winnipeg urban population base. Urban centres, particularly western cities like Winnipeg, Regina, and Saskatoon, have significantly higher shares of Aboriginal people among the younger age groups, and some research would suggest among the most marginalized (La Prairie, 1994, 2002; Siggner, 2001).

In Prairie cities like Edmonton and Regina, Aboriginal populations are clustered into core areas. This is not the situation in Halifax, Toronto, and Montreal, where Aboriginal people are more widely distributed throughout the general urban populations and are not concentrated in inner cores. In research undertaken in the early 1990s on Aboriginal people living in two Prairie (Edmonton and Regina) and two eastern (Toronto and Montreal) cities, it was also found that the most socially and economically marginalized groups lived in the two Prairie cities (La Prairie, 1994).

While there is a tendency, particularly among government bureaucrats, to talk about the 'urban Aboriginal issue' there is no single, representative urban area or issue, nor is there commonality in the approach to those issues. For example, even in the higher Aboriginal density centres in the western provinces there are different perceptions about these areas and the challenges they present. In this vein, Kaufman and Associates note that: 'In Manitoba, the Aboriginal situation in Winnipeg is the overwhelming preoccupation. By contrast, Alberta officials have much less of a sense of a distinct set of urban Aboriginal problems facing the province's major cities. Spokespersons in Saskatchewan and British Columbia, even though they have major concentrations of Aboriginal people in their cities, tend to take a province-wide view of issues and would want to see strategies tailored in this way' (2000: 21). In central and eastern Canada, Aboriginal populations in urban areas are not generally viewed as a distinct population, much less a serious preoccupation.

In part this diverse approach to the 'urban challenge' reflects the disparate nature of the urban Aboriginal experience. There are different 'types' of Aboriginal urban areas, ranging from the denser and more racially segregated inner city areas of Edmonton, Regina, Saskatoon, and Winnipeg to the smaller, less dense, less segregated, and more widely dispersed Aboriginal populations in Halifax, Toronto, and Montreal. There are also the Aboriginal populations clustering in medium and smaller sized cities like Thunder Bay, Brandon, Kamloops, and Prince Albert. Although Vancouver is a 'western' city, with a known Aboriginal population most often associated with the Downtown Eastside area, recent research reveals a smaller proportion of Aboriginal people living in the poorest economic conditions in that city as compared to the Prairie cities. These differences necessarily dictate variation in policy approaches.

Jeremy Hull's research (2001) on Aboriginal people and social class reveals the folly of treating Aboriginal people, and on- and off-reserve populations, as similarly disadvantaged. His findings about the class system that has emerged on reserves in Manitoba extends to off-reserve Registered Indians where control of local resources is concerned. Perhaps the most telling of Hull's findings in relation to the non-Registered or 'other' Aboriginal population is that their class structure more closely resembles that of the non-Aboriginal than that of the reserve population. These issues will come into relief in Part II, where we examine political realities of communities and their implications for successful restorative justice projects.

Quantitative descriptions of the 'communities' Aboriginal people experience, whether as 'legal categories,' a national population, or within smaller, more conventional on- or off-reserve groupings, paint an interesting and challenging picture. The 'Aboriginal community' appears increasingly urban, distanced geo-graphically and, in many cases, qualitatively, from the traditional cultural roots associated with a more rural lifestyle. And while Aboriginal people occupy positions across the economic spectrum and class structure, affluence remains elusive for many Aboriginal communities and people. For far too many, poverty and violence remain the dominant pressures of daily life. These experiences have come to define a popular stereotype of Aboriginal life and, together with issues of cultural erosion and culture clash, they have been linked with the over-representation of Aboriginal people in the Canadian criminal justice system.[13] Insofar as over-representation has provided much of the momentum behind the community restorative justice movement, it is impor-tant to engage the issue as a theory and a reality, and to critique its impact on the restorative justice movement within Aboriginal communities. It is to this task that we now turn our attention.

CHAPTER 2

Communities and Conflict: Offending Patterns and Over-Representation

> The current Canadian justice system has profoundly failed Aboriginal people. It has done so in failing to respect cultural differences, failing to address overt and systemic biases against Aboriginal people, and in denying Aboriginal people an effective voice in the development and delivery of services.
>
> Robert Mitchell, Q.C. (Canada, 1996: 28)

> ... the quantity and quality of law enforcement the citizens receive, both as victim and as suspect, reflects the underlying pattern of social stratification in society.
>
> (Norris et al., 1994: 62)

In the previous chapter we attempted to provide a deeper understanding of the Aboriginal community in Canada, looking to both the national 'macro-community' and the smaller micro-communities comprised of both the rural reserve community and the pockets of off-reserve residents who come together in urban centres. It is clear that these communities are far more complex than previously imagined, and that some of the popular stereotypes of the past no longer apply. For example, the assumption of the definitive 'Indian community' as a rural, reserve-based one is increasingly undermined by the reality that nearly three-quarters of Aboriginal people, especially Indian and Métis people, reside off-reserve, many in urban centres. It is also apparent that Aboriginal people occupy a range of positions in the socio-economic landscape. The largely non-Status Indians and Métis who have attained affluence constitute an important, albeit small, qualification on what continues to be the experience of the majority, namely, the life of the 'working poor' or unemployed, living near or below the poverty line, with limited opportunities through which to escape that reality.[1]

The relationship of life chances to the potential for conflict with the criminal justice system is relatively clear: 'when an individual's life chances are poor, their likelihood of coming into conflict with the law will be increased' (Comack, in La Prairie, 1994: 63). Whether that likelihood is influenced more by the biases and processes of the law, the risks implicit in a life lived on the margins, or some combination of these factors remains unclear. What is clear, however, is that, after decades of research into over-representation and a range of policy efforts to combat it, the latter have been doomed by the limited clarity in outcomes produced by the former. Drawing on both qualitative and quantitative reports, attempts to explain the high rate of conflict with the law experienced by Aboriginal people have focused on the possibility of higher levels of Aboriginal offending and victimization, on the one hand, and on possible discrimination in policing, charging, prosecution, bail, sentencing, and parole, on the other. Thus Weatherburn et al. (2003), examining police arrests, previous convictions, and self-reports of criminal activities for Aboriginal and non-Aboriginal groups, found that the leading cause of Aboriginal over-representation in prison is not systemic bias, but high rates of Aboriginal involvement in serious crime. The authors argue that future efforts at reducing Aboriginal over-representation should focus on reducing crime in Aboriginal communities, and that alcohol use, early departure from school, unemployment, and being taken away from one's family are the main factors distinguishing Aboriginal people who have been arrested from those who have not. At the same time, however, Fergusson et al., (2003) drawing upon the longitudinal Christchurch Health and Development Study in which one hundred individuals were followed from birth to the age of twenty-one, were able to engage a comparative analysis of the experiences of Maori and non-Maori in the New Zealand youth and criminal justice systems. Their findings constitute an important addition to extant research indicating that ethnic differences in officially recorded crime may be influenced by biases in the U.K. and U.S. justice systems. Fergusson et al. found that, after controlling for offending history and socio-economic background, there was 'a small bias in the arrest/conviction process which leads [to] Maori offenders having higher rates of conviction than non-Maori offenders' (2003: 354). This research, as an incipient step in linking the qualitative and quantitative reports, is significant; unfortunately, its value is somewhat qualified by the fact, acknowledged by the researchers, that the self-report data relied upon did not take into account the seriousness of the offence – a factor which we know plays a major role in the system response to offenders. As well, the researchers expressed regret that they did not pinpoint the location or locations in the system at which the bias occurs. This is disappointing from a policy standpoint, as it limits our ability to target measures to eliminate bias. The finding of statistically significant levels of bias in the New Zealand system in relation to Aboriginal offenders may, however, be taken as further evidence in favour of broad-based system reforms – after all, if reform is approached as an overall system project, it is bound to cover those areas which are most implicated in the perpetuation of bias.

While continued investigation of the causes of over-representation provides important insights into the nature of the forces informing it, we still have only a partial picture of the causes and thus only a limited sense of possible solutions. Based on the extant portrait, it seems likely that the most plausible explanation for the over-representation of Aboriginal people may fall somewhere between the two explanatory poles of the biases and processes of the law and the risks implicit in a life lived on the margins. It is equally clear that variations in the social and economic situation of Aboriginal people across the country, and the characteristics of Prairie and other cities, must also enter into any realistic expository framework.

Identifying the configuration of Aboriginal offending and criminal justice processing in Canada is difficult. We do not have data similar to that enlisted in the New Zealand research discussed above to inform our efforts: in Canada, there is a prohibition on collecting and reporting race data at the level of police and courts.[2] The research problem is compounded by the absence of national, provincial, and territorial data that are both comparable and standardized. What has been collected over the years is generally piecemeal and time and issue-specific; data revealing trends over time and jurisdiction-comparable data on criminal justice processing are generally not available. The discussion that follows, therefore, is limited in scope.

(i)   The Concept of Over-Representation: What It Is and How It Looks in the Canadian Criminal Justice System

The phenomenon known as 'over-representation' is much easier to define and document than it is to rectify. Stated simply, it occurs when the proportion of a given group represented in, for purposes here, the courts or prisons, is disproportionate to their numbers in the general population. Thus for example, it is argued that Aboriginal people, constituting roughly 2.8–3.0 per cent of the Canadian population, are vastly over-represented in the criminal justice system where, in some provincial prisons, they constitute upwards of 50 per cent of the inmate population (Canada, 1996: 32).

Over-representation has played a central role in the criminal justice agendas of other countries with significant Aboriginal populations: New Zealand, Australia, and the United States. Although there is some variation in the degree of over-

Table 2.1
Aboriginal incarceration: Canada, New Zealand, and Australia (2000)

Country	% Aboriginal in general population	% of total sentenced admission population	Aboriginal ratio in prison to population
Canada	2.5	18	7x
New Zealand	14.0	41	2.9x
Australia	2.1	20	9.5x

representation, in these countries, as in Canada, Aboriginal offenders are consistently over-represented at all stages of criminal justice processing. Table 2.1 reveals both the extent of and variations in over-representation.

While there are no comparable data for American Indians, official data from 1997 reveal that almost three times as many American Indians were imprisoned (per 100,000 adults) compared to whites, and eight times as many when compared to Asians. On an average day almost 4 per cent of American Indians aged eighteen years and older were under the care and control of the criminal justice system. American Indians comprise approximately 3 per cent of the U.S. population (Greenfeld and Smith, 1999). The only group with a higher rate of over-representation in the U.S. criminal justice system is African-Americans.

Comparing rates of Aboriginal incarceration in the four countries is informative. The trend in New Zealand is similar to that found in the United States and Canada. New Zealand, followed by Canada, has the largest and most urbanized indigenous population of the three countries. Its Maori population comprises 14 per cent of the general population, and 82 per cent of the Maori population live in urban areas. Criminal justice data from New Zealand reveals that Maori are over-represented at every stage of the criminal justice process. In 1998 they were 3.3 times more likely to be apprehended for a criminal offence than non-Maori; they were also more likely to be prosecuted, convicted, and sentenced to imprisonment. The result was that Maori made up 51 per cent of the prison population (Doone, 2000). And while the Maori prison population tends to continually increase, the percentage of offenders classified as Caucasian decreased from 56 per cent in 1988 to 49 per cent in 1999. Changes in the percentage of offenders are influenced to some degree by the different population growth rates of the ethnic groups. For example, the increase in the percentage of offenders who are Maori or Pacific Islander is partly explained by the fact that these groups comprise an increasing proportion of the population (New Zealand Parliamentary Library, 2000).

In Australia, on 30 June 2001 there were 4,445 indigenous prisoners comprising 20 per cent of the prisoner population. Indigenous persons were much more likely to be in prison than non-indigenous persons, with an imprisonment rate of 1,829 prisoners per 100,000 adult indigenous population – fifteen times the rate for the non-indigenous population. The highest indigenous imprisonment rate in Australia was recorded in western Australia (3,036 prisoners per 100,000 adult indigenous population). Changes in Australia's prison populations suggest that their over-representation problem differs from that evidenced in Canada. Thus for example, we see that between the 1991 and 2001 prisoner censuses in Australia, the prisoner population increased by 50 per cent, from 15,021 at 30 June 1991 to 22,458 at 30 June 2001. The proportion of prisoners who were Aboriginal and Torres Strait Islander also rose, from 14 per cent in 1991 to 20 per cent in 2001. In Canada, by contrast, the general prison population is decreasing, and while the Aboriginal one is increasing, it is not doing so at the same rate as in Australia.

The phenomenon of over-representation is entrenched and persistent, and it has proven remarkably resistant to a wide range of policies and programs directed to its amelioration. Over-representation has become one of Canada's most intractable social and political challenges and, as suggested by the Task Force on the Criminal Justice System and Its Impact on Indian and Métis People of Alberta, shows few signs of abating: 'by the year 2011, Aboriginal offenders will account for 38.5 per cent of all admissions to federal and provincial correctional centres in Alberta, compared to 29.5 per cent per cent of all such offenders in 1989 ... In some age categories, for example, the 12–18 years of age group, Aboriginal offenders are projected to account for 40 per cent of the admissions of population to correctional facilities by the year 2011' (Canada, 1996: 31). The continued problem of over-representation has impelled support for the community restorative justice movement in Aboriginal communities – communities, it is believed, are unlikely to do a worse job of social control and 'rehabilitation' than the state and its 'experts' have done to date. This support begs a number of questions, however, insofar as the various explanations of over-representation both acquit and implicate Aboriginal communities in the very problem that they are expected to remedy through restorative justice. We will turn to these questions momentarily; our immediate task is to elucidate the reality of over-representation, offending patterns, and victimization among Aboriginal people as a prerequisite to exploring system reforms and the challenges facing it.

There is little doubt that far too many Aboriginal people are in prison, and that their numbers in both federal and most provincial institutions are grossly disproportionate to their numbers in the Canadian population. Aboriginal women account for almost one-quarter of all female inmates and there is a higher proportion of Aboriginal than non-Aboriginal female accused in custody. Their children fare no better: Aboriginal youth are over-represented under community supervision, in custody, and in alternative programs. As we will see, the fate of Aboriginal men is similar. While these realities demand critical scrutiny on a number of levels, it important to resist the temptation to make generalizations regarding overall patterns of over-representation in Canada. The nature and extent of Aboriginal over-representation varies markedly. Regional correctional statistics establish that certain areas of the country are disproportionate contributors to the over-representation of Aboriginal people within the Canadian criminal justice system, while recent reports originating with the Canadian Centre for Justice Statistics (CCJS), and an article by Stenning and Roberts (2001), reveal that *there is virtually no over-representation of Aboriginal people in provincial correctional institutions in Prince Edward Island and Quebec,* but a quite remarkable over-representation in other jurisdictions. If we take as a baseline measurement the proportion of Aboriginal people we might expect to encounter in the system given the size of the general Aboriginal population (as indicated above, roughly 3 per cent of the Canadian population as a whole), we see that Nova Scotia and Newfoundland manifest the least degree of over-representation, registering an over-representation of 1.5 to 2 times the expected figures. From here, the numbers seem only to grow: British Columbia has an over-representation rate of five times the expected number, Manitoba and Ontario, have figures of seven and nine times the expected rates of representation, respectively. Alberta ties with Ontario; Saskatchewan, with ten times the expected number of Aboriginal people in conflict with the system, has the highest rate of over-representation.

A closer look at these numbers provides an even more stark picture of the regional variation. For example, an examination of the Aboriginal incarceration rate for Saskatchewan and Nova Scotia reveals that in the former in 1996, 154 Aboriginal persons for every 10,000 in the population were on register in a correctional facility, whereas in the latter, the comparable rate was 31/10,000 (Statscan, 2000). The data on correctional federal inmates are similarly varied, with over-representation considerably lower in the Maritime, Central Canada, and Pacific than in the Prairie provinces (Boe, 2000). This regional variation has been relatively constant over the past decade (La Prairie, 1996).

Few attempts have been made to explain variation in over-representation across the country, but La Prairie's 1994 research in two western and two eastern cities set out to explore this issue, as well as social stratification within the Aboriginal populations in the inner city cores.[3] Her findings suggest some interesting possibilities about differences in criminal justice processing of Aboriginal people between western and eastern regions, and while they shed light primarily on the experience of urban Aboriginal people, they may also assist us in understanding Aboriginal conflict with the law and over-representation more generally. This is especially so if we enlist as a broader context in which to understand La Prairie's findings the relationship between life chances and potential for conflict with the law, noted above.

La Prairie's research reveals that in the inner city, Aboriginal males are significantly more involved in the criminal justice system (both in charges and deten-tion) than females, and the greater their marginalization within the inner city social strata, the greater their involvement with the criminal justice system. Other factors related to the degree of involvement in the criminal justice system included high mobility in childhood, parental drinking, and parental unemploy-ment. Living in a foster home, or with a step-parent, was related to child abuse and family violence, and often to later involvement in the justice system, especially for males. In an illuminating coincidence, there was east/west variation in childhood experiences across Canada, with the western group revealing more severe childhood experiences and considerably more family disruption. If the life chances theory is correct, these factors may play some part in the east/west variation in over-representation.

La Prairie's 1994 findings have been supported by more recent research (Drost, 2001; La Prairie, 2002) which suggests that Aboriginal people in Prairie cities are most disadvantaged in terms of employment and income, and live in much more concentrated and racially segregated areas than do their further western city (Vancouver) or eastern city (Toronto, Montreal, Halifax) counter-parts. In this regard the inner cores of Prairie cities may share many of the characteristics of inner cities in the United States, which often have heavy concentrations of marginalized ethnic minority populations. It is interesting to note that the eastern cities in Canada, which also tend to be lower contributors to over-representation, manifest much less extreme and obvious differences between the Aboriginal and non-Aboriginal populations.

The genesis of regional and city, between and within-group socio-economic and other indicators of disparity and disadvantage in the Aboriginal and non-Aboriginal populations are still unclear, yet it seems undeniable that these patterns of exacerbated disadvantage bear some relation to regional variations in patterns of conflict with the law. Here the American literature on crime and communities may be helpful, insofar as Sherman et al. note that 'the causation of inner city crime has received extensive diagnosis' (1998: 75), especially in comparison to the much less well-developed Canadian literature. The U.S. research suggests that many factors are implicated in the commission of crime in neighbourhoods, including residential instability, and concentrations of poor, female-headed households with children, multi-unit housing facilities, and disrupted social networks. These factors, added to segregation of racial and poverty groups in the most marginalized urban areas, have been demonstrated to foster and support the rise of criminogenic structures and community cultures (Bursik, 1988; Sampson and Wilson, 1995). We see these linkages clearly in the work of Sherman, who observed, for example, that delinquency causation may be a function at least in part of its community context: 'A community with a high percentage of single parent households may put all its children at greater risk for of delinquency by reducing the capacity of a community to maintain adult networks of informal control of children' (1998: 79). In apparent agreement are the findings of Sampson and Wilson (1995), which suggest that structural social disorganization, cultural isolation, and racial segregation provide a context for understanding the adoption of antisocial attitudes and the prevalence of crime and delinquency.

This research implies that antisocial behaviour is, at base, largely learned behaviour. Social learning theory posits that individuals learn how to act by observing the world around them and how others – families, friends, and peer group – engage with that world. One learns different things in different places, and thus the logic follows that those who live on the lowest rungs of the social ladder, and in personal situations which are characterized by dysfunctional behaviour, are disproportionately vulnerable to the adoption of antisocial attitudes and activities. This vulnerability resides largely in the wide-ranging limitations that characterize the lives of the poor, as well as, for many, alienation from mainstream and community resources and a lack of individual and family resources to promote pro-social attitudes (Andrews and Bonta, 1994). It is important to note that these major correlates and predictors of criminal behaviour are unlikely to vary substantially from one cultural and/or racial group to another (Andrews and Bonta, 1994).

While these kinds of theories and attention to risk factors have long been part of the analysis of the crime phenomenon in American inner cities, they have largely escaped scrutiny in explaining Aboriginal over-representation in the criminal justice and correctional systems in Canada. This is a significant oversight, especially in an era of unprecedented Aboriginal migration to the cities. If American researchers are correct, and if their findings are applicable to the urban experience of Aboriginal people in Canada, the sad reality may be that Aboriginal people who have fled bad situations on reserves may fare little better in the cities, and may place their children at risk from the psychosocial impacts of poverty, segregation, and antisocial behaviour found in many inner city neighbourhoods. In other words, for some Aboriginal people, the city may offer an experience not unlike the ones on reserve from which they are struggling to escape, but absent the support of band and reservation-based programming or the comfort of kin. Indeed, if the research is correct, the city may be a worse place in many ways. Life in the urban core tends to be much more public and anonymous, offenders are and thereby more vulnerable to detection and reaction by police; the city also offers a wider range of influences and dangers, all of which may combine into a much more toxic social mix.

Notwithstanding the degree to which social learning may or may not explain Aboriginal offending patterns, as the urban migration of Aboriginals has intensified, so too has their rate of over-representation in Canadian prison populations, especially in federal prisons. In 1991/2, 11 per cent of the federal inmate population was Aboriginal; by 1997/8, it had increased to 17 per cent. The same trend is evidenced in admissions to provincial facilities in the Prairie provinces, where some of the most depressed and dysfunctional urban contexts are found. For example, from 1988 to 1998, the proportion of provincial Aboriginal admissions stayed the same or decreased in the Atlantic, the Central provinces, and British Columbia, but increased in Manitoba, Saskatchewan, and Alberta (La Prairie, 1996). Aboriginal offenders were similarly over-represented in probation rates, and the regional variation is similar to that of sentenced admissions (Canadian Centre for Justice Statistics [CCJS], 2000b). While data are not available for all jurisdictions, similar trends emerge in data tracking the over-representation of Aboriginal youth. For example, rates of over-representation for Aboriginal youth were highest in Manitoba, Alberta, and Ontario, and lowest in the Maritime provinces (CCJS, 2000b).

While a decrease in total numbers of offenders incarcerated may be a result of declining crime rates in the general population, largely owing to an aging non-Aboriginal population, the increase in the proportion of incarcerated Aboriginal offenders may be linked with a number of factors beyond those noted above. For example, it has been argued that higher Aboriginal incarceration rates may reflect higher Aboriginal birth rates, as well as a younger Aboriginal population with a larger percentage of people falling within that category most likely to experience conflict with the law (male youths between the ages of eighteen and twenty-five). More troubling is the possibility that the rates of incarceration of Aboriginal people have come about as a corollary to the increasing growth of an entrenched 'Aboriginal underclass.' It is clear that the most disadvantaged of Aboriginal people are Registered Indians, and that this group is characterized by greater have and have-not disparities not only within its on- and off-reserve membership, but also in comparison to other Aboriginal groups across the county. It is perhaps not surprising that this group, which contains the larger percentage of both working poor and those who are without work, also produces the majority of Aboriginal offenders. Taken together, the coincidence of long-term poverty and a disproportionate contribution to the number of Aboriginal people in conflict with the law has been argued by some to present the pathology of a growing underclass among Aboriginal Canadians. If true, this would seem to confirm the 'life chances argument' and suggest compelling policy issues both for Canadian governments and Aboriginal self-government (Hull, 2001).

(ii) The Reality of Over-Representation: Aboriginal versus Non-Aboriginal Offenders

Weatherburn et al. (2003: 14) make an important and telling observation on the etiology of offending research on reducing Aboriginal over-representation in prison in Australia. They claim that in urban and rural Australia the vast majority of Aboriginal people have never been arrested for any offence. This renders it imperative to distinguish Aboriginal people who come into conflict with the law from those who do not. As noted earlier, the researchers conclude that the main features distinguishing those who come into conflict from those who do not are alcohol use, early departure from school, unemployment, and being taken away from one's natural family. These findings are entirely consistent with what is known about the impact of family dissolution, poor school performance, unemployment, and substance abuse among non-Aboriginal populations. They reinforce the position that the factors that promote conflict with the law are similar across a range of social and cultural groups, who are at the same time distinguished and distanced by geography and cultural experience and exposure to mainstream society – elements which also distinguish Aboriginal offenders (La Prairie, 1996; Planning Branch, 1975; McCaskill, 1976; Waldram, 1992; Comack, 1993). For example, it is well known that young people between the ages of fifteen and nineteen are at the greatest risk for involvement in the criminal justice system and that most adult offenders begin their careers as young offenders. While these characteristics hold across both Aboriginal and non-Aboriginal offenders, they are exaggerated in the Aboriginal context. Demographic and criminal justice data reveal that the Aboriginal population is younger than the non-Aboriginal population (particularly in the Prairie provinces) (Siggner, 2001) and Aboriginal offenders manifest a younger age of involvement in the youth justice system. As well, Aboriginal offenders generally have more prior contact with the criminal justice and correctional systems, and come from more dysfunctional backgrounds than do the non-Aboriginal groups (Planning Branch, 1975; Irvine, 1978; Birkenmeyer and Jolly, 1981; Shaw, 1991).

While Aboriginal offenders are both younger and more disadvantaged, their distance from their non-Aboriginal counterparts does not end there. Aboriginal offenders generally have less education[4] and are more likely to be unemployed than are non-Aboriginal offenders, contributing to their generally higher need levels overall; they are also more likely to display attributes of foetal alcohol syndrome/foetal alcohol effects (CCJS, 2000b). These characteristics of the Aboriginal offender population contribute to a perception that they present a higher risk to reoffend[5] – a projection which is borne out in practice, as evidenced in higher recidivism levels among Aboriginal offenders in comparison to their non-Aboriginal counterparts. It is important to qualify this statement, however, as existing data on Aboriginal and non-Aboriginal inmate risk/need classifications are not comprehensive, and there is a lack of comparable data for Aboriginal offenders in different regions of the country. However, demographic data on employment, income, and education would suggest that of all Aboriginal offenders, those in the Prairie provinces have the highest risk/need levels. In support of this assertion, previous work on risk levels of offenders on conditional sentence orders in Manitoba and Ontario revealed some risk differences between Aboriginal offenders in the two provinces. In Manitoba, 45 per cent of Aboriginal offenders on a conditional sentence order were classified as high risk, compared to 33 per cent in Ontario (La Prairie and Koegl 1998). While the factors that produce higher levels of risk are probably similar,[6] they may be differentially distributed across the country.

The differences between Aboriginal and non-Aboriginal offenders, while compelling, may be qualified by the nature of the distinctions and disparities within the Aboriginal population. For example, and consistent with the demographic discussion contained in the previous chapter, it is clear that Status Indians are the most disadvantaged of the overall Aboriginal offender group. Research across a range of criminal justice system levels confirms this position. In her research in four inner city cores, La Prairie (1994) found that Status or 'Registered' Indians were disproportionately represented in the inner city regions and that those from the Prairie cities were particularly at risk for involvement with the criminal justice system. This risk assessment is confirmed by the Canadian Centre for Justice Statistics' 'one-day snapshot' (Finn et al., 1999) of the criminal justice system, which revealed that the majority of the Aboriginal population in Manitoba correctional facilities was Status Indian. Similarly, the work of Bonta et al. (1997) revealed that the majority of Aboriginal offenders in the probation sample were Status Indian. Furthermore, while the risk of reoffending has generally been shown to be higher for Aboriginal offenders (York, 1995), a 1996 analysis of Manitoba probation data (which included non-Aboriginal as well as on- and off-reserve Aboriginal offenders) found that the risk of reoffending was greatest for the Status group, whether on- or off-reserve (Bonta et al., 1997). To the degree that Status correlates with the most profound degree of disadvantage within the Aboriginal population generally, the higher risk profile of this group offers further reinforcement for the life chances argument. Life on many reserves is characterized by factors known to influence crime levels – high unemployment, poverty, family dysfunction, diminished social and community controls. Thus, the communities to which the Status groups return (reserves and inner cities) may be more criminogenic than those to which non-Aboriginal and Métis/non-Status offenders return. This is consistent with previous research about crime and disorder on-reserve and in inner cities, particularly those in western Canada.[7]

An alternative means of examining the issue of the vulnerability of Aboriginal sub-groups, such as Status Indians, to involvement in the criminal justice system was explored in a recent study of socio-economic characteristics of Aboriginal and non-Aboriginal and within-group Aboriginal populations in nine major urban centres across the country (La Prairie, 2002). Because some research findings suggest Status or Registered Indians are over-represented in incarcerated Aboriginal populations, it follows that the characteristics of the most incarcerated group (Registered Indians) in the nine cities should be different from the general Aboriginal population and parallel regional variation in over-representation. This research found that discrepancy in socio-economic variables is greater for Registered Indians than for the total Aboriginal group. In other words, on most variables the Registered Indian group is 'below' the total Aboriginal group mean scores, but there is considerable city-by-city variation.

For many years there was virtually no information to be had about the geographic location of the offences for which Aboriginal people were incarcerated. The question asked of Aboriginal inmates was usually 'where are you from?' (to which many replied, 'a reserve'), rather than, 'where did you commit the offence for which you are presently incarcerated?' When researchers finally began to ask the second question it emerged that the majority of offences for which Aboriginal offenders were incarcerated occurred in an urban area. In a ground-breaking study of Aboriginal offenders in Manitoba, McCaskill (1976) was the first researcher in Canada to note that the majority of Aboriginal offenders were incarcerated for offences committed in off-reserve areas. Twenty years later, in a Correctional Service of Canada survey, Johnson (1997) found that only 19 per cent of Aboriginal offenders were from reserves; of that 19 per cent, slightly over half (51 per cent) had grown up in their home community, which suggests that while many offenders were 'from' reserves, they had spent the majority of their lives off-reserve.

A one-day snapshot of Aboriginal youth in custody in Canada found that more than half (54 per cent) lived in a city during the two years prior to the current admission, while 23 per cent lived on a reserve, and 21 per cent lived in a town. These figures were even higher for the Prairie provinces. Fully 67 per cent of the Manitoba, 56 per cent of the Saskatchewan, and 54 per cent of the Alberta youth in custody committed their offences in a city. Fifty-six per cent of the total sample also planned to relocate to a city upon release (Bittle et al., 2000). Focusing on the shifting nature of Aboriginal residence patterns, Boe (2000) suggested that the young and rapidly growing Aboriginal population in urban areas may greatly increase the risk of contact with the criminal justice system.

It is not difficult to grasp the relationship between urban offending and regional variation in Aboriginal incarceration levels. For example, in one Saskatchewan study, Canadian Centre for Justice Statistics (CCJS, 2000a) researchers found that the Aboriginal crime rate per 10,000 population was eleven times higher than the non-Aboriginal rate. This trend is exemplified in the Aboriginal offending patterns manifested in the city of Vancouver. In 1998, Aboriginal people accounted for 8 per cent of all victimizations in Vancouver but represented only 2 per cent of the population; their violence was also predominantly intraracial, that is, Aboriginal people were victimized by other Aboriginal people (CCJS, 2000b).

Despite the apparent domination of the urban setting and patterns in Aboriginal offending, the rural or reservation context remains a significant site of Aboriginal crime and disorder. As the CCJS research into Aboriginal crime and victimization in Saskatchewan (2000a) noted, crime rates on reserves were double those in urban and rural areas. The same phenomenon was discovered by La Prairie (1992) in James Bay, Quebec, and by Auger et al. (1992) in Ontario. The possibility that the criminal justice system responds differently to offences and offenders on- and off-reserve may explain the finding that the majority of those incarcerated committed their offences off-reserve. We will return to this question later in the chapter.

While it seems clear that a range of social, economic, and political factors contribute to the high rate of conflict between Aboriginal people and the criminal justice system, an additional, obvious reason for over-representation is the use of carceral sentences and Canada's general over-reliance on imprisonment in comparison to other countries around the world (Canada, 1987; Christie, 1993; McMahon 1992). If, in fact, patterns of law enforcement tend to replicate the underlying pattern of social stratification in society, it would make some degree of sense that a general over-reliance on incarceration would fall disproportionately and more heavily on Aboriginal people, given their location in the social structure. Other characteristics of general incarceration patterns in Canada may have similar impacts. For example, the use of imprisonment generally is influenced by a combination of factors, including those related to criminal justice, such as the actions of criminal justice professionals, and societal factors,

such as general attitudes of punitiveness and towards offenders and their situations. The apparent absence of a relationship between crime rates and levels of
imprisonment, however, indicates that other sociocultural factors are involved
(Tonry, 1994). Particular attitudes and assumptions about Aboriginal people in
Canada may be argued to play a role, whether consciously or unconsciously, in
the over-incarceration of Aboriginal people. This hypothesis will be explored in
more detail below.

Although we tend to over-use prisons, the majority of Canadian sentences are
short – less than six months. Crime (both reported and victimization) increases
from east to west and there is some variation in use of imprisonment (CCJS,
2000a, 2001; Statscan, 2000). While there are no major differences in the type of
offences committed across the country, some of the provinces which show the
highest use of carceral sentences may be dealing with particularly difficult
populations (in socio-economic and offence terms). Without better data on
prior records and offender profiles, however, firm conclusions about the factors
leading to disparity are not possible.

For some offences, particularly fine defaults, the provinces of British Columbia, Quebec, and Ontario appear to rely less on imprisonment than do other
provinces (La Prairie, 1996). The Prairie provinces have the most marginalized
Aboriginal populations and the consistent use of imprisonment for lifestyle-
related offences, such as administration of justice, public order, and fine defaults,
results, in part, in high levels of imprisonment (La Prairie, 1996). The use of
imprisonment also reflects cultural attitudes and penal values, which may help to
explain variation across the country – the argument here suggesting that the
more 'conservative' Prairie provinces (especially Alberta) may manifest more
punitive attitudes towards offenders in general, and Aboriginal people in particular. While it may seem intuitively correct, however, this position is not borne out
in the research, which has revealed that more punitive public views on the need
for imprisonment, or on Aboriginal issues, do not necessarily translate into a
greater reliance on imprisonment or higher Aboriginal incarceration levels
(Reid, 1994a, 1994b). Thus once again we confront the probability that over-
representation, and regional variation therein, is the result of a complex interplay
of a multiplicity of factors, and any effective response to this phenomenon must
be multifaceted and interdisciplinary in nature.

While too great a reliance on imprisonment in Canada is the most obvious
reason for over-representation in correctional institutions, even if the use of
incarceration could be reduced Aboriginal people would still be over-represented in non-carceral criminal justice responses. Indeed, our focus on over-
imprisonment, while understandable, has served to distract us from the
over-involvement of Aboriginal people across a range of locations in the justice
system. And despite our focus, we have failed to reduce over-representation.

How is it that two decades of awareness, knowledge, and research have done nothing but document the fact that over-representation exists? Researchers appear like witnesses to a car accident – watching as it occurs, apparently powerless to stop it or to aid those caught in the crash.

(iii) Theorizing Causation: Searching for the Roots of Over-Representation

There is considerable literature on the issue of over-representation, the majority of which identifies racism and/or discrimination in the criminal justice system as the primary causal factor perpetuating this phenomenon. Much of this literature, while compelling and cogent, is essentially qualitative in approach and manifests limitations in method which render it difficult to generalize. As well, when quantitative research on over-representation leads to a conclusion focusing on racism, there are too often gaps in method that undermine the validity of the conclusions. These studies tend to fall primarily into the first of three broad 'categories of causes' into which most of the extant research on over-representation can be divided. These categories, developed by La Prairie (1990), include:

(a) differential criminal justice processing as a result of racial discrimination and 'legal cultural clash';
(b) higher Aboriginal offending levels and commission by Aboriginal people of the type of offences that are more likely to result in carceral sentences; and
(c) criminal justice policies and practices that have a differential impact on Aboriginal offenders due to their socio-economic conditions.

While the state of knowledge in each of these explanations is still almost as limited as it was a decade ago, it would appear that a higher offending rate probably explains more of the over-representation phenomenon than do the other factors, and insofar as higher offending rates can be linked to larger social justice issues, it remains clear that over-representation is a result of the complex interplay of factors stressed repeatedly above. As will be seen, recent research by the Canadian Centre for Justice Statistics supports this claim. We will consider each of these causal categories briefly, in turn.

(a) Differential Criminal Justice Processing as a Result of Culture Conflict and Racial Discrimination

As a potential explanation of over-representation, the 'differential processing' position is a familiar one, as it is the explanation most clearly articulated in reports of commissions of inquiry and in much media and scholarly work. The essence of the position is straightforward; it holds that over-representation exists because of a profound legal-cultural clash as well as outright racial discrimination on the part of criminal justice system actors and the state which employs and empowers them. This disquieting and compelling explanation is underscored by far too many qualitative reports of the experiences of Aboriginal people caught up in the wheels of a justice system which is often foreign to them and mired within an out-dated and inappropriate perception of an 'Indian Problem.' It is personified in the experiences of Minnie Sutherland, an Aboriginal woman left for dead by a hit-and-run driver, only to be discovered by police who, assuming her lack of consciousness to be caused by alcohol rather than an automobile, took her to a detox centre which refused to admit a 'drunk Indian'; she was later left in a jail cell to 'dry out,' and released. Sutherland died seven days later from head injuries caused by the accident. Greater media attention was garnered by the experiences of Fred Quilt, J.J. Harper, and Donald Marshall, Jr, the latter incidents inspiring two of the most extensive and thorough of official inquiries, the 'Aboriginal Justice Inquiry of Manitoba,' and the 'Inquiry into the Prosecution of Donald Marshall, Jr.' These documents influenced the most recent and most well-publicized Royal Commission Report, *Bridging the Cultural Divide*; all focus on the differential processing position as one of, if not *the*, central factor in explaining over-representation.

These qualitative reports have recently received important support in the work of Fergusson et al. in New Zealand, discussed above. Fergusson's findings, however, do little to elevate arguments of differential processing based on race to the prominent place many of their proponents believe such arguments should occupy in the over-representation discourse. For while it is unquestionable that discrimination and, in some contexts, outright racism, constitute *one part* of a larger configuration of factors feeding into over-representation, the current research indicates strongly that racism is not the sole or even the major part of the problem – at least in the justice system, if not in society. While information about the criminal justice processing of Aboriginal and non-Aboriginal offenders is limited, available data suggest the involvement of Aboriginal people in the criminal justice and correctional systems cannot be attributed to racial bias alone. For example, one of the most critical gaps in information about the causes of over-representation is the role of police in charging. While anecdotal information such as that provided above abound, there are very few data collected through participant observation or any other kind of systematic research strategy that could assist us in arguing for shifts in police practice. As a result, while reports of police wrong-doing emerge in the media, it is impossible to say much with confidence about the role of the police in *over-representation generally* or, more interestingly, whether they play a role in the regional variation in over-representation observed across the country.

As we move through the system, the data are either equivocal or challenge the differential processing position. The issue of bail is apposite here. The claim has often been made that Aboriginal people are more frequently held in remand than non-Aboriginal defendants (Hamilton and Sinclair, 1991: 221–4), but the data are both slim and open to question. Research by Kellough and Wortley in 2002 into the use of bail in Ontario revealed no significant difference for access for Aboriginal and non-Aboriginal accused.[8] This finding is challenged by the 1999 CCJS one-day profile, which showed more non-Aboriginal than Aboriginal accused on remand in Manitoba. In the same year, however, La Prairie and Koegl (1998) examined Manitoba offenders on conditional sentence orders and found no difference in the proportion of Aboriginal and non-Aboriginal offenders held on remand prior to sentencing (Finn et al., 1999). This is intriguing, as one of the first indictments of the use of remand against Aboriginal accused came from the Manitoba Aboriginal Justice Inquiry.

The situation facing Aboriginal accused at court is unclear, as research into such matters as prosecutorial decision making is largely absent. Where data does exist, it indicates that unintended discrimination may be a bigger problem than consciously racist tendencies on the part of system actors. For example, the evaluation of a mediation program in Saskatchewan revealed that the guidelines for referral to mediation excluded the types of offences most often committed by Aboriginal offenders, thereby denying them access to an important alternative program. The problem was not an intentional policy of restricting access by Aboriginal people to a system alternative, but rather a built-in bias in the guidelines for referral that had a discriminatory impact on Aboriginal offenders (Nuffield, 1997). This research, while apposite here, may also be included under that category of explanations focusing on the differential impact of criminal justice policies given the larger sociodemographic realities characterizing Aboriginal peoples' lives.

Sentencing, long assumed to be a hotspot for unfair treatment of Aboriginal accused in the criminal justice system, would likewise seem a logical focus for research attention. However, unlike the United States, the United Kingdom, and Australia, where race data are maintained and considerable research into possible disparity in sentencing has occurred, Canada has conducted few comparative sentencing research studies, primarily because of the cost and time involved in participant observation research. Even those forums with resources at their disposal to explore the relationship between Aboriginal people and the criminal justice system, such as the Canadian Sentencing Commission, the Standing Committee on Justice and the Solicitor General (Canada, 1988), and the Law

Reform Commission, are long on recommendations but rather short on data to support them.[9] This is also true of the numerous public inquires in Canada, especially the Royal Commission on Aboriginal Peoples (Canada, 1996). The best data on these issues emerged from research in the 1970s and 1980s (Hagan, 1975; Moyer et al., 1987), despite the fact that in those decades the resources devoted to the issue of Aboriginal people and criminal justice by the 1990s were not available. If one compares the state of research knowledge about possible disparity in the sentencing of minority groups, and especially Aboriginal people in Canada, to other countries with similar populations, it is obvious that despite a number of very expensive and prolonged public inquiries into Aboriginal justice, we still lag far behind. We remain without answers to the central questions concerning sentencing disparity, such as whether there is unwarranted disparity in the disposition and length of sentences given to Aboriginal and non-Aboriginal offenders, how we might explain such variation, and the nature of any social and demographic differences in Aboriginal populations across the country which may affect involvement in the commission of offences and sentencing. This situation is unacceptable, and is made that much more problematic by the tendency evidenced of late to rush head-long into policy reform notwithstanding how little we know about the practices the policies are to reform – the revisions to section 718 of the Canadian Criminal Code and the Supreme Court of Canada's decision in *Gladue* are pertinent examples here.

The absence of data on Aboriginal offenders and sentencing disparity should not be taken to mean that no research has been conducted into sentencing and Aboriginal offenders more generally – although even here the studies are limited. Again we see that important participant observation research is virtually non-existent in this context, and Canadian Centre for Justice Statistics adult criminal court data do not distinguish between Aboriginal and non-Aboriginal accused, eliminating a source of data that could form the focus of analysis on disparity. The limited studies of the sentencing of Aboriginal and non-Aboriginal offenders tend towards a common position that, while carceral sentences may be used more often for Aboriginal offenders, this may be more an issue of *risk* than discrimination. For example, York's research (1995) on federal offenders revealed that disproportionately more of this group were incarcerated while more of the non-Aboriginal group were placed under community supervision, even when controlling for offence type. While this finding may indicate the influence of discrimination insofar as different sentences were awarded for similar offences, it is equally plausible that the distinctions may have been tied to the prior offence histories of those sentenced. Since Aboriginal offenders are more likely to have longer records and therefore present higher risk profiles at sentence, they are more likely to receive incarceration at sentence. Unfortunately, the failure of the researchers to provide important information about number and type of previous offences – factors central to the determination of sentence – of offenders sentenced over the course of the study radically limits its value. A similar study of the provincial court in Manitoba conducted during the course of the Manitoba Inquiry produced parallel findings, namely, that more Aboriginal than non-Aboriginal people received incarceration as a sentence (Hamilton and Sinclair, 1991). The Manitoba research went further, however, incorporating some details of the offence and noting that the Aboriginal group also had more counts and charges, and had committed more offences against the person. The authors argue that overt discrimination explains the greater use of incarceration for the Aboriginal group, as both groups had an equal number of previous offences. Their position is weakened, however, by their failure to provide any information about possible differences in type of previous offences, despite the common knowledge that courts consider both the number *and* the nature of previous offences in determining sentences. Additional research of this kind is required, and it will be of greater value if researchers include more complete information about the factors that influence sentencing.

While there is little well-constructed research to support the differential processing argument at this time, a growing body of work challenges that argument and compels researchers to look for other explanations for over-representation. Research questioning the differential processing position includes that by Moyer et al. (1987), which analysed Aboriginal and non-Aboriginal adult homicide data from 1962 to 1984, and found that the outcome of preliminary hearings showed no difference by race or gender. Aboriginal offenders were more likely to be convicted of manslaughter, and non-Aboriginals of first- or second-degree murder. Almost half of the non-Aboriginal group received life imprisonment, compared to one-fifth of the Aboriginal group, and half of the Aboriginal group received sentences of less than five years, compared to less than a quarter (23 per cent) of non-Aboriginals (Clark, 1989: 22). In a somewhat different but related vein, the Cawsey Inquiry found that only 18 per cent of the new Aboriginal cases in community corrections programs in 1989 were on probation, as compared to 34 per cent of the new non-Aboriginal cases (Cawsey, 1991). However, nearly twice as many Aboriginal offenders were involved in fine option programs as were non-Aboriginal offenders.

Research focusing on sentence length as part of the explanation of over-representation has produced a substantial body of evidence that appears to confirm the somewhat unexpected possibility that Aboriginal offenders receive *shorter sentences* than non-Aboriginal offenders. This finding is consistent across both federal institutions and some provincially sentenced offenders. For example, as early as 1982, Correctional Services Canada (CSC) data '*showed that native admissions tended to be very similar or marginally shorter, than their non-Native counterparts with the same admitting offence'* (Moyer et al., 1987; emphasis added). Since that time, similar findings have been generated in other studies, particularly research involving federal offenders. For example, in their work on recidivism, Hann and Harman (1992) found that non-Aboriginal offenders generally receive longer sentence lengths than Aboriginal offenders. More recently, York (1995) found that non-Aboriginal offenders have a longer mean sentence length (5.2 years) than Aboriginal offenders (4.2 years). At the same time, York also found that 9 per cent more Aboriginal than non-Aboriginal offenders had served a previous sentence and that approximately 75 per cent of the Aboriginal offenders were among the most serious offenders in prison (compared with 59 per cent of the non-Aboriginal inmate population), factors which render the shorter sentence finding that much more curious. For federally sentenced females, the shorter sentence length finding also holds true. The mean sentence length for Aboriginal females was shorter in all offence categories, including total offences (York, 1995). In Ontario provincial institutions, Shaw found Aboriginal women to be serving slightly shorter sentences despite the fact that they had more prior incarcerations (1994: 80).

Disparity in sentence lengths among Aboriginal and non-Aboriginal provincial offenders is less obvious. The CCJS 1999 One-Day Snapshot of Inmates revealed that Aboriginal offenders receive shorter aggregate sentences in Nova Scotia, Manitoba, Saskatchewan, and British Columbia provincial institutions (sentences were the same in Alberta), even though the Aboriginal group committed a disproportionate number of violent offences and were a higher risk/need group (CCJS also found Aboriginal inmates had shorter aggregate sentences in federal institutions). Earlier provincial correctional data for the years 1988–95, collected from Ontario, British Columbia, Alberta, Saskatchewan, and Manitoba, show that sentences for Aboriginal offenders are only marginally shorter than those for non-Aboriginal offenders. Alberta had the largest difference between the groups, with only 9 per cent of the Aboriginal population receiving a sentence of 367 or more days, as compared to 15 per cent of the non-Aboriginal group. Information on sentence length by type of offence was available only for Alberta and Saskatchewan. In both provinces, non-Aboriginal offenders received longer sentences for prison, property, administration/public order, and weapon offences. In Alberta, Aboriginal offenders receive longer sentences for driving offences – a finding which is consistent with overall regional trends in incarceration patterns – but in Saskatchewan, Aboriginal offenders do not receive longer sentences in any of the offence categories, a finding which would seem inconsistent with regional trends (La Prairie, 1996: 42–3). Interestingly, the Manitoba Inquiry report stated that in their provincial court study, sentences for Aboriginal males for 'common offences' (mischief, wilful damage, common assault and theft under) were more severe than sentences for the non-Aboriginal group (Hamilton and Sinclair, 1991: 109). However, provincial data from Manitoba for the years 1988–95 shows that, on average, Aboriginal offenders received slightly shorter sentences overall than did the non-Aboriginal group (La Prairie, 1996: 172), which may suggest variations in sentencing patterns in relation to the offence involved. While the latter may prove to be true, it is nonetheless significant that the Cawsey Inquiry revealed that, in 1989, the average aggregate sentence to Alberta Correctional Centres for non-Aboriginal offenders was 149 days, as compared to 122 days for Aboriginal offenders; for females it was 80 days for non-Aboriginal as compared to 54 days for Aboriginal females (Cawsey, 1991: 1–89). Thus, while it is possible that variations across offences influence sentencing patterns, and may skew overall findings, it is difficult to challenge the quantitative evidence as it currently stands, and to reconcile it with qualitative reports that speak to a quite different reality.

That being said, Clark's qualitative analysis of judicial decision making in Nova Scotia suggested one possible explanation for shorter sentences for Aboriginal offenders: the majority of provincial court judges are aware of the difficult conditions experienced by Aboriginal accused, and this may influence the nature of the sentences they hand down (Clark, 1989). Previously, Hagan (1975) reached a similar conclusion. He found a difference in sentencing patterns among judges who may be characterized as 'law and order' types, and who are less concerned about these issues, and those with less conservative perspectives and greater knowledge, but he also found that advocacy of law and order did not lead to any abuse of discretion or differential treatment of minorities. While conservative judges did not appear to consciously engage in negative discrimination, Hagan found that those who acted outside law and order positions were likely to engage in positive discrimination: 'Judges who are less concerned about the maintenance of law and order appear to use part of their discretion to provide lenient treatment to Indian and Metis offenders. It can be hypothesized that this favourable treatment is intended to compensate for the differential life chances and cultural experiences of persons of native background' (Hagan, 1975).

The findings of Canadian research on sentence length as a factor in overrepresentation have been replicated in other contexts. Research in western Australia also revealed shorter sentence lengths for Aboriginal offenders but, as in Canada, members of the Aboriginal group are more likely to be sentenced to incarceration than community corrections (Harding et al., 1995). The authors note that 'Once convicted, Aborigines are about four to five times more likely to receive a sentence of imprisonment than non-Aborigines ... However, once a decision has been made to imprison, the Higher Courts are likely to impose shorter sentences on Aborigines' (Harding et al., 1995: 75).

At the same time, the western Australia research also documented extraordinarily high levels of intraracial personal victimization, high rates of family violence against children, and the prevalence of spousal violence among the Aborigine as compared to the non-Aborigine group. And, as in Canada, the use of custody is most often used in western Australian courts for person offences (Harding et al., 1995: 73). Thus it may be the case that what works most against Aboriginals in the system is not *who* they are (although the New Zealand research indicates that identity may be an issue at some points in the system), but *what* they have done in the immediate instance and over their personal offending history. This would seem to suggest that, while arguments blaming racism and discrimination in the system for over-representation may have only qualified support, this should not be taken as implying that these factors play no role whatsoever. That is, insofar as Aboriginal offending patterns may be linked with the socio-economic marginality which is very much a product of historic policies promoting assimilation and strategic underdevelopment of Aboriginal communities, the larger discrimination and racism that informed these policies, and which continues to influence Aboriginal lives may help to explain high rates of conflict and disorder, and in turn, over-representation. Once again, then, we are confronted with the possibility that racism and discrimination, like culture, are parts of a much larger, and much more complex, aggregation of elements which combine to foster over-representation. Seen in this light, it is not so much that culture clash arguments are somehow wrong, but rather that their reification of one factor to the detriment or apparent dismissal of others renders their explanation of over-representation too simplistic and limited to accurately represent a full understanding of a very complex reality.

While we have important qualitative and, thanks to the work of Fergusson et al. (2003) in New Zealand, some incipient quantitative evidence of racism and discrimination, at the present time the far greater bulk of the research indicates that Aboriginal offenders in the Canadian criminal justice system are more likely to experience positive rather than negative discrimination in regard to sentencing, especially in terms of such factors as sentence length. Again, however, it is important to look beyond the quantitative reports and to question the appearances they convey. For example, one possible qualification on this finding is the apparent trend within the Aboriginal inmate population to obtain parole later in their sentences than non-Aboriginal inmates, if at all. Parole release data from 1988 revealed that federal Aboriginal offenders were less likely than non-Aboriginal offenders to receive full parole (Canada, 1988b), but more likely to receive temporary absences (Grant and Porporino, 1992). A more recent study by La Prairie, conducted in 1996 for the Ministry of the Solicitor General, found parole rates to be the same for Aboriginal and non-Aboriginal inmates when controlling for violent offences, suggesting a positive shift in parole patterns (La Prairie, 1996). Where disparities in release do exist, they can be explained to some degree by the seriousness of offences committed by Aboriginal offenders (Hann and Harman, 1992), and the generally higher recidivism rates characterizing Aboriginal offenders (York, 1995), both of which speak to the perceived risks presented by Aboriginal offenders seeking early release. Risk profiles are further exacerbated by the sociodemographic realities to which many Aboriginal offenders return upon release, and which may influence the formulation of viable release plans, especially for the most disadvantaged Status Indian offenders. It may be the case that Status offenders, who are the most disadvantaged in the sociodemographic factors (poverty and blocked opportunities, early exposure to substance abuse and violence, etc.) that may encourage greater conflict with the law, are less likely to obtain early release by virtue of precisely the same factors that contributed to their landing in prison in the first place. These factors may also explain intra-Aboriginal disparities in release patterns. This would seem to be an important area for research and analysis, as discrimination may play a role in the awarding of release for Aboriginal offenders – although Clark's (1989) findings on judicial discretion may equally be replicated for parole board members and case management officials who assist in the development of release plans.

It would thus appear that the differential processing explanation for negative discrimination against Aboriginal people in the Canadian criminal justice system is not supported by the quantitative research, which appears instead to support either the absence of discrimination/racism or the possibility that its role is one of positive discrimination. This may be a difficult conclusion to accept, as it runs counter to the experiences of many Aboriginal people caught up in the system. While reports of these experiences constitute an important and compelling element of the over-representation debate, they cannot and should not be discounted. How, then, might we respond to the challenge to the quantitative researches levied by the qualitative reports? For some, the best response is simply to reject the challenge itself: these methods measure different things in different ways, and their outcomes simply reflect different versions of the 'truths' produced by those disparate methods. The problem with this approach, however, is that it tends to encourage a debate of two solitudes – advocates of each method viewing those of the other as somehow less informed or scientific, and thus having little to offer. And yet it seems likely that the most tangible truth resides somewhere in between the explanatory and methodological poles created and occupied by the qualitative and quantitative reports. For example, the qualitative reports consistently communicate that far too many Aboriginal people experience racism throughout the system, while the quantitative reports seem to report with equal consistency that there is either no racism or predominantly positive racism in the system. Lost in the arguments presented by these 'sides,' however, is the possibility that the latter 'truth' does not necessarily undermine the former one. It is possible to experience racism and discrimination notwithstanding whether others perceive it to be present; an offender who views his or her position in the larger society as resulting from racist processes and politics is unlikely to qualify that view based on experiences of positive discrimination in the system, which may well be viewed as simply another racist intrusion into his or her life. This perception is made that much more likely by the realities communicated by the qualitative reports, and exacerbated by the probability that acts of positive discrimination may not be apparent to that offender, who is unlikely to be in a position to compare his or her sentence against that awarded to other offenders, whether Aboriginal or non-aboriginal, for the same offence. Here the larger social realities pressing on Aboriginal lives, accompanied by the unqualified racism evidenced in such documented incidents as the deaths of Osborne or Harper, or 'starlight tours' in Saskatchewan, encourage perceptions of racism in other contexts. That racism is both real and imagined does not undermine its power, and we will avail ourselves little in attempting to overcome the role it plays in over-representation if we do not accept this fact.

Another strain of the differential processing argument emphasizes the role played by 'legal cultural clash' in many of the problems Aboriginal people experience in a non-Aboriginal system, including the over-representation which is a logical outcome of the 'lack of fit' between First Nations offenders and Canadian criminal justice processes and policies. Reflecting the 'debate of the two solitudes' discussed above, these arguments have generally ignored the quantitative reports, preferring instead to generalize a fact of discrimination based on qualitative studies, and focusing upon the very real cultural dissonance between Aboriginal and non-Aboriginal approaches to conflict. This position problematizes not only the notion of 'law,' but also legal processes, goals, and ideas of justice. For much of its history, the culture clash argument has focused upon the direct and negative impact of Western legal culture on Aboriginal experiences, especially in the courts. The most commonly cited example of this is the tendency of some First Nations peoples to show respect by lowering their eyes – a practice which, before a non-Aboriginal judge whose culture shows respect – and transparency – through direct eye contact, was believed to feed directly into assumptions of guilt by the court on the part of the accused. A similar argument has been made about the propriety of prison as a 'culturally apposite' response to wrong-doing. Here, the position is simply that prison is not an effective tool for 'behavioural modification' of people whose cultural background emphasizes restitution, apology, and the provision of an opportunity to demonstrate positive behavioural change. Prison is deemed to be a place that hurts rather than heals, and is thus profoundly unsuited to dealing with Aboriginal offenders.

While the culture clash argument at its core contains a significant and substantial element of truth, as a lever for system change, it is weakened not only by its unclear connection to over-representation, but also by the failure to fully establish that legal cultural clash actually influences over-representation. As if these problems are not sufficient to motivate those arguing legal cultural clash to adopt a more systematic approach, there are also larger difficulties with the position. Given the nature of immigration patterns and the overall heterogeneity of Canadian society, such difficulties include the very real possibility that Aboriginal people are not the only group which could claim a negative impact from culture clash, rendering Aboriginal community restorative justice program advocates vulnerable to the 'thin end of the wedge' arguments so popular with the Right. A similar, but different weakness resides in the reality that, as increasing numbers of Aboriginal people migrate to the cities, they are likely to be subject to a range of other-cultural influences and increasingly distanced from the 'traditional cultural context' experienced in a relatively isolated reserve setting. As Aboriginal people move off-reserve, the nature of their cultural experience may be expected to shift somewhat, and the repertoire of behaviours upon which they may draw to respond to the challenges of a heterogeneous urban environment may be anticipated to expand. In short, as the Aboriginal experience in Canada becomes more urban and exposed to previously remote influences, the legal-cultural clash argument may become more difficult to sustain. And while there is certainly an argument to be made that Aboriginal people, as the First Nations in Canada, have a special claim to policy considerations based upon culture, arguments that focus on culture clash tend to be limited in scope and method. Far more powerful and compelling arguments can be made in support of legal and social change.

In some settings, moreover, the direction and content of the culture clash is probably not what is anticipated by at least some of the literature, which inclines towards the view that the non-Aboriginal system is much more punitive than an Aboriginal one would be. Such assumptions must be challenged, as they do not always hold outside of the predominantly academic circles in which they are popular. In Aboriginal communities, it is not uncommon to hear – often from Elders and through translators – that the problem with the dominant justice system is not that it is unduly punitive, but that it is insufficiently so. Such statements both qualify and reframe the culture-clash position. The qualification resides in the reality not that an Aboriginal justice system is somehow ' kinder and gentler' than a non-Aboriginal one, but rather that there may be quite different perceptions of what constitutes punitive sanctions in the respective cultures. For those communities that remain small and relatively intimate, wherein what anthropologists once referred to as 'face-to-face' social relations persist, and individual quality of life depends largely on reputation and standing, the shame and sanction implicit in facing one's community to acknowledge and atone for wrong-doing may be significant. That this confession and compensation might be followed by reintegration and acceptance back into the community may signal either a profound qualitative difference in the practice of 'justice' in First Nations, or the possibility that they succeed in reintegration where similar non-Aboriginal mechanisms, such as parole or probation, fail. The essence of the position is not that one system is basically 'good' and the other 'bad,' but rather that they seek the same ends in different ways. Too much of the extant literature on Aboriginal justice – and especially that on restorative justice – engages in such a juxtaposition, and thereby impoverishes both the depth and nature of the differences that separate Aboriginal and non-Aboriginal approaches to justice and conflict resolution.

Focusing upon the perceived gulf between approaches to justice, and the oversimplification of that distance, has presented a number of problems both for communities seeking to reinvigorate local control over justice and those state representatives and 'influential outsiders' who would assist them. For example, as noted above, legal-cultural clash arguments have tended for the most part to define the difference as between a 'good' Aboriginal system focused on 'healing' and a 'bad' non-Aboriginal system based on guilt and punishment. This has fostered two tensions. First, insofar as 'healing' systems *are* perceived as kinder and gentler, they risk being viewed as somehow something other than real or serious justice systems, which by dominant – and some community – standards are tough. This has led to a second tension: such systems or programs, however respected and successful they may be, are viewed as mere 'add-ons' to the larger criminal justice system network. The danger is that Aboriginal restorative justice programs, the origins of which are rooted in larger self-government projects, not only run the risk of failing to live up to those roots, but are open to criticisms that they constitute tacit legitimation of the system to which they are attached, notwithstanding resource limitations that may render any other approach practically unfeasible. Thus, for example, sentencing circles, viewed by many commentators as infusing Canadian justice with Aboriginal sentiment that profoundly alters the process of justice for accuseds and victims, may also be seen as essentially accommodationist insofar as the fundamental power relations among system, victim, and offender persist within the circle, and are in fact reinforced as they are obscured by the appearances fostered by the circle process. In like fashion, the system as a whole gains much from an appearance of openness to alternative mechanisms, as the incorporation of restorative justice or conflict resolution processes not only enhance the perceived legitimacy and fairness of the system, but also permit the extension of culpability for that system and its failings beyond the system itself.

Such criticisms may be countered by the assertion that restorative justice is less about changing the system as a whole than about improving the experience of conflict resolution for individuals, one case at a time. However, given that much talk about restorative programs – including sentencing circles – involves grand claims about the social transformation of entire communities, it may be difficult to convince either the sceptics or those communities most in need of such transformation that a piecemeal approach is the preferred strategy.

(b) Higher Aboriginal Offending Levels and Commission by Aboriginal People of the Type of Offences That Are More Likely to Result in Carceral Sentences

Research documenting higher Aboriginal offending levels as well as the commission by Aboriginal people of more serious offences overlap considerably. As noted above, there is, unfortunately, much quantitative support for these explanations. The Aboriginal population does appear to manifest a higher per capita involvement in conflict and disorder activities, including those much more serious offences. For example, on the two factors that are most likely to result in carceral sentences (seriousness of offence and prior record), Weatherburn at al. (2003) found Aboriginal people in Australia much more likely than non-Aboriginal people to be arrested for offences likely to result in imprisonment, and to have a prior record of serious offences. A self-report study of Aboriginal and non-Aboriginal secondary school students corroborated the offence and prior history data. Aboriginal students reported committing significantly more offences over a twelve-month and five-year pe-riod than their non-Aboriginal peers, and this was the case in every category of crime (2003: 7–11).

It is difficult to counter such facts, and yet the numbers must be contextualized within the larger sociodemographic situation of Aboriginal people. Although such a contextual analysis cannot alter the data, it does add two important dimensions to the discussion. First, it is important that Canadians be persuaded out of a common misperception that the problems that render too many Aboriginal communities inherently more criminogenic than non-Aboriginal communities are essentially 'of their own making,' and thus successive Canadian governments, and those who support them and their policies, have only limited responsibility for solving them. Second, it seems quite clear that more than two decades of research on the system and system reform have availed us little. Attending to the sociodemographic elements of offending patterns may shift the focus on criminal justice to a focus on social justice – or more specifically, to a recognition that the absence of the latter leads to over-representation in the former. For while it is difficult to understand or develop ameliorative policy based on the quantitative picture of over-representation, when the numbers are informed by knowledge, for example, that disproportionate numbers of Aboriginal youth fall into the age range most likely to encounter conflict with the law, and that these youth face poverty, blocked opportunity, and early exposure to violence, we can move beyond them to develop policy aimed at the situations which encourage those numbers. In fact, when one looks at the overall portrait of certain communities in Canada, it seems logical to enquire why offending rates are not higher.

An additional difficulty with focusing on offending rates to explain over-representation lies in the fact that the problem may not be offending per se, but rather how we choose to respond to offending. That is, over-representation is caused when we choose to respond to offending in a particular way. Aboriginal offenders present different profiles in comparison to non-Aboriginal offenders, thus they tend to be responded to differently by the justice system, and this leads to over-representation and perceptions of bias. However, inasmuch as the differences arise from the application of similar criteria (offence type, prior offending history, etc.) and processes to all offenders, this begs the question of the direction and shape that should inform efforts to reform, especially given the putative absence of negative discrimination indicated by the quantitative research.

System reform seems to have had little impact, and as we will see, it is too early to judge the impact of community and restorative justice programs. To the degree that critics of such programs have expressed concerns about the potential for net-widening, an important qualification on restorative justice as a 'better way' is thrown into relief, namely, it is unlikely that communities differ greatly with respect to the sort of offences they wish to see addressed. If the findings of La Prairie's research into the Cree can be generalized, devolving control over justice to communities may well result in a rise in local 'crime rates,' as historic tendencies to absorb crime and conflict to keep community members out of the dominant system are averted. We may see an explosion in offending rates owing not to actual increases, but to the arrival in the community of a more user-friendly form of redress. Thus the problem is indeed not offending, but how we respond to it – and our responses to date have been less than fruitful because we have not effectively targeted offending, which is essentially a social justice problem.

(c)   Criminal Justice Policies and Practices That Have a Differential Impact on
Aboriginal Offenders Due to Their Socio-Economic Conditions

Explanations of over-representation that fall within this category generally assert
that the phenomenon is caused at least in part by discrimination, as opposed to
racism. Such explanations are superior to many of the differential processing
arguments, which often fail to distinguish between the two forms of prejudice.
Racism involves overt and conscious attitudes of bias which are willingly and
knowingly translated into both physical and psychological violence against
members of targeted groups; discrimination, while no less devastating in impact,
tends to arise from the unconscious implementation of structures or policies
which were not intended to be discriminatory but which, owing to the manner
in which they interact with larger social structures, have a negative impact on
members of certain groups. The distinction, then, is akin to that between stealing
and borrowing – what makes the difference is the intent behind the actions, the
'mindset' impelling the actor. And while the impacts of discrimination and
racism are equally devastating for those on the receiving end, different types of
prejudice may require quite different policy approaches to ameliorate them.

The differential impact category of efforts to explain over-representation falls
very much in line with the 'life chances arguments' that opened this chapter.
Here, what is of note is the larger sociodemographic context in which far too
many Aboriginal children are raised, which is characterized by poverty, early
exposure to violence, substance abuse, and generally more dysfunctional social
patterns. Such a context not only encourages the likelihood of conflict with the
law, in some cases it may render the choice of a criminal lifestyle a fairly rational
one. Thus the sociodemographic argument not only informs the 'why' of much
Aboriginal offending, wherein the absence of social justice paves the way for a
far greater intrusion of criminal justice agencies, but also explains the differential
impact of those agencies' activities in Aboriginal lives. Such an impact is apparent
in the example of Aboriginal offenders who were found not to qualify for access
to alternative dispute resolution (ADR) processes in one Saskatchewan program,
or who are denied bail or early parole, owing to sociodemographic backgrounds
that encourage higher risk profiles.

While it cannot be doubted that factors such as poverty affect access to justice,
quantitative data indicating positive discrimination against some Aboriginal offenders in regard to some aspects of the system suggests two considerations that
must inform efforts to explain over-representation within this category of explanations. First, it may be that, in some jurisdictions at least, judges are not only
aware of the disadvantaged backgrounds of Aboriginal accused, but take those
factors into account in their sentencing of these offenders. Thus it may be that

sociodemographics are to some degree already controlled for in terms of their contribution to over-representation. Second, if this is indeed the case, our most productive reform efforts may now be directed to a much earlier point in the process. That is, if sociodemographics influence not only the decision – or lack of choice – to engage in acts of conflict and disorder, we may wish to target sociodemographic change and not the criminal justice system. Explanations of over-representation that focus on criminal justice system reform may be distracting attention from the much more necessary reform of the very factors to which much of the responsibility for rates of conflict and disorder among Aboriginal people is attributed. Of course, effecting sociodemographic change would involve massive social policy changes and the meaningful redress of historical treaties and human rights among Aboriginal peoples, and is thus unlikely to find favour with the state and many of those it represents. It may be in that space between criminal justice reform and social justice reform that we can locate the origins of restorative justice – the reform that promises to restore and transform entire communities by changing the way criminal justice is administered to Aboriginal communities in particular.

Explanations in this category require us to redirect our focus outside the justice system to consider larger social and structural elements that may contribute to over-representation, and they offer the most compelling and broad-based critique of both the system and the society with which it interacts. As such, they have played an important role in the genesis and support of community alternatives, while also, sometimes inadvertently, profiling the challenges that may fall against those alternatives. We will turn to a consideration of those challenges later in this text; in the chapter which follows, we discuss and critique the reforms proposed to date to address the problem of over-representation.

CHAPTER 3

Severing the Gordian Knot: Efforts at Institutional Reform and the Rise of Restorative Approaches

Federal expenditures for the 1992–93 fiscal year amounted to $129.6 million, divided between spending on Aboriginal policing ($44.7 million) and correctional services ($84.9 million). The policing component includes $12.3 million to the RCMP and a little over $30 million for First Nations-specific programs, employing 609 First Nations police officers. The correctional component includes costs for the 2,300 self-identified Aboriginal offenders in federal correctional institutions in 1992, together with some $3 million for institutional programs such as Aboriginal spirituality, inmate liaison and substance abuse programs.

Goss Gilroy (Canada, 1996: 294)

Because research is often negatively perceived by Aboriginal people and is of sporadic interest to government, its history of shaping justice projects and influencing policy decision-making has been marginal at best ... despite claims that 'Aboriginal people have been researched to death', the amount of primary and evaluation research funded, when compared to funding allocated to programs, projects, conferences, consultations, workshops, and government structures, has been minimal.

(La Prairie, 1999)

The state has not remained mute in the face of the increasingly intractable problem of over-representation, and the past three decades have witnessed a range of important reforms in the area of Aboriginal criminal justice, reforms which have in turn stimulated a much more broad-based reform of the system as a whole. Initial ameliorative efforts rarely went beyond the piecemeal and limited addition of an 'Aboriginal perspective' to extant justice structures through 'indigenization' and cross-cultural training for predominantly non-Aboriginal system personnel; such reforms were largely cosmetic and did not challenge either the existing monopoly over legal services enjoyed by the dominant system or the discriminatory or myopic manner in which those services were administered. However, in the wake of the 1969 White Paper and the rise of a new Aboriginal consciousness, the drive for more meaningful and substantial reform, situated increasingly within a self-government paradigm, was initiated.

Common to virtually all reform efforts, past and present, however, has been the concept of culture, articulated most recently within restorative justice projects as a thing known and understood only by communities and thus best expressed within community justice projects. The emphasis on culture as the justification for, and blueprint of, criminal justice reform is grounded in two rationales. According to the first, over-representation is the product of discrimination in the criminal justice system resulting from culture conflict. Cross-cultural or cultural sensitivity training for criminal justice personnel are believed to promote a greater understanding of Aboriginal culture and thus to reduce the potential for culture conflict and discrimination. The second rationale emerges in programs directed to Aboriginal offenders and inmates (and in some cases, would-be-offenders) that contain significant 'Aboriginal culture components,' which are believed to render that programming more relevant, comprehensible, and thus effective for Aboriginal peoples in the system.

Although these rationales have informed a wide range of reforms, little of that reform can be clearly linked with research outlining the nature and location of the primary challenges within criminal justice in relation to Aboriginal people, nor has there been significant evaluation of many of the resultant changes in policy, processes, or programming. These weaknesses may have rendered neuter many of the reform efforts of the past thirty years and, insofar as we appear to be repeating the same mistakes in regard to the rise and implementation of restorative justice, more recent reforms may risk similar failures.

(i) Changing the Psyche to Change the Cycle: Cross-Cultural Training, Cultural Sensitivity, and Indigenization

Consistent with perceptions that Aboriginal people experience discriminatory treatment in the criminal justice system largely as a result of ignorance or racism on the part of those administering the system, much early reform effort was directed to educating justice personnel about Aboriginal culture and traditions, in the hope that knowledge of First Nations would effectively redress the particular forms of ignorance that inform racist attitudes and discriminatory practices. Since ignorance was perceived to penetrate every level of the system, such programming rapidly infused training and practices across criminal justice personnel.

Police, as the largest and most visible component of the criminal justice system, were among the first recipients of 'cultural education' programs. That the police were in need of such training was clearly evidenced in the documentation of systemic racism and discrimination central to the reports of the inquiries into the wrongful conviction of Donald Marshall, Jr, and the deaths of J.J. Harper and Helen Betty Osborne. While the errors and failings documented in those reports were unambiguous, their qualitative, case-based approach made a focus on personnel almost unavoidable. The compelling first-hand reports from Aboriginal people of the racism they had experienced at the hands of police and courts personalized not only the victims but the perpetrators of the wrongdoing. And in the general absence of social science research that might have informed this focus, the problems of Aboriginal people in the system were seen to be created by personnel, rather than by the nature and structure of the system and society within which they functioned. The consequences of this approach for reform were significant. If 'people' were the problem, no significant alteration to the larger system and structures was required. If those people were taught the error of their ways through continued education and training, reform would inevitably follow. Equally, if the problem was the people in the system, consideration of the role of dysfunctional communities and the contribution of criminogenic environments to placing many Aboriginal people in this particular sort of harm's way need not inform policy efforts. It is thus not surprising that the state directed its reform efforts to improving personnel. Aboriginal leaders, however, acknowledging education and training as an 'immediate step in the right direction to changing the perception of Native justice issues by justice officials' (MacGregor, in Canada, 1996: 99) also argued for much more broad-based system and social reforms.

Consistent with the assumption that ignorance lay at the heart of the problem, virtually all components of the system began to emphasize cross-cultural or 'sensitivity' training in both their training of new personnel and as part of the longer term professional development of more senior actors. This initial reform thrust was quickly followed by a second wave of reform tied to the cultural awareness approach: indigenization. Recognizing that cross-cultural training could only be expected to reach so far towards reform targets, the next best approach was felt to be the recruitment of Aboriginal people for criminal justice roles that were previously the sole province of members of the dominant culture. Through indigenization, and subsequent efforts to develop fully Aboriginal police forces and courts, criminal justice was to be rendered more relevant, sensitive and efficient for Aboriginal peoples and communities.

(a) Cross-Cultural and Cultural Sensitivity Training Programs

Cross-cultural training is perhaps best understood within the larger 'intercultural education' movement that emerged within policing in the early 1980s and was intended to assist police forces to respond to the changes to their function necessitated by the growing multiculturalism of Canadian society (Stenning, 2003: 12–13). Intercultural training was directed toward four objectives:

1. To encourage interaction and understanding between members of the police department and members of the racial and cultural minority communities.
2. To develop understanding of and sensitivity to the values, beliefs and behaviours of people from racial and cultural groups different from one's own.
3. To assist the police to utilize minority community resources and apply strategies which will work effectively in policing minority communities.
4. To provide members of minority communities with an understanding of how the police department operates, what community service programs it provides, and how minority communities can relate to the police department (Miner, 1984: 88, in Stenning, 2003: 12)

In essence, these programs were aimed at altering the beliefs underlying prejudicial attitudes by attempting to provide awareness and understanding through the provision of information (Hill and Augustinos, 2001). As such, and with some modifications consistent with the target group of the training, cross-cultural awareness and education programs manifested – and continue to manifest – similar founding assumptions feeding into similar training structures: 'this information is typically proffered in a seminar or workshop style group via readings, films, and discussions on the target outgroup's history, achievements and contributions. Some programmes also incorporate an intergroup contact element, using members of the target group to administer the intervention' (Hill and Augustinos, 2001). Such training is commonplace in the current Canadian criminal justice system, and is probably best exemplified in the approach taken by the RCMP. Even a brief visit to their website provides ample evidence of their commitment to become more 'Aboriginal-friendly' through the education of non-Aboriginal officers and the recruitment of Aboriginal ones. The RCMP Native Spirituality Guide, for example, offers information 'to help police officers gain an understanding of sacred ceremonies practised and sacred items carried by many Native people across Canada' (RCMP, 1998: 1). To this end, the guide describes 'the circle of life,' sweat lodges, and 'spiritual artifacts.' While the direct relevance of much of this to the police function is initially unclear, readers are subsequently given direction regarding the 'policing' of sacred articles and officers are warned that they may see more of these sacred items in carring out their duties: 'Male enforcement officers may conduct a search of someone wearing these [sic] without incident if they ask the wearer to open the bundle. If the person is genuine, then the request will be granted ... What is important to remember is that in ever increasing numbers, Natives are returning to their own heritage in expressing their religious beliefs. These sacred objects may be encountered with greater frequency now that spiritual Elders often travel great distances to conduct their sacred ceremonies. While keeping public safety in mind, security personnel should endeavour to make themselves more aware of these traditions and the artifacts involved through increased cross-cultural awareness' (RCMP, 1998: 11–12). This direction reveals the inherent contradictions of cross-cultural training, which seems as much about expanding and enhancing efficiency of the police function as it is about more informed and aware administration of justice. Insofar as the former goal may have more to do with net-widening and the improvement of charging and clearance rates in policing Aboriginal peoples and communities, the latter may prove elusive.

Judges too may attend cultural awareness workshops, while lawyers can access such training through their local bar associations as well as a range of conferences on Aboriginal justice offered by government, academics, and private educational institutes. Even prisons have embraced more 'culturally informed' approaches to incarceration. For example, in the five-year review of the *Corrections and Conditional Release Act* released in February of 1998, Correctional Services Canada boasted that:

> Over the past few years, the Board has used General Board meetings and regional meetings as opportunities to provide members and staff with information and sensitivity training on various Aboriginal issues. Aboriginal workshops were a significant part of the 1990, 1991, 1992, 1995 and 1996 General Board meetings. In addition, one day at the 1997 General Board meeting was devoted to Aboriginal issues. Topics at these meetings covered: native perceptions of the parole process, family violence, Aboriginal traditional treatment, risk assessment and violent offending, substance abuse and reintegration ... Newly appointed Board members are provided with an Orientation Manual, which includes a chapter on Aboriginal offenders ... Several cultural workshops for Board members and staff have been held. Specifically, national office Board members have attended: a 2 day session in March, 1994 on self-esteem and Aboriginal offenders as it relates to risk assessment; a two-day workshop in January, 1996 in Belleville to provide first-hand experience and knowledge of the realities of life on a reserve, the role of elders, and ceremonies; and

a 2 day session on Aboriginal institutional programming and the assessment of risk. In addition, Regional Board members and staff have also participated in several cross cultural workshops. (Canada, 1998: 6–7)

The state and the justice system have embraced cross-cultural training with a degree of enthusiasm rivalled only by the affection of the courts for sentencing circles, and probably for the same reasons. Cultural awareness programs require comparatively limited resources and foster an appearance that the state is reforming the system when, in fact, the programs in question involve little, if any, significant change to the larger system and structure. Limited in vision, these programs appear equally limited in impact. Indeed, it may be within the vision that we find the seeds of an explanation for that limited impact: like the 'Indian policy' that created dysfunctional communities and unacceptable levels of Aboriginal conflict with the law, cross-cultural training is based on misguided assumptions. The limited efficacy and negative, unintended effects of policies of civilization and assimilation were seen not as the result of any weaknesses in the policies themselves, rather, in the nature of the recipients. The problem with Indian policy, that is, was the Indians, not the policies. If cross-cultural training is any indication, Aboriginal justice policy does not seem to have moved beyond such perceptions. This approach too appears to be based on a belief that 'culture,' rather than the nature of the system or the society in which it operates, is responsible for the dissonance between Aboriginal people and the criminal justice system. And yet, there is limited evidence to suggest that traditional culture is, in fact, the larger part of the problem Aboriginal people currently experience in the dominant justice system.

Given that a large percentage of Aboriginal offenders reside in urban environments and may have limited contact with, or awareness of, their traditional cultural heritage, 'culture' would seem at best a very partial explanation of those problems. It is difficult to see how culture conflict can be such a violent part of the equation when so many Aboriginal inmates, for example, credit 'cultural awareness programs' and Elders' visits in prison for their initiation into traditional culture. This seems especially so in regard to conflicts between police and Aboriginal people in an urban context, where differential policing may have as much to do with the urban Aboriginal reality of poverty, visibility, and marginality as it does with Aboriginality per se. In this context in particular, it seems likely that what is as necessary as education about the 'differences' between Aboriginal and non-Aboriginal cultures is an understanding of the similarities across the life circumstances of those people who live on the margins of our society, and who face clear and negative consequences from agents of authority for doing so. Thus to really understand the circumstances of many Aboriginal people in the city, for example, we must work through the layers of their experiences of poverty, powerlessness, substance abuse, personal histories of abuse and loss, social dislocation, *and* racism, and attempt to determine which are the most potentially effective targets for reform efforts. The challenge, of course, is that a determination that the problem is largely rooted, for example, in poverty, involves a much different focus and direction of reform, and notwithstanding the fact that Aboriginal poverty is a consequence of historic state policies of deliberate underdevelopment and marginalization, there may be little motivation to treat it differently from the poverty of any other group. Conversely, should we discover that ethnicity plays a role in how Aboriginal people are policed, and yet there seems little reason to interpret that role as fundamentally one of conflict between *cultures* (as opposed to more 'simple' issues of intolerance of difference), the problem may be one of racism.

If racism is the problem, attempts to encourage understanding of Aboriginal peoples and cultures on the part of system actors would seem valuable. There is little research, however, to suggest that cross-cultural training actually works; we have little systematic evidence, that is, of the efficacy of cross-cultural or sensitivity training as mechanisms for undermining prejudice in the administration of justice. Evaluations of Canadian cross-cultural and intercultural training programs have been somewhat discouraging: 'While evaluators found there have been some benefits from the interactions between police personnel and representatives of minority groups participating in the courses in terms of communication and sharing of information, they were skeptical about the impact of the courses on police attitudes and practices. In particular, evaluators noted "that the 'power' of the workshop experience was insufficient to counter the 'power' of the social forces which shape attitude development." within the police' (Stenning, 2003: 13). This conclusion is echoed in evaluations of cross-cultural education programs targeting Aboriginal cultural awareness: 'While it is usually found that participant-knowledge about the target group and related social issues increases, there is scant evidence that the programmes produce a change in attitudes or behaviour. Moreover, even when effects due to the programme are found, there has been no research as to how enduring these effects are' (Hill and Augustinos, 2001: 247).

This finding was prominent in a recent evaluation of an anti-racism education course that comprised one part of the staff training program given to the Courts Administration Authority (CAA) in southern Australia. Consistent with the goals of cross- and inter-cultural training, the program was intended to 'increase knowledge about indigenous history and culture and to reduce prejudice towards Aboriginal Australians' (Hill and Augustinos 2001: 247). The CAA cross-cultural training program was delivered in a series of workshops conducted over three days. Attendance was mandatory, and each day was dedicated to a particular subject, including Aboriginal history from an Aboriginal perspective, stereotyping and prejudice, and 'racism role-plays,' which had trainees experience racism as perpetrators, recipients, and witnesses. All workshops incorporated videos and small group activities, as well as debate and discussion between students and facilitators (Hill and Augustinos, 2001: 247). The goals were essentially consistent with cultural awareness training more generally, and included the development of a broader understanding of Aboriginal peoples and their cultures, past and present, as well as an appreciation of stereotypical or prejudiced attitudes and advice on how to eliminate them and reinforce positive attitudes. Central to both these goals and the strategies designed to achieve them was contact with members of the 'target outgroup' as a primary means of combating stereotypes.

The evaluation focused on assessing the CAA training in terms of three of its goals: changes in knowledge, attitudes, and stereotyping. To this end, they assessed participants' knowledge, attitudes, and stereotyping before the training, immediately after the conclusion of the workshops, and three months later. They expected to find significant positive changes at all points of evaluation; as it turned out, those expectations were too high.[1] The evaluation revealed that the cross-cultural training program had a significant impact in the immediate aftermath of the workshops. That is, all participants indicated an increase in knowledge of Aboriginal Australians' history, culture, and current circumstances, as well as *some degree of reduction* in negative attitudes and stereotypes *over the immediate short term*. At the three-month post-training assessment, it was found that, while most program participants had retained the knowledge they had been given about Australian Aboriginal peoples, similar persistence in reductions in negative attitudes and stereotyping did not endure. In fact, it was only among the most pronounced 'red-neck'[2] racists that a significant, sustained decrease in 'old-fashioned prejudice' was apparent (Hill and Augustinos, 2001: 258). As well, there is some reason to be sceptical about the nature of the knowledge retention. As noted by the researchers, the 'General Knowledge Device' enlisted to assess persistence of knowledge gained in the training program is highly vulnerable to practice effects, and thus it may be that taking the same test three times in three months may have had more to do with the retention of knowledge about the test than either the training provided or the nature of the knowledge it presented. Insofar as logic would seem to suggest that knowledge of a marginalized group may encourage understanding of that group and their circumstances, ideally leading to a reduction in negative attitudes towards, and stereotyping of, that group, the fact that prejudice reduction did not seem to persist suggests that we ought not to assume too much about the nature and quality of the knowledge taken away from the CAA course. One also cannot help but query whether, when it comes to prejudice reduction, it is less difficult to soften the edges of the extremes than to challenge the unconscious prejudice of the mushy middle.

It should also be noted that the cross-cultural training given to the CAA employees not only failed to reduce negative stereotyping among the majority of trainees, it was similarly unable to increase endorsement of the positive stereotyping that is one part of modern racism (Hill and Augustinos, 2001: 258). This is interesting, as a central component of much cross-cultural training involves bringing together trainees and members of the target outgroup, Aboriginal peoples, to direct and participate in workshops intended to combat stereotypes. The rationale for this approach is that intergroup contact encourages prejudice reduction, that is, the facilitation of positive interactions between groups will render the tenability of negative stereotypes increasingly weak, thereby reducing racism. However, while participants in the present study initially deemed the Aboriginal facilitators to be typical of Australian Aboriginals, over the post-program evaluation period this perception seems to have altered such that, by the three-month post-test, the Aboriginal facilitators were clearly deemed to be atypical (Hill and Augustinos, 2001: 259). This finding suggests that a particular conundrum affects cross-cultural training programs focusing on an intergroup contact approach. Stereotype reduction requires that one challenge that stereotype as befitting all members of the target group; however, as the researchers note, 'the stereotype of Australian Aboriginals is overwhelmingly negative ... making it extremely difficult to locate "typical" Aboriginal Australians who would still disconfirm the stereotype' (Hill and Augustinos, 2001: 259). Hence a paradox emerges for cross-cultural training programs – how can you show that stereotypes do not hold by exposing people to individuals they can easily perceive as the exception to that stereotype, rather than the rule? To state it another way, while almost everyone is racist in general, very few people are racist in particular – we all know someone who contradicts the stereotype, but that does not seem to undermine our more general perspective. This someone does not make us question the stereotype; we instead view the individual as an aberration who reinforces our negative general prejudice. If my friend could 'rise above it,' why can't 'all the others'?

The fundamental problem with cross-cultural training programs is that, simply put, they may have underestimated the toughness of the nuts to be cracked. For example, research into stereotyping behaviour strongly suggests that stereotyping is *functional* – that is, it serves a particular purpose for those who engage it. Social psychologists looking at stereotyping and prejudice have recently confirmed just how resistant stereotypes are to change. First, stereotypes help people to make sense of an often confusing and contradictory world. That is, stereotyping is an adaptive behaviour that serves a useful purpose for those who engage it – 'stereotypes must be resistant to change, or undermine their own role as relatively stable structures to make sense of the world' (Hill and Augustinos, 2001: 259). Second, and in our view more compellingly, it has been argued that stereotyping serves important social functions, insofar as stereotypes contain 'useful' information about the nature of intergroup relations. As observed by Hill and Augoustinos in their evaluation: 'The content of stereotypes is, then, both descriptive and explanatory, and hence functional in that it provides the perceiver with information that describes, explains, and rationalizes existing social arrangements. Stereotype change becomes difficult from this perspective because the stereotype is useful to the perceiver. Any immediate short-term changes from stereotype change interventions are not sustained because participants emerge from the programme to find that the world remains unchanged and that the beliefs they went into the programme with are still *useful*' (2001: 259). For the police officer on the inner city beat, stereotypes of the Aboriginal people he or she encounters permit the development of almost reflexive strategies for dealing with those encounters, enabling the officer to avoid the risks associated with the development of empathy or sensitivity to the circumstances of those being policed. If one assumes, as one police officer of the Winnipeg Police Department did, that Aboriginal people are found 'on Main Street and that's what they do with what they get [waste benefit entitlements on a marginal lifestyle]' (Aboriginal Justice Implementation Commission [AJIC] 1999), policing becomes a relatively unproblematic activity – the stereotyped and negative experiences inner city Aboriginal people have with police become the well-deserved consequences of their own choices, as opposed to the result of ignorance or racist choices on behalf of police officers. Insofar as this manner of perception is, as Hill and Augoustinos observe, 'functional' for the perceiver, the degree to which it promotes dysfunction in the administration of justice will remain a secondary consideration for those implementing those services, and thereby that much more difficult to reform.

Evaluations of cross-cultural training in both Canada and Australia suggest that such programs present very limited potential for securing significant, sustainable reform of justice services to Aboriginal people. Stereotypes are remarkably intractable, and institutions appear to have a very limited commitment to providing the sort of the training that might erode them. For example, cross-cultural training in most locations in the criminal justice system is voluntary, and those most in need of that training are the least likely to volunteer for it. Participants who recognize the importance of such training and the issues which impel it, as well as the possibility that they may be improved by participation, are invariably those least in need of such programming in the first place. Retired Supreme Court Justice Bertha Wilson observed that even those judges who fall short of holding overtly negative views of others tend not to perceive themselves as prone to stereotyping or similar 'limitations in perspective' (Wilson, 1990). If one does not perceive a lack or need, where is the motivation to fill it?

The general lack of commitment to serious cross-cultural training is indicative of the challenges characterizing Aboriginal justice reform approaches generally. On the one hand, such training is probably less costly to the system in monetary and political terms than many other reforms. It also has the added benefit of being conspicuous and thus reinforcing a perceived commitment to reform. And it may, despite its failings – most of which are institutional in creation – have an impact on at least some personnel some of the time, which is better than doing nothing. On the other hand, evaluations of extant programs have strongly indicated that they do not have a sufficient impact to make them worthwhile. Such outcomes have led, in turn, to a frantic search to find an approach that does have such impact, producing a proliferation of methods and approaches directed to ever more wide-reaching goals – all of which seem ultimately to be ignored in favour of the workshop, target-group facilitator approach which has been shown to be problematic. Given the disparities between approaches and their tendency towards multiple and often unclear goals, standardized evaluation becomes difficult, if not impossible. We tend, therefore, to remain focused on 'original models' not because they work, but because we are at a loss regarding what will work. In the face of such uncertainty, we pursue a wide variety of strategies at once – not necessarily a bad way of proceeding, if those strategies are fully informed, supported, and sustainable. The problem with regard to cross-cultural training, however, is that the current approach 'falls so far short of what is needed, in both design and delivery, that it is not only inadequate but may also result in reinforcing stereotypes' (Ontario Race Relations and Policing Task Force, 1989: 97).

It seems, then, that if we are truly committed to cross-cultural training, we must either step up to the plate or abandon the game. As it now stands, we are investing a not insignificant measure of human and monetary resources into the widespread mobilization of a program that appears to have only modest impacts on most participants for a very limited time, and significant impacts on only a few extreme cases for any length of time. Certainly there is an argument to be made that the resources consumed by such programs may be better channelled towards more promising program directions. Given the limited evaluation of most Aboriginal justice programming, however, it might be difficult to determine the appropriate direction. Assuming that we are not prepared to abandon cross-cultural and cultural sensitivity training as it is currently conceived and delivered, we must at the very least be mindful of its limitations, and of the warning expressed by the Ontario Native Council on Justice to the Royal

Commission nearly a decade ago – that we may be doing little more with this reform than 'creating culturally aware racists' (Canada, 1996: 100). If this is true, the potential of such training even to provide an effective 'band aid' on the way to better justice through Aboriginal self-government is called into question.

(b) Indigenization

The conviction that culture is the key to unlocking a superior system of justice for Aboriginal people is also evident in the movement towards indigenization of many aspects of the system. Indigenization is premised upon the notion that the juridical experience of Aboriginal people can be fundamentally altered by slotting Aboriginal personnel into the various roles of the justice system previously filled by non-Aboriginal personnel, thereby 'indigenizing' or 'indianizing' the 'white' system. Indigenization – like cross-cultural training – is thus based upon an assumption that the system is basically 'good,' and only minor reforms are necessary to render it equally 'good' for all people. As framed by the Royal Commission on Aboriginal Peoples: 'Philosophically, these programs start from the premise that all people living in Canada should be subject to the same justice system, but that special measures may have to be taken to make that system understandable and comfortable to Aboriginal people who come to it from a different perspective' (Canada, 1996: 93). As noted earlier, there is an argument to be made that it is these defining principles which doom indigenization and cross-cultural training to limited impacts and outcomes, insofar as they appear to share a belief that the problem is people, not structures and processes. System personnel require enlightenment, and Aboriginal and non-Aboriginal facilitators and educators must provide it. Similarly, in the realm of indigenization, the burden of reform is placed squarely on the shoulders of those Aboriginal people who consent to participate in an indigenized program. Here, it is the Aboriginal police officer, lawyer, judge, or correctional officer who must 'break the psyche' of colleagues and justice administration, and thereby somehow alter the cycle of Aboriginal over-representation. Is it fair to place this responsibility on Aboriginal people? Can these programs work?

As a means of reform, indigenization has a range of targets. Within the system, this approach articulates the same essential assumptions of the culture contact and prejudice change hypotheses contained within cross-cultural training, as it brings Aboriginal people into the system to work alongside non-Aboriginal personnel in the administration of justice. The expected result of such contact is that non-Aboriginal system personnel will be exposed to Aboriginal people in a context and capacity that will force the questioning of stereotypes and a subsequent alteration of pre-enlightenment practices. In essence, indigenization creates a sort of long-term, intensive cross-cultural training program as Aboriginal and non-Aboriginal people work together in police cars, courtrooms, and correctional facilities. As with more conventional cross-cultural training, however, indigenization suffers from the paradox of typicality, wherein non-Aboriginal police officers, for example, may simply come to see their Aboriginal colleagues as aberrations which do not suggest any great need to rethink pre-existing stereotypes of Aboriginal people 'in general.' At the same time as perceptions of Aboriginal justice personnel as atypical are problematic, so too is the very real possibility that such personnel will be perceived by non-Aboriginal colleagues not as aberrations, but as threats to established system cultures and structures, resulting in the rejection of the Aboriginal justice worker as either colleague or agent of change.

The experience of some indigenized police officers strongly suggests that this outcome is a common one in indigenization, and a significant barrier to the success of such initiatives. The problem, moreover, is not limited to the internal workings of agencies experimenting with indigenization: the indigenized 'cop' in particular may face rejection also by the Aboriginal community he or she is expected to police. The rejection of indigenized justice workers is often the result of a perception by some community members that these personnel are 'turncoats' or 'apples' – red on the outside, white on the inside. Clearly, indigenization is not without costs, and those costs may well fall disproportionately on those their very ambiguous effects are intended to benefit.

Probably the most well-known and oft-cited experiment in indigenization is that of the RCMP's 'special constable program.' The largest such policing initiative, the special constable program was implemented in 1973 following the report of the Federal Task Force Report on Policing on Reserves. This report had proposed and considered three models through which the policing of Aboriginal people and communities could be achieved. Two of these options focused upon the development of autonomous police forces on reserves, which would be administered and staffed by community members. Citing an absence of local expertise and agency to make such an approach workable, the report opted instead for the development of the special constable program within the RCMP. Many felt that this choice was *fait accompli* long before the report was released, given the proximity of senior and former RCMP members to the Task Force, and it essentially placed the responsibility for reforming the problems with Aboriginal policing to the very body which had been credited with creating most of those problems in the first place. While this may seem odd, and perhaps misdirected, Harding argues that, given the exigencies of the moment, it was the perfect choice: the development of a special constable program created within the RCMP a new mechanism for extending social control on reserves

and of Aboriginal people, obscured within a rhetoric of 'mentorship' and facilitation of self-government (1992: 631). Like cross-cultural training, the special
constable program seemed much less about improving the way Aboriginal people
were policed than it was about enhancing the efficiency of that policing function –
two very different ends. Notwithstanding these tensions, by 1989 there were 189
Aboriginal special constables participating in the RCMP initiative.

Problems with the program emerged fast on the heels of its implementation.
At the most basic level, while the program was often linked to self-government,
band councils had little role in, and no control over, the program or those who
participated. Aboriginal constables were recruited by the RCMP, and were
answerable to the detachment to which they were assigned. The special constables were trained by the RCMP, but the training provided was inferior to that
given to 'regular' members and clearly, if not intentionally, designed to facilitate a
subordinate status. While non-Aboriginal recruits received twenty-five weeks of
training at the RCMP training facility in Regina, the Aboriginal special constables – who were subjected to less rigorous entrance standards – received only
sixteen weeks of training, followed by six months of 'field training' not required
of regular members. As well, although the special constables were given full peace
officer status on and off reserves, they were paid less, faced highly circumscribed
potential for advancement in the ranks, and tended towards very different types
of duties (Hamilton and Sinclair, 1991: 612–13). Aboriginal special constables
found themselves disproportionately directed to dealing with acts of conflict and
disorder on reserves, and to situations that regular officers found unduly dis-
agreeable. As reported by the Royal Commission on Justice and Aboriginal
People, 'Chief Enil Keeper of Little Grand Rapids was a special constable at one
time. He spoke of being called names and being given the dirty jobs to do. He
said that he did not have the same privileges as the white officers. He was called
"Blood" and his partner used to say things like "let's go shoot another Indian"'
(Hamilton and Sinclair, 1991: 612–13).

Given that the primary goal of the program was to render policing services
more 'appropriate' by having Aboriginal officers police Aboriginal people and
conflicts, the direction of the special constables towards such ends was perhaps an
understandable turn of policy. However, the practice rapidly proved to be
extremely stressful for the special constables who, in policing their own, met
with criticisms for ethnocentrism from their clients that non-Aboriginal officers
could avoid, and judgment by colleagues who assumed all special constables
would tend towards positive discrimination in policing Aboriginal communities.
Many Aboriginal participants in the program also reported experiencing racism
and intolerance from their non-Aboriginal colleagues.

Pressures such as these motivated many Aboriginal special constables to leave the force, and in the face of these defections, and increasing public pressure, the RCMP disbanded the Indian Special Constable Program in 1990. It was replaced by a program of 'structured entry' for Aboriginal recruits, whereby deficiencies in qualifications such as educational requirements will not stand as a bar to recruitment, and Aboriginal recruits will have two years to upgrade. Once accepted into the force, Aboriginal RCMP will have the same powers, potential, and levels of compensation as regular members. While this approach may alleviate some of the problems inherent in the special constables' inferior status and opportunities, it arguably does little or nothing to resolve concerns about community input or control over policing administered by the RCMP, or to ameliorate the racism and discrimination experienced by Aboriginal RCMP. It is also important to remember that the evident failings of the special constable program have not led to the dismantling of similar special constable programs in other policing agencies: the Ontario Provincial Police Force, for example, continues to offer a special constable program.

While the RCMP's initiative is the most notorious, indigenization of the policing function has also transpired under a range of arrangements made pursuant to federal and provincial agreements, *Indian Act* by-laws, and provincial legislation. These arrangements vary across communities, but they remain re-markably consistent in their general tendency to adopt a mainstream approach to policing which is animated and administered by Aboriginal people. For example, since 1978 the Amerindian Police Council has operated in Quebec as a non-profit corporation with a federal charter to police approximately twenty-three First Nation Communities in that province. In the same year, the Sûreté du Québec established an Aboriginal Police Program for those communities associ-ated under the James Bay and Northern Quebec Agreement and the Cree and Naskapi Northeastern Agreement, including nine Cree communities, the Inuit, and the Naskapi of Kawawachikamach (Canada, 1996: 84).[3]

In June 1991, the federal government announced the implementation of a new First Nations Policing Policy, transferring authority for this function from the Department of Indian Affairs and Northern Development to the Ministry of the Solicitor General (Solicitor General Canada, 1992). Under this policy, policing of reserves was to be determined through tripartite negotiations involv-ing the community and the federal and provincial/territorial governments, who were to offer expertise and funding at rates of 52 and 48 per cent, respectively, to support the on-reserve policing arrangements. While the government boasted that this policy would 'provide 80 percent of the on-reserve population with First Nations policing service by 1995–96,' insofar as the exodus from reserves was well underway even then, it is doubtful that a majority of Aboriginal people experienced more 'culturally relevant' or indigenized policing in the wake of the implementation of this policy in 1992. Given that the majority of Aboriginal people now live in cities, on-reserve policing is increasingly irrelevant. The best chance of being policed by an Aboriginal person for these off-reserve individuals, resides in the success of urban, non-Aboriginal forces to attract Aboriginal people to join their ranks. While these chances are not good, they appear to be improving. In Montreal in 1996, for example, Aboriginal people constituted 0.3 per cent of the city's population, and 0.4 per cent of the Montreal Urban Police; in Vancouver in the same year, Aboriginal people constituted 2.2 per cent of the urban population and 3.8 per cent of the provincial population, and they comprised 3 per cent of the recruits receiving training at the British Columbia Police Academy (Stenning, 2003: 12). It would seem, then, that at the level of both governments and police institutions, indigenization remains the primary focus in First Nations policing.

The fundamental raison d'etre for indigenization was to empower Aboriginal people to police their own communities. In so doing, indigenization would, in one fell swoop, mend much of the rift between police and Aboriginal people. An indigenized police force would eliminate 'culture conflict,' as the police and those they serve would share the same traditional and community culture, and encourage a more 'traditional' type of social control. Insofar as control over the local, indigenized force resides in the band council or similar body, the police would also become more accountable to, and under the control of, the community. In short, through indigenization, Aboriginal communities would receive better policing than they had previously received from non-Aboriginal forces.

There can be little question that those more rural or isolated communities that received police services from a distant RCMP detachment and who rarely saw police in their proactive capacity, and only long after the fact of an emergency in reactive mode, obtained more immediate and informed policing insofar as the police were now localized and, in most cases, came from the same community. However, beyond this benefit, it seems clear that, like much policy in Aboriginal justice, indigenization was informed by a number of unfounded assumptions. While culture might have been one part of a much larger and more complex set of challenges facing policing and Aboriginal people, it was by no means the only – or perhaps even the largest – part of those challenges. Being policed by people from one's own community greatly enhances the possibility of overlap in language and culture, and thus eliminates the barriers to effective interaction or communication created by gaps in these things. However, indigenization in its permutation as band policing runs the risk of exchanging one set of cultural problems for another. That is, it is possible to share language and locality, but to participate in very different – and possibly dysfunctional – community cultures. In their examination of patterns of conflict and disorder among the James Bay

Cree, La Prairie and Leguerrier found a significant asymmetry among the rates of requests for the police to respond to violent interpersonal events and the numbers of charges laid by those police, as well as the degree of importance they assigned to such conflicts. They note that: 'The official data do not provide an accurate accounting of the actual events in most communities … The way spousal assaults are dealt with by police in the Cree communities exacerbates the problem of recording (and does not reflect the provincial charging policy as not all Cree officers were even familiar with the policy)' (La Prairie and Leguerrier, 1991: 159–60). This statement offers critical insights into the challenges facing community policing in First Nations. Accepting that the policing of interpersonal and family violence is a difficult task, and that state policies in regard to domestic violence are often ineffectual and less than victim-friendly, La Prairie and Leguerrier observe that '[i]n interpersonal disputes (particularly assaults) there is a strong correlation between what victims want to do and opening a file' (La Prairie and Leguerrier, 1991: 156). While this would seem to suggest that, in policing domestic conflicts, Cree police are prepared to adopt a more victim-friendly approach, other findings from this and related studies suggest that the benefit may not be an unqualified one. For example, while respecting some degree of victim control over the decision to proceed is important, it fails to consider that victims may require a significant degree of support to proceed, and communities may be unable to provide the support necessary to facilitate action by victims who might otherwise choose to proceed. Reports from James Bay suggest that police often tell victims that, should they request that police lay charges against an abusive spouse or partner, 'the victim will have to go all the way with it, which clearly discourages victims from proceeding further' (La Prairie and Leguerrier, 1991: 156). And while such advice may simply reflect the frustration many police agencies experience when dealing with domestic violence, in the Cree context the reluctance to charge seems to be the result of a much more complex interplay of factors. Among these factors is the finding that police were also often less willing to lay charges where there was a perceived 'repetitiveness of incidents' (La Prairie and Leguerrier, 1991: 157), as if the frequency of violence somehow rendered it more mundane and less important to redress. Brodeur noted a similar tendency to view these sort of offences as 'seasonal, time-sensitive and alcohol-related,' and family violence in particular as 'serious' but generally beyond the power of Cree police to resolve (Brodeur and Leguerrier, 1991: xi). A further, interesting, addition to the mix is the different charging rates in Cree communities, depending upon whether the police are local or from outside the community: 'Opening official files for interpersonal reports (assaults, "getting mad," fights, family and private disturbances, threats) varies from 73% in Nemaska to 10% in Mistissini with the other [seven] communities between these two extremes. It is noteworthy that the two communities with the lowest attrition [in charging rates] are those with a policeman not from the community (Nemaska) and with a constant S[ureté du] Q[uébec] presence (Whapmagoostui)' (La Prairie and Leguerrier, 1991: 156).

While, as La Prairie and Leguerrier note, this finding lends additional credence to the ongoing concern about the difficulties experienced by Aboriginal police in their own, often small, isolated communities, it also suggests a very important issue which has remained largely on the margins of discussions of Aboriginal policing. That is, when it comes to maintaining their communities as secure, peaceful places to live, Aboriginal people want and deserve at least the same quality of policing as non-Aboriginal communities demand and receive. Too often, Aboriginal people turning to police, whether their own or non-Aboriginal outsiders, simply want their complaints and concerns to be taken seriously; they want meaningful reactions from police and actions from courts, commensurate with the nature and degree of the victimization experienced. In James Bay, a common concern expressed by the consumers of indigenized policing is that 'police do not investigate fully and may not want to find offenders' (La Prairie and Leguerrier, 1991: 156). More seriously, Cree people expressed concern the local police become caught up in local politics, such that allegations of favouritism are not uncommon. In the absence of any 'formal mechanisms to make Cree constables accountable to their communities' (Brodeur and Leguerrier, 1991: xiv), community policing does not seem to improve the quality of policing the people receive, nor does it appear to improve the lot of the police, who feel insecure and unsupported by councils with which they often have, at best, an ambivalent relationship (Brodeur and Leguerrier, 1991: xiv).

While indigenized policing purports to offer a more relevant and effective police service, in the Cree context at least, it appears to offer little more than a shift in the nature of the problems Aboriginal people experience in their relationship with police. As with cross-cultural training, the ambiguous success of these programs should be taken not as sufficient excuse to bin them and start afresh, but rather as a plea for greater understanding of the complexities of such programs. We have tended to assume that focusing on culture as the troublesome variable would resolve much of the difficulties inherent in Aboriginal justice reforms to date; however, as these program initiatives indicate, this assumption may be off the mark. This seems especially so in regard to indigenization. It seems an oversimplification to assume, as indigenization appears to have done, that being arrested by an Aboriginal cop if one is an Aboriginal offender is somehow better than being arrested by a 'white' cop. Barring racism on the part of the latter, it may in fact be more troubling to be arrested by someone who is perceived as sharing your background and culture, just as making the arrest may be more troubling for the Aboriginal officer. Given the ongoing tensions within many communities, the pressures on officers and those in conflict, and on the leaders who must make community programs work, community policing in reserve communities is a far from simple or uncomplicated undertaking. While community policing has strong potential to improve communities, in the absence of full attention to the complex matrix within which Aboriginal police must function, it is far from clear that community policing can create a more secure environment or offer a better quality of policing. It may simply create a different quality and direction of discriminatory treatment, arising from the nature of the class system on many reserves and the political and social tensions that characterize these communities.

The uncertain promise of indigenization is underscored when attention is directed to the experiences of Aboriginal people in the urban context. Here, once again, we encounter a very complex reality. The deeply troubling cases of 'starlight tours' in Saskatoon and rates of abuse and death in custody (or following release from police custody) indicate that there is something very wrong in the relationship between police and Aboriginal people in many jurisdictions. However, the research by La Prairie on Inner City Aboriginal people provides some important qualifications on this conclusion. For example in response to queries about their general treatment by police, a majority of Aboriginal inner-city dwellers reported that their dealings with police were generally 'respectful or matter-of-fact': 'In cities, 41% of the total responses reflected respectful or matter-of-fact treatment, 18% rude treatment, 17% verbally abusive treatment, and 24% verbally abusive treatment' (La Prairie, 1994: 62). While the reports of abusive treatment signal a clear need for improvement in the way Aboriginal people are policed in the inner city, it is interesting that almost half of the sample saw police conduct as respectful or 'matter of fact.' This might suggest that at least some urban Aboriginal people receive the same type of policing received by some urban non-Aboriginal people. More importantly, when respondents were asked to describe their experiences with policing 'at home,' comparable figures were 55 per cent for respectful/matter-of-fact treatment, 14 per cent rude treatment, 13 per cent verbally abusive treatment, and 18 per cent physically abusive treatment (La Prairie, 1994: 64). While the degree to which home communities and reserves were policed by community police or the larger non-Aboriginal provincial policing body is not clear, the sample likely encompassed respondents with experience with both indigenized and non-indigenized forces. This raises the issue of where those respondents might have fallen in the response categories. If individuals from communities with indigenized policing were distributed relatively consistently across all reported categories, indigenization may be an equivocal success at best.

Finally, while non-Aboriginal policy makers have tended to persist in an assumption that culture is the key to improving relations between Aboriginal people and the justice system, the viewpoints expressed by inner city Aboriginal people would seem to underscore previously mentioned concerns about this direction. In the city, Aboriginal people were remarkably consistent in asserting the importance of poverty and lack of education as central in how the police in particular dealt with them. When asked about the general police treatment of Native people, nearly one-third of respondents expressed a belief that poor treatment of Natives by police was an issue of class – 'that is, more affluent, better-dressed, and well-off Native people were treated with more respect' (La Prairie, 1994: 68).[4] Thus, once again, we are confronted with the dangers of viewing 'culture' as the essence of the issue; in neglecting such factors as class and the clustering of negative consequences that accompanies poverty for many people, we may have undermined the potential for success of much justice reform. And lest we assume that class is only a problem in the city, it is important to bear in mind the findings of Hull (2001), who has documented a complex and changing class structure on Manitoba reserves, and that of Andersen (1998), who argues forcefully for the importance of understanding class and politics in implementing community-level justice reforms. Clearly, whether a program's focus is urban or rural communities, governments must move away from the one-trick pony approach to Aboriginal justice reform – the need for reform has emerged out of a highly complex interplay of historical, political, economic, cultural, and social forces, and any reform initiative that rejects that complexity and targets single parts of that whole cannot hope to achieve sustainable or significant impacts.

The trend towards indigenization has not been limited to the police. Depending upon how one chooses to define the term, it is possible to view the majority of reforms at a range of locations in the system as involving indigenization. The insertion of Aboriginal lawyers into the system is certainly a crowning achievement in indigenization, especially given that even non-Aboriginal people undergo a significant transformation into the homogeneous creature known as a lawyer by benefit of law school. Perhaps more overt are those acts of indigenization implicit in the promotion of Aboriginal lawyers to positions on the bench, where, in the same fashion as indigenized police services, they are expected to administer 'white man's law,' but filtered through (to reverse Rupert Ross's now famous line) 'their non-white eyes.'

At the level of corrections, where indigenization was once confined to efforts to recruit Aboriginal jailers, today this approach has manifested an intriguing turn. While there are certainly arguments to counter the view of this trend as truly one of indigenization, it is possible to see the development of 'healing lodges' as a manifestation of indigenization of prisons. Here, however, we see the indigenization of the physical structure of the prison as well as the employment of Aboriginal people to the greatest extent practicable to perform the range of services, both control and curative, these 'neo-prisons' are intended to offer. Thus guards are known by other names, less punitive in tone and implication, and in an interesting twist on the indigenization process, non-Aboriginal staff must also become, in effect, as 'indigenized' as the structure within which they now function. According to the Commissioner of Correctional Services Canada: 'we have increased Aboriginal programs, increased the number of Aboriginal staff ... The goal is to create programs linked to the Aboriginal community and Aboriginal culture, and a restorative healing approach to the management of conflicts ...' (Ingstrup, 1998). Boasting the appointment of 'Aboriginal Wardens' and a commitment to 'focusing on Aboriginal issues particularly for the next three to five years' (Ingstrup, 1998), it appears that Corrections is poised to surpass the police as the leader in indigenization of the criminal justice system. The question then becomes, in terms of both Corrections and the system as whole, to what end?

Whether one views indigenization as a successful type of reform will depend largely upon how success is defined. What is this approach intended to achieve? We suggested earlier that, in the policing context at least, indigenization was initially intended to achieve greater efficiency in the administration of justice services to Aboriginal people through increasing the 'shared cultural space' between Aboriginal people and the system. Yet this offers little insight – does efficiency relate to crime control? Has indigenization led to a reduction of crime rates among Aboriginal people? Or should we be defining efficiency, and thus success, in terms of the underlying motivation for reform in the administration of justice to Aboriginal people generally: the reduction of over-representation of Aboriginal people at every level of the system? If we choose the latter measurement, then clearly indigenization is a failure at all levels of the system. Over-representation levels appear to be remarkably robust despite indigenization and cross-cultural training. With the exception of Quebec and Prince Edward Island, where, as we have seen, there is little over-representation of Aboriginal people, rates have remained the same or increased, a fact which begs the question whether, if an effective response to over-representation is what is desired, we should perhaps stop focusing solely on what is wrong, and attempt to discover what these jurisdictions are doing right in criminal and/or social justice – bearing in mind that jurisdictional differences may also reflect history and varying patterns of settlement.

If, on the other hand, indigenization is about efficiency, there is some evidence to suggest that, at the level of policing, indigenization does indeed produce the sort of results desired by 'crime control' approaches. That is, whereas it was intended that indigenization ought, at least in part, to render policing more culturally informed and appropriate, it seems also to have resulted in a rise in reported rates of crime and victimization, and, by implication, in net-widening as well. As observed by Harding: 'One Ontario evaluation of Option 3(b) [special constable program] found a definite increase in reported crime, and hence an increased involvement of Aboriginal people within the criminal justice system (Harris, 1977). This is not to suggest that any more conflict existed with the involvement of the special Native constables. It is quite likely that these Native police were intervening in real problems in Aboriginal communities. But the outcome was more criminalization of Aboriginal people, and not necessarily the strengthening of the communities to address these problems ... As such, special constables may just be furthering the systemic discrimination ...' (1992: 632). If crime control is the purpose of the police, indigenization is a success; if indigenization was intended to improve the detection and processing of more Aboriginal crime, success is evident here, too. And if, as seems to be the case with indigenization of court personnel, representation or prosecution by an Aboriginal lawyer or determination of guilt and sentencing by an Aboriginal judge renders that process somehow fundamentally different from its non-indigenized counterparts, then again, we have some success. And if we convert prisons to places where we attempt to 'heal' rather than 'correct' residents – notwithstanding the shared approach of an implied medical model here – there is an assumption, as yet unproven by evaluation, that indigenization is successful here as well. One cannot help but wonder, however, about the 'success' of a program of reform which has had the effect, whether intended or not, of improving the administration of justice to Aboriginal people by employing Aboriginal people, history, and culture to draw ever larger numbers of them into police custody, courtrooms, and prisons. If a reduction of over-representation is truly the goal, then indigenization is rather like a duck-blind. We have merely disguised the system to make the pursuit more effective. Seen in this light, indigenization appears to be a greater part of the problem than it is a potential solution.

(ii) Beyond Indigenization? Sentencing and Other System-Based Reforms

While cross-cultural training and indigenization seem to have targeted the attitudes and approaches of personnel, other attempts at reform have focused upon those locations in the system that constitute particular 'hot-spots' in feeding the over-representation phenomenon. While policing can certainly be seen as one such location, at least two others have attracted the attention of reformers: prosecutors and their use of prosecutorial discretion, and judges in the act of sentencing. Reforms in the former category have focused largely upon the education and encouragement of prosecutors to use their discretion positively, and to divert appropriate offenders out of the system where the circumstances of the offence permit and where there is a program available to accept and support the diverted offender. In large measure the practice of diversion is dependent upon the presence of community programs that offer viable alternatives to mainstream traditional justice processing, and it is difficult to discuss diversion in detail without attention to the programs that make it possible. Since the bulk of the next section of the book focuses on such programs and their linkages with the system, we will leave the discussion of diversion and diversion programs to that context. Suffice to say at this juncture that probably the single most important aspect of both pre-trial and pre-charge diversion resides in the potential of this reform to reduce the number of formal contacts some Aboriginal offenders have with the system, and which thereby feed directly into their receipt of sentences which, while seeming disproportionate to the offence at hand, are in keeping with the overall record of the offender. In this light, diversion has the potential to direct a real challenge to over-representation, as it provides an opportunity to keep an offender out of the system in the immediate context as well as mitigating against future processing and incarceration. Of course, insofar as the latter possibility is bound up with both the presence of quality, sustainable community projects to receive divertees and a reasonable rate of success within those programs, diversion may be a good option at risk. We will return to this issue in the next section.

The view that sentencing is a particular 'hotspot' in the over-representation phenomenon has inspired a range of attempts at reform. Among the earliest of such reforms were the putative precursors of the modern sentencing circle (discussed in detail in the next chapter), Elders' Panels. These bodies were initiated in some communities as a way of injecting community interests and input into the sentencing of, in most cases, judgments of itinerant courts. Official endorsement of such advisory panels can be traced to a 1974 Law Reform Commission of Canada (LRCC) Report that acknowledged the success of such initiatives in some European contexts and encouraged their development and active support in an Aboriginal context (LRCC, 1974). As observed by Ross Green, such panels were evident in some communities, such as Rousseau River, around the mid-1970s, and they continue to offer a relatively attractive program option for many First Nations and the courts that serve them (1998: 104). In some communities the panels have expanded to involve larger community representation, sometimes through the personnel of the local Justice Committee, and thus move ever closer to a sentencing circle format.

As with many such 'add-on' programs, the Elders' or Community Sentencing Panels manifest a number of weaknesses which, depending upon one's perspective, may also be viewed as strengths. Like indigenization and cross-cultural training, sentencing panels do not in any way alter the fundamental flow of pre-existing power relations within the criminal justice structure. The judge, and thus the system, remains firmly in control, notwithstanding the appearance of possibly genuine consultation which may be disregarded by the judge, if he or she feels this to be appropriate. In addition, while true consultation would seem to imply a relatively open and broad-based form of interaction, this, too, is often structured by the judge, who may limit the nature and direction consistent with the questions he or she poses to the panel and the assumptions regarding relevant and important information that inform those questions. Thus not only might the panel be restricted, to some degree, in their input, they may also face the possibility of advising on options posed by the judge, none of which seem appropriate. The example of an exchange between the judge and a panel cited by Green is apposite here: 'The judge said that he viewed any sexual assault to be serious ... [T]hen he stated to the justice committee, 'I feel that in this case jail is appropriate, but I want you to tell me whether you think I should give him a really high fine, around $1000, or whether I should send him to jail.' And then he conducted a poll or a vote and the justice committee voted and decided that the man should get a $1000 fine in addition to probation terms ...' (Green, 1998: 104). In this context, while the judge chose to follow what was essentially consistent with the advisory panel's recommendation, the panel was limited in their consideration and input to basically two options, both posed by the judge. It is difficult to see how being required to select the lesser of two evils constitutes either real choice or genuine input, and one wonders what might happen in another context with a different judge. It is here that one of the basic conundrums of such reform options resides – as will be seen, it applies equally to sentencing circles – the potential for similar offences to carry disparate sentences, depending upon the proclivities of the judge and the agency and politics of both panels and communities, as well as across individual offenders. This is not to suggest that sentencing should be a 'one-size-fits-all' exercise, but the importance of certainty and predictability in the law may require that greater attention is paid to the impact of such variance on fairness across offender categories overall. As well, it is important to recall here the complaints made by some Aboriginal communities in relation to policing, namely, what matters is not necessarily who is doing the policing, but that the police treat victims' complaints seriously and courts provide redress commensurate with the seriousness of the offence. Insofar as panels and sentencing circles tend towards the determination of community-based and, in some contexts, questionable sentences for serious offences, there is a genuine risk that such initiatives may be as unfair to victims as they are uncertain for offenders.

An additional difficulty with initiatives such as this resides in the fact that sentencing advisory panels have the questionable effect of transferring responsibility for the weaknesses of the system onto the very people those weaknesses have most deleteriously affected. Because panels are only advisory, and do nothing to alter the fundamental power relations between the community and the criminal justice system in any real way, two dangers arise. First, the system secures the complicity of the community in its activities under the guise of consultation, with a number of potentially problematic results. Consultation implies 'buy-in,' and for many First Nations peoples, buy-in to a system which they believe has had highly problematic impacts for their communities is not a feasible political or personal choice. More importantly, buy-in means that if the people accept the system when the panel 'works,' when one more Aboriginal person is kept out of jail or directed to meaningful training or healing programs, they must also accept the arguably numerically larger and more frequent failures of that same system. That the program and its benefits may be one part of the reforms that will ultimately usurp the larger system and its high costs may not be sufficient to sustain this uncomfortable trade-off, even in the short term.

Equally problematic, consultation is not control, and such reforms do little, if anything, to move communities towards true self-governance. One qualification on this concern may be found in the admittedly significant enhancement of feelings of agency and importance which accrue to those on the advisory panel or justice committee, cited by Green and others (Green, 1998; Ross, 1992), who assert that the impacts of this empowerment cannot be underestimated. While that may be true, these effects can certainly be overestimated, and one wonders whether the positive impacts will persist over time. Furthermore, this form of empowerment, while fundamentally a good and worthwhile thing that may assist communities to take the first tentative steps towards true self-governance, may prove inadequate compensation for supporting a system that does not serve them well, or which is not capable of addressing the larger community problems that feed into high levels of crime and disorder; it may also serve to divert the attention of communities seeking self-governance from that larger, longer term goal.

While reform efforts such as Elders' and community advisory panels are largely complementary to the sentencing process, focusing on enhancing judicial knowledge of offenders and options at sentencing, other attempts at reform have been more specific and directive. Central among the latter were the amendments to the Criminal Code sentencing provisions that came into force in September 1996. These reforms were broad-based and went straight to the heart of the sentencing process, 'setting out the purposes and principles of sentencing and codified jurisprudence regarding the objectives of sentencing' (Stenning and

Roberts, 2001: 138). As noted by Stenning and Roberts, while these changes directed restraint generally in the use of imprisonment, they went beyond this in regard to Aboriginal peoples, including in section 718.2(e) a clear directive to judges to take extraordinary measures to counter the over-representation of First Nations within Canadian prisons:

> 718.2. A court that imposes a sentence shall also take into
>   consideration the following principles:
>
> . . .
>
> (e) all available sanctions other than imprisonment that are reasonable in the circumstances should be considered for all offenders, *with particular attention to the circumstances of Aboriginal offenders.*

Just as cross-cultural training and indigenization are premised on a mistaken assumption that 'culture' is the predominant factor responsible for Aboriginal conflict with the law and over-representation, the changes to sentencing law assume that over-representation is largely a result of judges placing Aboriginal people in prisons. While this is what judges do, to place the blame for over-representation upon the judiciary overlooks at least two fundamental facts. First, as we argued in chapter 2, judges are constrained by a number of factors in determining sentences for criminal offences, including the necessity to consider such factors as severity of the offence and prior offending history. Since Aboriginal offenders commit a disproportionate number of serious crimes against the person, and tend to have longer and generally more serious histories of involvement with criminal justice agencies, they are more likely to receive longer sentences of incarceration. This makes all that much more curious the second fact that must qualify our reception of the changes in section 718, namely, that research indicates that on average, both male and female Aboriginal federal offenders are more likely to receive more lenient treatment than non-Aboriginal offenders manifesting the same offending history and seriousness of offence.[5] Although the disparities are less obvious at the provincial level, Clark's investigation of judicial decision making in Nova Scotia determined that the shorter sentences awarded to some Aboriginal offenders was a function of judicial awareness of the difficult circumstances of Aboriginal accuseds. Thus it appears that at least some judges in some jurisdictions were already doing what section 718.2(e) requires them to, with the result that whatever discrimination in sentencing appears to exist works to the benefit, rather than the detriment, of Aboriginal offenders.

The implications of this latest misdirection in Aboriginal justice reforms are not small, and it is important to contextualize the sentencing changes. The majority of serious offending in Aboriginal communities is intra-Aboriginal; Aboriginal offenders, that is, usually leave a trail of Aboriginal victims in their wake, and those victims are most commonly women and children. When one looks at the lesser sentences given to these offenders, it is difficult to determine which of two equally unacceptable mindsets is at work. Is Aboriginal offending somehow less serious because, for some reason, Aboriginal offenders are not as culpable for their actions as others? Or are their victims somehow less in need of the system's albeit limited protections? Are their injuries and needs less deserving of serious attention and response? That Aboriginal offenders are often the product of profoundly stressful and dysfunctional environments should not be taken to reduce either the seriousness of their actions or the rights of their victims to protection and justice. Before racing too quickly to endorse the sentencing reforms, we would do well to remember that, in the way that most Aboriginal people seek only the level of policing services that the non-Aboriginal population takes for granted, so too do they wish no more from the courts. In this regard, we may once again be heading in the wrong direction. If we are committed to this direction, we must also recognize that this path has implications well beyond Aboriginal justice circles. That is, if we are going to establish a precedent that demands that poverty, marginalization, dysfunction, and despair be actively accounted for in determining culpability, there are few arguments to deny that consideration to all offenders who have such backgrounds. Are we prepared to go this far, and if we are not, what does this say about our perception of Aboriginal offenders and victims?

While section 718.2(e) certainly seems to run the risk of entrenching the unfairness to Aboriginal victims, and to those non-Aboriginals who share similarly dysfunctional backgrounds, the problems do not end there. According to the interpretations given them by the courts, judges are to work to keep Aboriginal offenders out of prison wherever possible (Roach and Rudin, 2000). In practice, this is likely to translate into more conditional sentences for Aboriginal offenders, as judges try to divert these individuals into putatively more appropriate healing or community programs. While not necessarily a bad thing in themselves, conditional sentences are arguably conducive to net widening as opposed to decarceration. Aboriginal offenders who might once have been given relatively succinct periods of, for example, probation, now find themselves sentenced to the 'quasi-incarceration' of a healing program:

> With over 28,000 conditional sentences being ordered in their first two years of existence, prison populations have not been reduced to nearly the same extent. In some and perhaps the majority of cases, conditional sentences are being ordered where probation orders, fines and suspended sentences would normally have been

ordered. Conditional sentences can be considerably more coercive and intensive than these other sanctions. The process of net-widening affects Aboriginal offenders who make up a significant percentage of those offenders subject to conditional sentences, especially in the western provinces and who may be disproportionately subject to having their conditional sentences breached. For Aboriginal offenders who breach conditions, a conditional sentence may very well mean jail. (Roach and Rudin, 2000: 369)

While Roach and Rudin make a compelling case, some important qualifiers are absent from their arguments, without which we cannot fully appreciate the implications of the expanded use of conditional sentences. There are clear indications in the research that Aboriginal offenders who present higher risk profiles disproportionately receive conditional sentences for crimes against the person, and that those sentences are likely to be shorter even when the offences are more serious than those committed by non-Aboriginal offenders with similar offence histories and risk profiles. As well, follow-up of Aboriginal offenders serving such sentences appears to be very limited, and the incarceration rate for these offenders is extremely low (La Prairie, 1998). Too often, an Aboriginal offender receiving a conditional sentence will return to his or her community, where there is minimal supervision. Such offenders will drift away from the terms of their sentence into a state of breach, and nothing really happens. The lack of consequences for offenders is a source of aggravation for the community, whose perception of the justice system as ineffectual and insufficiently punitive is reinforced, and for the victims, who cannot help but feel the system is unconcerned with their experiences and needs.

Roach and Rudin are also concerned that, following the Supreme Court ruling in *Wells*, which reinforced the position of the court in *Gladue*, where serious or violent offences are involved, sentences handed down to Aboriginal and non-Aboriginal offenders are likely to be the same or similar, notwithstanding the 'unique circumstances' of the former. The authors express concerns that this may restrict the use of conditional sentences for Aboriginal offenders who have committed violent offences, arguing that a rejection of section 718.2(e) in such cases would deny the Supreme Court's clear rejection of 'crude just desserts understandings of proportionality that automatically tie punishment to the seriousness of the offence' (Roach and Rudin, 2000: 367). Unfortunately, once again, their argument is substantially weakened by the quantitative evidence that Aboriginal offenders are *more likely* to receive conditional sentences for violent offences and, as noted above, are *much more likely* than similar non-Aboriginal offenders to obtain such a sentence (La Prairie, 1998). What, then, can we make of the court's direction that section 718.2(e) should lead to similar sentences for

Aboriginal and non-Aboriginal offenders convicted of serious or violent offences? Either the courts will be forced to extend the same approach to sentencing non-Aboriginal offenders as they did to Aboriginal ones in a pre-section 718.2(e) context, or they will have to find compelling ways to distinguish these categories of offenders. The difficulty here is that, outside of Aboriginality, there may not be too much to distinguish the majority of serious and repetitive violent offenders, and what there is (i.e., longer offending histories) may offer little support for positive discrimination regarding the most intransigent Aboriginal offenders.

If current trends persist, however, increasing numbers of Aboriginal offenders will receive sentences which are to be served in their communities, under some manner of local supervision. Given this likelihood, the issue of high quality, sustainable programs for Aboriginal offenders serving conditional sentences is a major factor mediating the success of the sentencing reforms. To be viable as alternatives to open court or custody, such programs must provide not only for the 'healing' and supervision of offenders, but for the security of victims and the larger community. This would seem to entail, at a minimum, a coherent program base and sustainable funding, as well as support and 'buy-in' by the local community. The challenge is that these requirements are not met in many community programs, especially in rural contexts. It is to these community programs that we now turn our attention.

PART TWO

Restorative Justice: Theory and Practice in Aboriginal Communities

Ameliorative responses such as indigenization and cross-cultural training, which are inherently system-based, have had little, if any, positive impact on either over-representation or the relationship between First Nations citizens and the criminal justice system. The rates at which Aboriginal people are entering the system have not been reduced in the wake of such programming; in fact, they seem to be rising and, if the trends of the past twenty-five years are not arrested, may continue to do so. Clearly, something has to change, and many commentators and social activists view the primary vehicle of that change to be restorative justice – the panacea which can not only resolve conflicts between individuals, but transform communities and heal and rebuild nations. The question, of course, is whether restorative justice – or, for that matter, any criminal justice program – can possibly achieve such goals. And what are the implications for communities who choose to believe in the promises of restorative justice?

This part explores the philosophy and principles of restorative justice generally, and the way in which these have come to be articulated in community justice programs within First Nations. Restorative justice can be traced back to the informal justice movement and, according to some commentators, to much earlier forms of dispute resolution practised by some Aboriginal peoples in the traditional historic period. While the latter suffered significant erosion over the period of colonialism and colonization, they and the informal justice movement share the notions that justice must have a truly community character in order to resolve disputes meaningfully and fully for parties to conflict. That is, the structures and processes of justice must be accessible and open to the participation of community members, who can engage them to provide justice to each other, thereby encouraging community cohesion and restoration following acts of crime and disorder. Within restorative justice, then, we see a putatively more intimate form of justice that tends to be presented in stark contrast to the mainstream system, which is both authoritarian and hierarchical and distant from those whose conflicts it claims and purports to resolve.

Restorative justice is thus most often contrasted with retributive justice, and celebrated by its proponents as a distinctly superior way of achieving justice. Such informal justice practices, however, have also been criticized on the grounds of legal principle and the potential for unchecked power imbalances. Opponents stress the lack of formal safeguards in informal processes and question the optimism of the advocates. Once again the truth undoubtedly resides somewhere between these extremes. Our pursuit of that location is made difficult by the lack of systematic empirical work in the area (Daly, 1996: 13), and the tendency on both sides to frame 'complex legal relations and justice modalities in oppositional, dichotomous, and hierarchical terms' (Daly, 1996: 13). The simplification implicit in this tendency towards polarization in the field is counterproductive. Not only does it distract us from moving towards a balanced understanding of how justice is, could, and should be done in communities, but the focus on contrasting restorative with retributive justice tends to result in the latter persisting as the definitive form of justice against which others must be measured. The terms of the debate remain inherently those of the dominant system, its values and cultures, the bulk of which have long been documented as out of sync with First Nations. As Daly frames the problem: 'We would do well to learn some lessons from the previous decade on informal justice: to transcend the idealism–impossibilism duality, to see the interweaving of formal and informal elements in law and legal process, and to recognize the falsity of pitting restorative justice values against those that are termed retributive. The character of the debate in some quarters today suggests that we remain unable to "unthink" the adversarial, oppositional frame that so many wish to abandon in favour of a kinder, more responsive justice' (1996: 13). This book is intended to encourage attempts to understand restorative justice from the perspective of community, and thereby to step out of the restorative–retributive dichotomy characterizing much of the extant literature. Community restorative justice projects must be measured by the degree to which they are truly grounded in the community, 'fit' with the culture of that community, and are effective at resolving conflict and encouraging greater peace and health in communities. As will be seen in this Part and Part III, such measurement is made difficult by the attitude of the state towards restorative projects in First Nations, evidenced in part in the apparent reluctance of governments to engage in serious and sound evaluation of the majority of community justice projects.

Understanding restorative justice approaches within Aboriginal communities thus requires a grasp not only of the general theory and practice of restorative justice, which can provide a reference point outside the mainstream system for

Aboriginal restorative projects, but also of the shifts and development of that theory and practice within an Aboriginal context. It is towards such an understanding that chapter 4 is directed, as it traces the origins of restorative thought and practices, both in Canada and internationally, and then narrows to a focus on similar trends in First Nations. Chapter 5 engages in the difficult but necessary task of outlining the nature of the challenges to which Aboriginal community restorative justice projects must respond. A compelling case can be made that restorative practices may not only have a tough time dealing positively with crime and disorder in First Nations, but are unlikely to keep the grand promises of community restoration and rebuilding made by many of its proponents.

From this foundation we turn to a detailed examination of three dominant restorative practices in Aboriginal communities. To this end, chapter 6 discusses the origins and remarkable rise in popularity of sentencing circles. This restorative initiative is dealt with independent of other reforms not only because of its popularity, which has spawned a significant literature, but because sentencing circles are the only restorative program that functions within the criminal process. That is, while sentencing circles lay claim to community origins and boast considerable community input and control, they are, in fact, a formal sentencing process in which the community is given the opportunity to speak to sentence to a judge who, consistent with mainstream sentencing processes, retains full control over, and responsibility for, determining and imposing sentence. What is perhaps most interesting about sentencing circles is that, while embraced by communities as mechanisms of self-government and control over justice, they leave the fundamental power relations of state legal structures virtually untouched. As well, insofar as this initiative appears to act as a conduit into communities for the interests and preferences of outside elites, it seems logical to query precisely where we might encounter the 'community' in a sentencing circle. Too often, the community bears the burden for sentences and offenders in cases which, given their not uncommonly serious and violent nature, could reasonably be questioned as appropriate for a circle in the first place.

Chapter 7, the final chapter in this part, provides more in-depth analysis of the development of community conferences in First Nations. Drawing on extant research and field experience, the discussion outlines how this program, which originated in New Zealand and is attributed by government as being consistent with the beliefs and practices of the Maori people, has been modified to respect the differences in traditional cultures of Aboriginal communities in Canada. Here the question is necessarily raised whether once again we have not stumbled forward with a pan-Indianism which is out of place. Does a practice that purports to be Maori-derived have greater relevance to, for example, Quebec

Cree cultures of conflict management, than do dominant Canadian practices? This is not a small matter, and in seeking the answer to this question we uncover the unique nature of conferencing as it has emerged in the Canadian context.

Also considered in this chapter are healing circles, an additional restorative initiative and one which, it would appear, has a truly Canadian and community origin. The most well-known program, the Community Healing Circles of Hollow Water, forms the focal point of our discussion. Like that of most such programs, evaluation of the community healing circles has been limited and problematic, and yet the program claims astonishing rates of success in healing sex offenders and their victims, and continues to receive considerable state support. Examination of the issue of evaluation in Aboriginal community justice provides the bridge into the final part of this work, which looks to what we can state with confidence about restorative justice, what appears to work, and what does not. This leads into a discussion of the characteristics, according to the current research and our experiences in communities required of a community and its justice project to allow the project to succeed and to effect the positive social transformation of communities.

A final note of caution as we enter this part: the chapters in this section critique current restorative justice initiatives – and it is clear from the bulk of the extant literature in Aboriginal restorative justice in particular that critique is not a common occurrence in this field. Many reasonable and informed commentators and community people who have embraced and support community justice have shied away from raising the myriad questions they have about restorative justice generally and community projects in particular, fearing backlash and allegations about the motivations that inform their criticisms. We are among these cautious supporters of restorative justice in Aboriginal communities, and while we will raise many difficult questions about these initiatives, we believe that this is a necessary prerequisite to the development of solid, sustainable programs that respect communities and cultures, and the integrity and security of those who reside within them.

CHAPTER 4

Restorative Justice in Aboriginal Communities: Origins and Early Developments

The rise of restorative justice within First Nations has transpired in a context of conscious opposition to mainstream retributive justice. Perceiving the dominant system as, at best, foreign and distanced from their communities and cultures, and at worst, overtly biased against and unduly punitive towards, Aboriginal people, restorative justice is rooted in the belief that communities can provide better justice through restorative practices. In much Aboriginal restorative programming, however, this 'better justice' is not confined to the limited arena of conflict resolution. Here, we see very clearly the theme evidenced in much of the literature and case law around sentencing circles in particular, that restorative justice is transformative justice; that is, restorative justice is not only about criminal justice – it is the means by which social justice will be achieved and communities almost 'magically' transformed.

It is not clear that the early development of restorative justice as theory or practice manifested such high goals and claims. Rather, it seems that, in its earliest incarnations, restorative justice was primarily about opening the dominant system to greater citizen participation, especially for victims, and thereby moving criminal justice away from its hierarchical, adjudicative focus to a more balanced, participatory focus on resolving conflicts and restoring relationships. Given this, most mainstream restorative justice projects are system-appended, and maintain linkages with the extant system. In the Aboriginal context, while many early restorative programs were similarly system-based, there was also a focus on the rejection of the mainstream system and its programs in favour of the development of separate and independent Aboriginal justice systems. While this goal remains one part of the dialogue of Aboriginal justice, it is increasingly lost in the din of state and community responses to restorative programs that hold out the potential for self-government and, depending on the project and the community, state funding. This trend is important, as the increasing distance in

Aboriginal justice between community and separate justice assumes that restorative justice is both a viable mechanism of conflict resolution and capable of realizing its proponents' promises of social transformation. As will be demonstrated in this and subsequent chapters, both these propositions are, and should be, open to question.

(i) Restorative Justice: Origins in Theory and Practice

Restorative justice finds its contemporary roots in the 1977 work of Norwegian criminologist Nils Christie, who argued that criminal conflicts have become other people's property – primarily that of lawyers – and advocated that offenders should take some responsibility for their actions through a process of mediation with the victim and/or the affected neighbourhood (Christie, 1977). Christie's views were given support and elaboration in 1989, when Australian criminologist John Braithwaite (1989) introduced the notion of reintegrative shaming, which he claimed is more supportive of controlling crime and reoffending than is the commonly practised process of stigmatization. Braithwaite argued that the alternative to stigmatic humiliation is to condemn the crime, not the criminal. According to Braithwaite, shame is accompanied by social integration, whereas stigmatization is accompanied by social exclusion. The proper use of shame gives offenders the opportunity to reintegrate into their community but, in order to earn the right to a fresh start, offenders must express remorse for their past conduct, apologize to any victims, and repair the harm caused by the crime (Sherman and Strang, 1997). In many respects, the work of Christie and Braithwaite, building upon previous advances in popular justice, laid the foundation for what is known today as 'restorative justice.'

As a way of conceptualizing restorative justice, Braithwaite and Strang (2001) argue in the introduction to their book, *Restorative Justice and Civil Society*, that restorative justice is now conceived in the literature in two ways – as a 'process' for resolving conflict, and as a 'value system' about restoration and 'healing.' From the first perspective, restorative justice is a process that brings together all stakeholders affected by some harm that has been done, and returns to them the power and responsibility to respond to, and recover from, acts of crime and disorder in their community. As a value system, restorative justice is about healing both those who engage acts of crime and disorder, and those who are touched by the harms these create, both directly and indirectly, rather than hurting them through punishment or alienation from the system. Within this value system, responding to the hurt of crime with the hurt of punishment is rejected, as is the value of proportionality, that is, meting out punishment that is proportionate to the wrong that had been done (Braithwaite and Strang, 2001). This 'eye-for-an-eye' approach, so much a part of the mainstream justice system, is viewed by those embracing restorative values as counterproductive to meeting the needs of victims or offenders, and thereby unlikely to reduce recidivism or overall rates of crime and disorder in communities.

Whether one views restorative justice from a process or a values perspective, it is clear that the policies it promotes 'are being advocated as a benevolent means of addressing the crime problem' and reducing offender recidivism (Levrant et al., 1999: 9, 17). Underlying the crime prevention goals of restorative justice is the desire to reduce prison populations and formal criminal justice processing through the rehabilitation or 'healing' of offenders (by assuming greater accountability and sensitivity to victims), and by responsibilizing and empowering individuals and communities to deal with many of the crime and disorder problems normally dealt with by the state's criminal justice system. Like crime prevention and community-based policing, which share many of the same underlying principles as restorative justice and have similarly captured the Canadian imagination, restorative justice emphasizes the solving of crime and justice problems through the delegation of many aspects of criminal justice decision making to the local level. It also supports the use of 'partnerships' (where desirable) between the private (individuals and communities) and public (state agencies such as police and probation) spheres.

For the past decade, the restorative justice movement has been attracting considerable attention both nationally and internationally (Galway and Hudson, 1996; CCJC, 1996; Messmer and Hans-Uwe, 1992). Like Christie and others, Levrant et al. (1999) suggest that the primary focus of restorative justice is on the way crime disrupts relationships between people within a community. Its approach is informal and seeks to repair these relationships. Restorative justice, we are told, can rebuild and rejuvenate communities and strengthen the bonds between their members; it can hold offenders accountable through shaming and reintegration, and 'restore' victims through the provision of an opportunity to regain their personal power. Restorative justice has 'rediscovered' the victim and moved justice towards a more victim-oriented system (Weitekamp, 1993).

In Canada, restorative justice has been identified as a new 'paradigm' in justice and become integrated with and, in many respects, indistinguishable from, other current justice initiatives such as safe communities, crime prevention, Aboriginal justice, victim- and other locally/community-oriented justice initiatives. Restorative justice is the stated new justice wave for several provinces, including Saskatchewan, British Columbia, Alberta, Nova Scotia, and New Brunswick, all of which have formally announced their provincewide adoption of this approach. That the provinces should have embraced the promise of restorative justice is not surprising. The increasing shift to the right evidenced in provincial politics, which shares with a less baldly conservative federal administration a rhetoric of financial retrenchment and 'responsible citizenship,' renders the Canadian justice landscape ripe terrain for a restorative shift. The realization that incarceration is both expensive and of limited efficacy in reforming offenders, and the fact that, to date, restorative justice projects appear to be fuelled largely by volunteers, makes restorative programming an attractive option indeed. Add to these very practical attributes the unique blend of conservative ideas of social responsibility (whereby crime and social control may be devolved from the state to citizens), with attractive and easy-to-sell notions of 'healing,' restoring, and rebuilding communities riven by the 'old ways' of doing justice, and it is clear that restorative justice has little downside for cash-strapped governments looking to offload increasing amounts of programming and state responsibilities to the voluntary and private sector. Whether these programs 'work' for offenders and communities may be less important than their ability to meet current state needs for service offloading and financial retrenchment.

The apparent dovetailing of the interests of the modern state in Canada and restorative justice principles and approaches is consistent with what have been identified as the local governance/responsibilization movements described by Garland and Crawford. Adam Crawford concludes that, when considering the emphasis on 'community' and 'partnerships' in restorative justice '[r]esponsibility for the crime problem, according to current government strategies, is now everyone's. It is shared property' (Crawford, 1997).

This shift is explained by sociologist David Garland (1996), who argues that a major dilemma facing governments in contemporary Western societies is the combination of the normality of high crime rates and the limitations of criminal justice agencies to deal with them. The response to these realities has been contradictory and ambivalent crime control policies and official discourse. Thus, in England and the United States, there is evidence of both an increase in punitiveness in criminal justice and a move towards the 'responsibilization' or sharing of crime control responsibilities with private partners. This contradiction has come about as a result of government awareness of its limited capacity to be the primary and effective provider of security and crime control combined with its recognition of the political disaster of withdrawing from the 'sovereign state' role in criminal justice. One way to deal with this dilemma has been to create 'partnerships' with agencies, organizations, and individuals 'which are quite outside the state and to persuade them to act appropriately.' Garland notes that 'the current message of this approach is that the state is not, and cannot effectively be, responsible for preventing and controlling crime' (1996: 452–3). This approach fits well with other government strategies geared to greater privatization and reductions in public expenditures.

The state focus on partnerships and 'offloading' may have significant implications for the development of Aboriginal community restorative justice projects. A true partnership would seem to require some degree of equality, however tenuous, and there may be little balance between the extant resources of the community and the power of the state. Thus, for example, while the state has entrenched the idea of community restorative justice in law through the formalization of alternative measures for adults within the Criminal Code of Canada (s. 777), and in its clear direction to the judiciary to actively incorporate restorative principles in their determination of sentence, especially in regard to Aboriginal offenders (s. 718(2)e), restorative justice in an Aboriginal context has become synonymous with community justice – thus placing a considerable burden on communities to seek out state partnerships and enter the realm of justice services. Recognition that such partnerships require considerable knowledge on the part of the state of the capacity of communities to carry such burdens, and considerable agency and other-than-monetary resources on the part of the community, seems a small part of the restorative justice equation in Canada, possibly for the same reasons that lead to state reluctance to evaluate restorative justice programs.

Given the state's apparent enthusiasm for restorative justice, it is important to query the nature of its role in restorative justice. In supporting a system of justice based on the belief that the approach to crime should be one of collective problem solving and not of blaming the offender and coercion, Weitekamp (1993) suggests that one important role for the state would be to oversee arrangements in communities to make sure that justice and fairness are maintained by local groups responsible for restorative justice. The challenge here, of course, lies in the apparent reluctance of the state to enquire too deeply into Aboriginal community restorative justice programs, out of concerns that any such evaluation would impinge upon the self-governance these programs represent. As will be discussed in chapter 5, however, there is reason to question the degree to which the most common projects, such as sentencing circles, truly constitute exercises in self-government. And while the government may step back from evaluation for fear of violating community autonomy in justice matters, the degree to which the state may have vested interests in seeing communities succeed in managing offloaded responsibilities in processing and 'correction' of offenders makes their reluctance to evaluate suspect. It is also important to bear in mind that avoiding the determination of whether a community project is working in order to respect the 'community' may easily equate with the abandonment of individuals in that community who are either not well-served or, worse, further harmed, by a project which is not functioning well and has not been evaluated.

The Centre for Restorative Justice and Mediation (CRJM) suggests that the state maintains a number of important responsibilities in regard to community restorative justice (CRJM, 1996). These include (1) making sure offenders are held accountable for their behaviour and ensuring there is a response to criminal behaviour; (2) passing laws and providing resources to support victims, communities, and offenders; (3) supplying uniform ways of tracking information; and (4) monitoring restorative processes and results. While these would seem to constitute a minimum responsibility, close scrutiny of state involvement in restorative justice indicates that, with the possible exception of what appears to be uneven and inconsistent funding to community projects, there is little evidence that the modern state has embraced its responsibilities as outlined here. Bayley (2001) takes a broader view of the role of the state in restorative justice. He argues that the character of justice provided by the state is being challenged by the restorative justice movement, but that even if the restorative justice paradigm realizes all its promise, sound state policy will continue to have a central role in confronting crime. States must maintain the capacity to be the 'police of last resort' if responsibilizing neighbourhoods does not work out, and consistent with this function they should coordinate and standardize communication and information systems, create national databases, and maintain forensic laboratories and research facilities. As well, states must be able to monitor and evaluate public safety throughout their jurisdictions or territories, and they must also be prepared to act on the analyses they make. As will be seen, this does not seem to be the case to date in most jurisdictions, especially in regard to Aboriginal community restorative justice projects.

What is intriguing about the gravitation of the state towards restorative programming is the fact that, in many respects, it is hardly the new or revolutionary idea so many commentators argue it to be. The principles upon which restorative justice rests, and to which it lays claim, have long been a part of the juridical landscape in Canada, and have been seen in alternate dispute resolution, community justice, and popular justice movements. These have been present in one justice form or another for at least thirty years, possibly more, depending upon the processes and mechanisms one chooses to include under the rubric of restorative justice. In fact, the 'restorative revolution' is really less that than a somewhat logical progression of previous movements which has been accelerated by larger social changes in the direction of devolution and demands for more active citizenship. The observations of Llewellyn and House are apposite in this regard. In their 1999 report for the Law Commission of Canada, these researchers, citing Van Ness and Strong (1996), identified five movements or principles which they believe were central contributors to the phenomenon that is known today as restorative justice. Among these is the informal justice movement, which emphasized informal procedures for increasing access to, and participation in, the legal process for victims in particular, thereby anticipating the subsequent demands of victim's rights movements which not only echoed these positions, but went further, pressing the state to formalize victims' rights to be present and participate in legal proceedings pertaining to their victimization and the processing of those responsible. As the needs and rights of victims gained voice and presence in the popular imagination, calls for greater attention to restitution emerged. Proponents of restitution, which focused on the needs of victims, maintained that meeting the needs of victims would serve the general interests of society, and in this regard may be linked with the rise of the reconciliation/conferencing movement. This latter movement had two foci or strands, including victim/offender mediation, which dates back to the 1970s and as such has the oldest restorative pedigree and degree of evaluation, and the family group conferencing movement, which is more recent and focuses on the gathering of those involved in a conflict to address the needs of victims and offenders. Finally, restorative justice is seen to have been influenced as well by the much broader social justice movement, which involves different groups working in a context that is concerned with social well-being. Insofar as justice is both a social and legal construct, and one which is an integral part of a healthy community, the principles and foci of the social justice movement most certainly appear to have linkages with the restorative justice movement (Llewellyn and Howse, 1999: 8). They may all be seen to have informed and shaped the contemporary articulation of restorative justice, and are evident in the foundational attributes of the general restorative justice approach. According to Ferguson, this approach is an alternative way of understanding and responding to crime and conflict, and is informed by three central principles: (1) crime results in harms to victims, offenders, and communities; (2) not only government, but victims, offenders, and communities should be actively involved in the criminal justice process; and (3) in promoting justice, the government should be responsible for preserving order, while the community should be responsible for establishing peace (2001: 13). These principles are seen to emerge from a larger restorative justice framework or philosophy that is highly victim-centred, both in terms of rights and accountability, and which defines crime and its victims quite broadly and differently from the mainstream system. Thus, within a restorative framework, crime is not seen as an attack on the state and its monopoly on social control and the legitimate use of force, rather, it is a violation of victim and community. The community must therefore be made accountable through the person of the offender, for whom it must accept some broad responsibility for creating and rehabilitating, and who in turn must be accountable to the community and the individual victims for the harms implicit in the offending. This responsibility is articulated through a response to crime which is grounded in the group rather than the state, and which demands the active participation of offenders, victims, and community to 'restore' the community and personal relationships by repairing the harms caused by the crime. Within this community process, accountability of all parties is measured by their clear and definitive assumption of responsibility as evidenced in the actions they take to repair the harm implicit in the criminal act. While the offender is probably the most important player in this revised morality play, and his or her assertions of responsibility, accountability and, perhaps most importantly, apology, tend to constitute the focal point of restorative justice in practice, the victim is also seen to occupy a central function in negotiating restitution and the terms of the 'healing' to be undertaken by the parties and the community. Thus what may be seen to set this process apart from mainstream criminal justice is the parity of rights of participation shared by victim and offender, and the community context and process in which those rights are vindicated and 'healing' begun.

In developing a framework for restorative justice Llewellyn and Howse (1999) suggest that it should come into play only when a wrong has been committed. But even in situations of wrong-doing, restorative justice should ask critical questions about the meaning of justice and in doing so, challenge the fundamentals of the current system. While Llewelleyn and Howse suggest that a restorative theory of justice borrows elements from restitution, corrective justice, and retributive justice, a distinguishing feature of restorative justice is that it is inherently relational, taking relationships and human connectedness as the starting points for justice reasoning transforms the traditional picture of justice. They argue that models of restorative justice are context-dependent and, therefore, restorative justice processes may be fundamentally different in design and still restorative in nature. Common elements will exist; these include a wrong-doing that has caused harm to a relationship; a perpetrator of the wrong doing; a victim or a sufferer of wrong; a community, however defined; and a restorative process. The parties are seen to come together voluntarily in an encounter that is driven by the participants and overseen by a facilitator who will structure the discussion, assist in the creation of guidelines for the process and ensure they are followed, and assist in the formulation of a mutually acceptable and viable outcome.

(ii) Restorative Justice, Principles, and Potential: Trends in Canadian and International Practice

Restorative justice principles and programs can be applied at various stages of the criminal justice process, and the means of accessing them will differ across different types of programs and according to the size and nature of the community involved. It is important to note that in many Aboriginal communities, community restorative justice programs function primarily through the vehicle of a community justice committee, which receives and filters referrals and requests to access restorative programming, notwithstanding the origins of the referral. Thus, for example, a judicial or defence request for a sentencing circle will often go through a justice committee as one part of the process for accessing a circle; it is this committee which is generally made responsible for organizing the circle, working out the logistical details, and ensuring that the community is 'on board.' While not all communities have such committees (a sentencing circle, for example, does not require the services of such a committee to become part of a circuit court session in a rural community), they are important aspects of the community development component of restorative justice. As will be seen in the chapters that follow, and discussed explicitly in chapter 8, the constitution and practices of these committees are important factors facilitating program sustainability and success in communities.

Consistent with the range of combinations and permutations of restorative justice programs, there are a range of capacities and modes of access functioning across them. For example, some restorative programs do not require contact with the criminal justice system as a precondition to accessing their services. Thus we see that, in some communities, a restorative justice project may be accessed by parties who wish a conflict to be resolved before it escalates to the point of involving police or other formal justice system agencies. For example, a family and community of care of a youth who is engaging in increasingly problematic behaviour in the home or at school may request a facilitated dialogue with the youth to try and deter him from the path he has chosen. A community conference or healing circle may provide the context for such a dialogue. In this manner a local justice project may manifest a clearly preventative focus which, while it may have implications for the rights of the youth, nonetheless does not constitute net-widening in the common usage of that term, as it does not involve formal criminal justice processing.

A similar, but more formalized, function occurs through restorative programs that operate as a diversion program prior to the laying of a criminal charge. Here, an offender may be diverted out of the system to engage in a restorative process that will work with the offender, victim, and their communities of care to devise a program of restitution and 'healing.' If not completed within a statutorily defined time frame, a criminal charge may be laid. Restorative programs may also work with offenders following the laying of a charge, but before trial. They may comprise one (or an entire) part of those actions taken in parallel with court decisions, and they may also provide a forum for meetings between victims and offenders at any stage of the criminal process. Alternatively, restorative programs may operate as part of the sentencing process once an accused has pleaded guilty or been found guilty at trial. Here we encounter a controversy discussed in greater detail later in this part, whereby the primary route to a restorative option may be through a guilty plea, with obvious implications for due process considerations and offender rights. Finally, a restorative justice program can operate after a sentence has been imposed, whether as a community-based sentence, a sentence of imprisonment, or as part of a parole release process. Latimer et al. have summarized the entry points to restorative justice programs from the criminal justice process as (2001: 2):

(1) Police (pre-charge),
(2) Crown (pre-trial),
(3) courts (pre-sentence),
(4) corrections (post-sentence), and
(5) parole (pre-revocation).

Although not widely conceptualized or applied to the area of corrections, Bazemore and Schiff claim that 'restorative justice opens up a new horizon of possibilities for changing the nature of correctional intervention and for increasing and changing the quality of the community's involvement in the corrections process' (1996: 317). However, they also admit that because restorative justice is generally strong on vision and relatively weak on the specifics of policy, practice, and implementation, considerably more work needs to be done on thinking through its value in the correctional field. These observations are especially important in regard to Aboriginal participation in the restorative justice movement, as it is clear that, in the context of sentencing circles and healing circles such as that in Hollow Water, Aboriginal restorative justice programs are very much involved in the business of corrections. As will be seen in the chapters that follow, many sentencing circles lead to sentences which are to be served entirely or in large part in the community, under the supervision of largely untrained community and family members who may not realize the full implications of their responsibilities when they are thrust upon them in a circle. Through the circle the community may become responsible for supervising an alcohol prohibition, or overseeing the 'healing' of the offender by accompanying him or her on a trapline for a number of months. If this is not a 'corrections function,' it is difficult to say what would qualify as such. Similar queries may be raised in relation to healing circles such as Hollow Water, where the community assumes control over the rehabilitation of one of the most intractable categories of offenders, paedophiles, and responsibility for controlling recidivism. Again, these functions are reminiscent of what might be termed 'restorative corrections,' and given the concerns expressed by Bazemore and Schiff, they constitute one more context in which Aboriginal communities are providing a 'laboratory' for restorative experiments not yet seen in the non-Aboriginal context. While a potentially important and ameliorative experiment, Aboriginal restorative corrections are an experiment nonetheless, and apparently one with limited controls and uncertain impact on communities. Aboriginal communities may by now be weary of providing a laboratory for such experiments, and it is incumbent upon outside experts and influential others to enquire deeply into the degree to which those experiments are truly welcomed and accepted by the majority of community members, not to mention adequately resourced and supported by the state when they are so-accepted.

Notwithstanding the preceding, and despite the limitations in moving from vision to practice, most theorists and practitioners agree that restorative justice is a malleable concept and may be adapted to suit a wide range of social and criminal justice needs and contexts.[1] Thus it is argued that restorative justice programs may be used across a range of adult and criminal matters, as evidenced in the use of sentencing circles in cases involving such serious matters as assault and arson. Restorative justice is also suggested as an appropriate vehicle for the resolution of a range of civil matters, such as family welfare and child protection, and disputes in schools and workplace settings.

Internationally, restorative justice has emerged at a range of junctures and manifests varying forms and foci. Thus we see that, while justice practices in premodern societies may have contained elements of restorative principles (such as restitution and compensation), current applications of the idea began to develop and proliferate in the 1970s in North America, beginning with a victim–offender reconciliation program in Ontario, Canada, in 1974. Hundreds of similar programs subsequently emerged in other North American sites and in Europe. A somewhat different model of restorative justice surfaced in the Antipodes. Here restorative programs, first introduced in New Zealand in 1989, were based on what were understood to be Maori approaches to family group decision making and applied to child protection and juvenile justice cases. The conferencing idea was subsequently borrowed and adapted by jurisdictions in Australia, the United States, Canada, the United Kingdom, Ireland, Singapore, and South Africa.

Family Group Conferences in New Zealand grew directly out of a concern that the criminal justice system was not culturally sensitive to the needs and circumstances of Maori communities and youth. By contrast, conferences were seen to mesh with traditional Maori culture and offer communities the opportunity to provide support and guidance to youth (Alder and Wundersitz, 1994). In Family Group or Community Accountability Conferences victims and offenders and their supporters (family, friends) come together using a defined process to discuss the nature of the offence, the harm done to the victim, and what should be done to repair the injuries caused by the crime. The arresting police officer and other community representatives may be present as well. A trained facilitator who ensures that the conference follows the designed format conducts the proceedings.[2] An apology by the offender to the victim made in front of the people who are most important to him or her is an integral part of the healing, rehabilitation, and reintegration process. The facilitator assists the participants to reach a decision that is agreeable to all. Once a decision is taken, a contract that sets out the terms and conditions of the agreement is written up; the offender is required to sign this contract as a confirmation of his or her commitment to seeing through the terms of the resolution. The group decides the nature of the follow-up and who will assume responsibility for ensuring the agreement is followed. If there is a breach of the agreement, the conference may reassemble to decide what more to do and/or a charge may be laid (AJIC, 1999: 2–5).

As will be seen in chapter 7, conferences can differ from victim-offender mediation schemes in that they bring more community people into the discussion, acknowledge a wider range of victimized people, and emphasize participation by the family members of offenders. Mediation programs involve victims and offenders coming together with a trained mediator to begin to resolve the problem and the harm the offence has caused, and to construct their own approach to achieving justice. These programs seek to empower the victim and offender to resolve their conflict, but in a setting where the mediator provides structure and guidance while allowing the victim and offender to resolve the dispute together. The mediator imposes no specific outcome; the goal of mediation is to empower participants, promote dialogue, and encourage mutual problem solving. However, the mediator can balance power differentials between the two participants to ensure that no coercion occurs and that the outcome is agreeable to both parties. Evaluation results from mediation programs suggest that they are beneficial for many victims and offenders, and encourage offender responsibility and accountability to the victim, and by inference, to the broader community.

A third, less widely used, approach that falls under the banner of restorative justice is the sentencing circle. As will be seen in the next chapter, sentencing circles have found favour in some parts of Canada, primarily Yukon and Saskatchewan, and in the case of Yukon, were designed and implemented at the instigation of the local judiciary and one judge in particular. Sentencing circles are based on many of the same principles of restorative justice but occur after adjudication of the offence, and where a finding or an admission of guilt has been entered. The purpose of the sentencing circle is to bring the community, broadly defined, into the sentencing process. The judge usually acts as the facilitator and the purpose of the circle is to reach an agreement about what should constitute a reasonable sentence. It is important to keep in mind that these circles take place after the offender has been through the criminal process, and they can involve people who have no particular relationship to either the offender or the victim. How follow-up is pursued, or the benefit of sentencing circles to victims, offenders, or communities, is not clear, because no external, objective evaluations have been made, nor has there been any ongoing and systematic monitoring. These matters are explored in greater detail in chapter 5.

Increasingly, commentators who work in the field in Aboriginal communities, and many Aboriginal participants in restorative justice, are beginning to question not only sentencing circles but restorative processes more generally, and the promises these make to vulnerable individuals and communities. Concerns are emerging about the nature of the interests restorative justice serves, and, increasingly, about the visibility and transparency of restorative projects. Questions about accountability abound. In attempting to address accountability issues in Family Group conferencing (FGC), Roche argues for an expansion of the concept to include what he refers to as 'deliberative accountability' (2003: 79–80). Deliberative accountability is regarded as 'inherent in the sort of deliberative process' central to a family group conference, and is comprised in the 'mutual accountability [that] is built into meetings where participants provide verbal accounts of events which are then scrutinized and assessed by other participants, whose own accounts are in turn scrutinized' (Roche, 2003: 79–80). While such accountability may indeed form one part of the deliberative processes common to many restorative processes, the viability of deliberative accountability in at least some contexts is uncertain. For example, within certain Aboriginal contexts, the issue may be less whether the open sharing of stories provides a check on veracity and perceptions than whether those stories will necessarily emerge in the first place, and whether parties to the process are prepared to challenge each other on the versions provided and any contradictory facts. The possibility that restorative processes cannot transcend dysfunctional power relations within communities or families, and the implications for 'healing,' have been well-documented by researchers such as Crnkovich (1995; 1996), Green (1998), Anderson (1998), Clairmont (1994a), and others.

While a facilitator may be in a position to challenge open contradictions or apparent untruths in the process – assuming he or she is able to detect them – doing so may well risk the perception of bias by the party whose version is questioned. Many restorative processes tend to require some degree of neutrality by the facilitator, and implementing accountability through this individual may be problematic. In short, then, deliberative accountability would seem to rely on the presence of a level of trust that may be absent in many processes and within the relationships of the parties to them, such that contradictions in stories may not always be challenged. As well, not only may parties feel insufficiently safe or empowered to challenge contradictions in each others' stories, they are not actually required to tell any story at all. None of the participants in an FGC can be forced to give an account, let alone one that meets minimum expectations as to its content. 'Deliberative accountability' lacks enforceable obligation, and thus it may not really qualify as 'accountability' this term is commonly understood.

While accountability remains a difficult and elusive concept in much restorative justice, this seems particularly the case in Aboriginal communities, which often manifest asymmetrical power structures and authority patterns (Polk, 1994; Crawford, 1997; La Prairie, 1998; Moyer, 2000; Anderson, 1998). Politics too often enter circles and other restorative processes and exert negative and counterproductive pressures on the process. Thus for example, Moyer, in her analysis of sentencing circles, echoed participants' concerns about abuses in sentencing circles, which included marginalization of the victims and an undue weighting of the circle towards the offender's family and friends (2000). Similar concerns have been expressed regarding healing circles, especially Hollow Water, discussed below. Participants in the process consistently reported that while much was done for offenders, victims received little assistance and sometimes seemed marginal to the healing exercise (Lajeunesse, 1996; Couture et al., 2001). Ryan and Calliou (2002) and Crnkovich (1995; 1996) further underscore the impacts of both local and family politics in responding to the abuse cases that form much of a community justice process's caseload. Crnkovich, for example, observed first hand the implications of family politics, and the power of the offender, for the free-flow of information and 'deliberative accountability' in a sentencing circle dealing with spousal assault (despite judicial concerns about the use of restorative processes in such cases). Ryan and Calliou (2002) reinforced the implications for community justice and accountability in their case studies, remarking that community politics were such that despite relatively widespread knowledge of sexual abuse in the community, convictions were unheard of. Similar concerns have been expressed about spousal abuse cases. We will return to these issues later; for present purposes, it is important to recognize that while deliberative accountability is good in theory, it is probably unfeasible in practice.

(iii) Restorative Justice Projects in Aboriginal Communities: A Primer on Form and Focus

Some of the early Aboriginal justice initiatives characterizing the period 1970–90 arose primarily in response to the emergent 'over-representation problem' and were, understandably, focused on law rather than restorative justice; they also tended more towards indigenization than truly autonomous programming. The Native Courtworkers Program, the most nationally implemented and well-known of these initiatives, was established in the mid-1970s on a federal/provincial cost-shared basis to assist Aboriginal accused. It was implemented in the belief that culture, language, and other Aboriginal-specific factors disadvantaged Aboriginal people who became involved with the criminal justice system. Aboriginal courtworkers were retained and trained to provide information and support to Aboriginal people through the criminal trial process, offering translation not only of the language of the courts, but also of their structures and processes. The intention of the Native Courtworker Program was primarily to render the dominant justice system more transparent and comprehensible to Aboriginal accused and, to a lesser degree, victims, and thereby render their participation (such as it was) more meaningful. Like most of the system-based reforms discussed in chapter 4, this program was designed to enhance the expedience and smooth functioning of the system, as opposed to fundamentally altering the way justice is done in relation to Aboriginal people.

Other models focused on the provision of legal services to Aboriginal people and communities emerged in the wake of the Native Courtworker Program, often in specific geographic areas. For example, the Nishnawbe-Aski Legal Services Corporation provides legal services to a large number of tribally affiliated communities in the Treaty 5 and 9 areas in northern Ontario, many of which are isolated or 'fly-in' access only, and all of which are small and rural. The Nishnawbe-Aski Legal Services Corporation was established following years of negotiation between the Nishnawbe-Aski Nation (NAN) and the governments of Canada and Ontario. Formally incorporated in 1990, it was set up to deliver a wide range of services, including legal, paralegal, and law-related services, to the First Nations of the Nishnawbe-Aski Nation. Legal and paralegal services included criminal, family, administrative and civil legal aid, interpreter services, referrals, public legal education generally and more specifically regarding the rights of accused before the law. The corporation also had a research arm, which examined Aboriginal systems of justice based on custom (Campbell Research Associates, 1994). A similar, geographically wide, system-focused initiative was the Dakota-Ojibway Probation Service, implemented in 1985. It differed from the Nishnawbe-Aski Legal Services Corporation approach by virtue of the fact that, like many initiatives in policing, it was 'indigenized' in nature and involved attaching an Aboriginal probation service to the existing one, as opposed to the creation of an autonomous and distinct Aboriginal service that could stand alone (Bracken, 1994).

The constitutional discussions on Aboriginal rights in the mid-1980s, and the emerging interest around the world into customary law, led primarily by legal anthropologists, meant that no newly funded Aboriginal justice projects implemented since that period have escaped attention to larger matters of public education and social justice. Even the law-focused programs implemented before the mid-1980s had strong orientations in this regard, which were consistent with the emerging Aboriginal self-government agenda. That the early attention to customary law and popular justice often took the form and title of alternate dispute resolution only reinforced those interests. Popular justice increasingly gave way in title, if not form, to restorative justice, and counselling and attendant activities to what is now commonly described as 'healing,' 'reintegration,' and 'reconciliation' – the most oft-cited objectives of Aboriginal projects. For example, in developing a manual for front-line community workers dealing with sexual abuse disclosures, the authors, Bopp and Bopp (1997), suggest that one of the main reasons Aboriginal communities want to assume control over incidents of sexual abuse is because these are viewed as a sickness needing healing, rather than crimes that call for punishment.

Although the three types of projects discussed above (victim-offender reconciliation, family and community Conferencing, and sentencing Circles) are commonly described as 'restorative' approaches, a reading of descriptions for Aboriginal community justice projects reveals a range of projects that do similar things and which have a common focus. These are variously described as diversion, alternative measures, healing circles, family group conferences, mediation, and dispute resolution. Most existing projects are pre-adjudication and may be pre-or post-charge, although pre-charge is clearly a preferred. Most target both adults and youth, although some, mainly those described as alternative measures or diversion, target one or the other. Those identified as 'diversion' are the most commonly identified type of project, but their descriptions and objectives are little different from those for alternative measures, family group conferences, healing circles, or dispute resolution. There is a strong focus on acquiring control over justice matters by collaborating with the mainstream system (via sentencing panels, sentencing circles, advisory panels, supervision of probationers and parolees) or by taking direct responsibility, at least in the first instance, for particular groups such as youth.

Culture is an important component of many projects, which often refer in their descriptions to being or incorporating 'traditional' responses, 'culturally relevant' interventions, and activities that reflect and support cultural traditions. Sometimes 'culture' can refer to meetings and other justice forums held in an Aboriginal language; some may open with prayers and the use of sweetgrass. Traditional lore is sometimes used to encourage offenders to change their behaviour, and Elders often advise on the cultural components of projects.

However, Clairmont notes that 'there is some question to the substance of the native distinctiveness that characterizes these initiatives' and there is 'some ambivalence among community and panel members concerning the relevance and appropriateness of traditional values and especially native spirituality' (Clairmont, 1994a). Obonsawin and Irwin (1992) also questioned tradition as an acceptable ingredient in community justice projects, given the vast changes in communities since 'traditional' times. However, 'healing,' and attendant traditional and cultural activities, are no longer even questioned for Aboriginal justice projects and have become a central element of mainstream restorative justice and New Age ideology.

Neilsen notes that the first Youth Justice Committees were set up in Alberta in the fall of 1990 in Fort Chipewyan, a small community in northern Alberta (Neilsen, 1995: 18). The committee concept was initiated by members of the local community and the criminal justice system who were concerned about youth getting into trouble. The idea was supported by the local courtworker and judge, and the collective efforts of the interested parties resulted in the establishment of a Youth Justice Committee. A second committee was implemented a few months later and since that time both Alberta and Manitoba have witnessed the proliferation of these committees.

Perhaps the most famous and frequently cited community 'restorative' justice project is the Hollow Water Community Holistic Circle Healing Program. Initiated in 1986 by the Hollow Water First Nation in Manitoba in response to problems of sexual abuse and family violence, it involves thirteen steps, from disclosure through various victims/offender and community activities, concluding with a healing contract and a cleansing ceremony (Griffiths, 1996: 202–3). The Hollow Water project (discussed in detail in chapter 7) has been the subject of virtually all restorative justice discussions that involve Aboriginal people and communities and is regarded by government and other agencies and commentators as the epitome of a successful restorative justice program operating in an Aboriginal community. The Canim Lake Violence program in British Columbia, designed for the management and treatment of adult and youth sex offenders and for the victims of sexual abuse, is also considered an example of a successful restorative justice project. The treatment interventions blend modern clinical techniques with traditional Aboriginal healing practices. The offender must sign a contract agreeing to complete the treatment program; if this is breached, formal prosecution follows.

While most of the projects funded by large initiatives like the Aboriginal Justice Strategy of the federal Department of Justice or provinces are reserve- or small community-focused, there are also projects that address the criminal justice problems and needs of Aboriginal people in urban centres. The most well known of these is the Toronto Aboriginal Legal Services Community Council Program (Campbell Research Associates, 2000a). This is a diversion program whereby an offender who admits an offence receives a 'community' disposition such as counselling, treatment, and/or restitution. Similar programs have been implemented in Vancouver and Winnipeg. The Vancouver Aboriginal Transformative Justice Services offers an alternative to the formal court process for Aboriginal accused, also involving the use of a community council which is responsible in part for developing healing plans for offenders; a similar project has been implemented in Winnipeg. In Saskatchewan, the Regina Alternatives Measures Program, which is Aboriginal administered and staffed, diverts adults and youth to family group conferences and mediation. Smaller urban centres have also witnessed the growth of Aboriginal justice projects. For example, the Tsimshian Tribal Council operates a diversion program for Aboriginal youth in Prince Rupert and Prince George in British Columbia, and has implemented an Urban Aboriginal Justice alternative measures program for adults and youth.

While some projects in urban areas are not Aboriginal specific, their location indicates that they may serve a large Aboriginal clientele. For example, the Yukon Domestic Violence Option is a court alternative to formal justice processing for victims. The offender is encouraged to accept responsibility and become involved in a program of treatment in order to 'unlearn' violent behaviour. Treatment personnel, probation services, and the court closely monitor the performance of the offender. Like the drug treatment court model now in vogue in Canada and elsewhere, if the offender successfully completes the period of treatment, the sentence will be less than would have been imposed by the mainstream process and will not include jail.

At the present time, three issues dominate the Aboriginal community justice agenda. The first is youth and youth offending, the second is sexual abuse (and often related to that, family violence),[3] and the third is crime prevention, broadly defined. However, underlying the attention to these kinds of specific issues is, for many communities, the exercise of control over justice matters. This is often described in terms of community institution building, community empowerment, and/or community development and self-government. While specific problems often provide the justification for specific projects, the complementary agenda is frequently community control and decision making over justice matters as part of a broader transition to self-government.

The disproportionate numbers of children and youth in the Aboriginal population is a critical factor in understanding the disproportionate number of Aboriginal youth in custody or under the supervision of the youth justice system. Griffiths suggests that the over-representation of Aboriginal youth may be even more pronounced than that of Aboriginal adults, and that they may be less likely to be referred to alternative measures than non-Aboriginal youth (1996: 150). In large measure, therefore, justice projects are often implemented in order to keep Aboriginal youth offenders in their home communities, or at least out of custody. Aboriginal youth in Australia and New Zealand are likewise the focus of many of the existing alternatives to formal criminal justice system processing (Alder and Wundersitz, 1994; Morris and Maxwell, 1998). In Canadian Aboriginal communities, the objectives of many projects with a focus on youth are twofold: (1) to reduce the numbers of Aboriginal youth involved in the mainstream criminal justice system; and (2) to promote the engagement of youth with Elders, even though language and communication may be difficult (Obonsawin-Irwin, 1992; Neilsen, 1995).

Relying upon intergenerational connection and support to respond to youth conflict with the law is far from unproblematic in Aboriginal communities, where children have often experienced victimization and abuse at the hand of caregivers and older community members. For example, it is now apparent that the magnitude of sexual abuse in Aboriginal communities is disproportionate to that found in non-Aboriginal communities. In her inner city research, for example, La Prairie (1994) found that 11 per cent of the males and 30 per cent of the females interviewed had experienced child sexual abuse, and nearly half (42 per cent) of the reported abuse was severe. Those figures can be contrasted to the 10–15 per cent reported by Mullen (1990) in his review of research on the prevalence of child sexual abuse in non-Aboriginal society. But they relate only to child sexual abuse and do not include the sexual assaults where adults are victimized. While no reliable studies have been conducted on Aboriginal victims, the fact that Aboriginal offenders are disproportionately incarcerated for sex offences, and that most Aboriginal crime is intraracial, would suggest a disproportionality in adult victimizations as well. Given this reality, community justice programs face the not inconsiderable task of ensuring that those whom they recruit to work with their troubled community members in a healing capacity are themselves 'healed,' and that vulnerable youth in particular are not placed in situations of further risk through restorative programs that do not carefully screen volunteers and employees.

An additional dimension challenging Aboriginal community justice programs resides in the fact that Aboriginal communities manifest disproportionate levels of family violence in comparison to non-Aboriginal society. Aboriginal women and women's groups have been vocal in their concerns about the level of family violence, and of their own victimization (McGillivray and Comaskey, 1999). Data from the United States indicates that 80 per cent of Indian families in urban areas had a history of family violence including incest, sexual abuse, and battering (Carter and Parker, 1991). Three-quarters of La Prairie's inner-city sample reported violence in their families 70 per cent of the males and 75 per cent of the females (La Prairie, 1994). These realities create significant challenges for any restorative justice program, whether sentencing circles that attempt to respond to family violence, or community and family group conferences that rely on families and associated communities of care to assist those in conflict to resolve their difficulties and heal.

The disproportionate levels of incarceration of Aboriginal people, and the levels of crime and disorder that afflict Aboriginal communities, are the primary rationales for identifying crime prevention as a legitimate focus for community justice. However, at the same time that these challenges have initiated a focus on Aboriginal communities as in need of support and repair, and encouraged the development of restorative justice, the very dire situation impelling these reforms renders them difficult to realize in practice. Too often, the influential others and outsiders who promote restorative measures in First Nations, while quick to recognize the depth and nature of the need, do not extend that recognition to include the impacts on reform initiatives these needs are likely to create. Thus communities are placed in the untenable position of being presented with program options intended to address a range of community dysfunctions that fail to take that dysfunction into account in their implementation and effects. The critical issue of the magnitude of the challenges, both in terms of offences and offenders, facing community restorative justice projects is the subject of the next chapter. We will also raise the difficult matter of whether 'tradition,' as the crucial and definitive element of Aboriginal restorative justice programs, is capable of meeting these challenges or, indeed, if the programs it claims to inform are, in fact, 'traditional.'

CHAPTER 5

Providing a Context for the Challenge of Community Justice: Exploring the Implications for Restorative Initiatives in Disordered Environments

Restorative justice has been widely heralded as the most traditionally practised and appropriate response to crime, disorder, and disputes in Aboriginal communities. Because of the amount of attention it captures, we felt that it was critical to the general 'community' thrust of this book to explore the concept in some detail. In this chapter we begin that process by examining the existing literature to document the kinds of disputes and offences that commonly occur in Aboriginal communities, and to identity some of the characteristics of disputants, victims, and offenders. If we are to understand the value of restorative justice to Aboriginal communities, we must examine the kinds of problems restorative justice projects would be expected to resolve and how they would resolve them.

Following that discussion we will attempt to assess how 'traditional' restorative justice is in the context of contemporary Aboriginal communities, and perhaps of most importance, how appropriate it is to these communities and the resources required to support and sustain it. The issue of appropriateness is critical, given the nature and scope of disputes and offences, and the characteristics of victims and offenders that a restorative justice system will have to address. The changed and changing nature of contemporary Aboriginal communities in Canada will be the subject of a later chapter. The intent of these discussions is not to reach a final conclusion about restorative justice in Aboriginal communities, but to raise and highlight some of the issues we feel should be taken into account when considering the use of restorative practices in these communities, and when evaluations of restorative justice programs are being conducted.

(i) The Challenge of the Nature of Disputes: Violence and Victimization in Aboriginal Communities

As mentioned in chapter 2, the criminal justice research literature now accepts the fact that interpersonal violence, property crime, family problems, and other forms of social tension, friction, and disorder occur in Aboriginal communities at levels far exceeding the national and regional ones. Research in four countries with significant Aboriginal populations – Canada, the United States, Australia, and New Zealand – reveals a consistent pattern of elevated levels of Aboriginal offending and victimization and disproportionate levels of interpersonal offences. Aboriginal victimization, in these countries presents a disturbing picture of extreme levels of violent victimization often involving Aboriginal females.[1] In Canada, the 1999 General Social Survey (GSS) on victimization collected data on race and cultural status, including Aboriginal status. An analysis of the data found that approximately 35 per cent of the Aboriginal population reported having been the victim of at least one crime in the twelve months preceding the survey, as compared to 26 per cent of the non-Aboriginal population. Aboriginal people were also more likely to be victimized more than once and to be victims of violent crime. While the rates of theft of personal property were similar for both Aboriginal and non-Aboriginal people, Aboriginal people experienced violent crime at a rate that was nearly three times greater than for non-Aboriginal people. For visible minorities the rates were similar to those of the general population; for the immigrant group, the rates were lower. Aboriginal people, and particularly Aboriginal women, were found to be at much greater risk for spousal violence (CCJS, 2001).

Research into the victimization of Native Americans in the United States reveals an equally disturbing picture. Analysing five years of data, U.S. researchers found that the rate of self-reported violent victimizations for American Indians was well above that of other U.S. racial or ethnic groups, and more than twice as high as the national average. This disparity in violent victimizations occurred across age groups, housing locations, income groups, and sexes. While the rate of violent victimizations was highest for the group aged 18 to 24 (as expected), the rates of violence for every age group of American Indians was higher than for all races. American Indian males and females were disproportionately victimized in relation to all other races, and American Indian women experienced 50 per cent more victimizations than that reported by Black men. American Indian victims also disproportionately report that the offender was drinking at the time of the offence (Greenfeld and Smith, 1999).

The crime and victimization picture for Aboriginal people in Australia is similar. In a nationwide victimization survey conducted in Australia in 1999, approximately 13 per cent of Aboriginal persons aged thirteen years and over had been physically attacked or verbally threatened in the twelve months preceding the survey. This compares with 2.5 per cent of all Australians aged fifteen years and over who were assaulted, threatened with force, or attacked. Seventeen per cent of females had been victims ten or more times, as compared to 14 per cent of males.

In New Zealand, Maori and Pacific Island people are more likely to be victims of violent crime than are Europeans/Pakeha people, and Pacific Island people have particularly high victimization rates by people well known to the victim (New Zealand Parliamentary Library, 2000: 9). A major survey of victimization conducted in 1996 and reported by the Ministry of Maori Development (MMD) showed that Maori were much more likely to be victims of assaults and threats, and to be repeat victims, than were non-Maori. Where 9 per cent of New Zealand Europeans surveyed had experienced some form of violence (including sexual violence), the figure for Maori was 16 per cent. The number of offences/incidents of victimization per one hundred respondents for Europeans was thirty three, while for Maori it was seventy two. The figures for violence against women by their partners showed a huge disparity between Maori women and New Zealand women, with Maori women experiencing up to three times more injuries that required medical or hospital attention (MMD, 2002).

The nature and scope of crime, and of disorder and disputes, that characterize Aboriginal communities have important implications for using restorative justice practices to resolve them. The characteristics of Aboriginal offenders and victims, and the kinds of offences with which communities will have to deal, are other important aspects to consider when contemplating appropriate community justice responses. In this regard, Depew comments: 'It is striking that variable and changing patterns of Aboriginal crime and disorder tend to be more social than strictly criminal in nature, although there may be significant comparative differences between rural/remote and urban areas along these dimensions. This finding stems, especially in rural and remote communities, from intense kin-based interaction, proximity and familiarity within a broader context of structural disparities. High levels of interpersonal violence, including assaults and the victimization of women, children and the elderly commonly occur between spouses and relatives. Furthermore, they often involve repeat offenders' (1994: 25).

Thus we see that rates of crime and conflict in the lives of Aboriginal people are higher than, and disproportionate to, their counterparts in the non-Aboriginal population (CCJS, 2000b; Roberts and Doob, 1994; Trevethan, 1991). As a practical reality, this finding means that local justice initiatives in First Nations communities will have to deal with a volume of offences, offenders, and victims that is considerably higher than that facing similar initiatives in non-Aboriginal communities. Aboriginal crime is also predominantly intraracial; that is, notwithstanding location, Aboriginal people most commonly victimize other Aboriginal people (Silverman and Kennedy, 1993; Griffiths et al., 1995; Trevethan, 1991; Roberts and Doob, 1994). At the same time, much more of that crime is violent in nature (Moyer, 1992; Silverman and Kennedy, 1993), and a significant proportion of those victimized by violent crime are female victims of domestic abuse (Comack, 1993). These last two findings suggest that Aboriginal communities will have to deal with a larger volume of crime and trouble involving families, familiarity, and interconnectedness than would be the case for most non-Aboriginal communities.

A number of other differences distinguish Aboriginal and non-Aboriginal crime and victimization. Aboriginal women are much more likely than non-Aboriginal women (relative to men) to be involved as accused and victims in reported crime (Roberts and Doob, 1994: 13), and to be under the influence of alcohol at the time of the offence (Moyer, 1992; Phillips and Inui, 1986). In addition, the use of alcohol distinguishes Aboriginal crime from non-Aboriginal offending (Roberts and Doob, 1994: 14). In the case of homicides, for example, research by Doob et al. (1994) in Ontario revealed that more than half the homicides involving Aboriginal victims (54 per cent on- and 52 per cent off-reserve) involved alcohol on the part of both the offender and the victim. The comparable figure for non-Aboriginal homicides was 11 per cent. Research in the Prairie provinces shows that Aboriginal victims are much more likely to be assaulted by someone they know than are non-Aboriginal victims (Trevethan, 1991).

The differences do not end there, as research data reveal intragroup age, socio-economic, risk/need, and Aboriginal status differences. As noted in previous chapters, it is now well known that young people between the ages of fifteen and nineteen are at the greatest risk for involvement in the criminal justice system, and most adult offenders begin their careers as young offenders (Surgeon General, 2001). Community-based and other research reveals that the vast majority of Aboriginal offenders are between the ages of eighteen and thirty-seven years and are males who have victimized other Aboriginal people (NCPC, 2000: 5), frequently their partners or spouses. Adult Aboriginal offenders are generally younger, have less education, and are more likely to be unemployed than are non-Aboriginal offenders. They also manifest higher risks to reoffend and have higher levels of need, that is, substance abuse, personal/emotional, marital/family and employment problems. These factors may vary across the country. For example, Aboriginal offenders in the Prairie provinces are most likely to exhibit the highest risk/need levels, and this is reflected in their hugely disproportionate incarceration levels.

Many aspects of Aboriginal crime and disorder in Canada, including the use of alcohol, and the characteristics of offenders cut across international lines. In Alaska, Philips and Inui found that both Native and white offenders were predominately unmarried adult males. However, the Native offenders had higher than expected levels of unemployment and of living alone when compared with non-Native offenders. While the 'never married' status was a stronger indicator of legal problems for Native than for white Alaskans, unemployed Natives were less likely to become offenders than unemployed whites, perhaps because unemployment was already a more chronic situation for the Native Alaskan group (Phillips and Inui, 1986: 130). This finding has some resonance in Canada. One justice official in a Dene community in northern Saskatchewan remarked that alcohol is the greatest problem in the community, and that this problem is compounded by unemployment, childhood violence, and generally negative experiences. He added, however, that he had seen significant reductions in both alcohol and crime problems when people find jobs (La Prairie, 1997).

Tatz argues that in Australia there is abundant evidence of a great deal of personal violence and child neglect within Aboriginal groups, a marked increase in Aboriginal deaths from non-natural causes, and that the vast quantity of alcohol consumed generally explains these behaviours (Tatz, 1990: 249). Phillips and Inui found that, compared to white Alaskans, Native Alaskans were 2.2 times more likely to get arrested; 3.3 times more likely to be arrested for a violent felony (murder, rape, aggravated assault, armed robbery); 2.9 times more likely to have a psychiatric hospitalization; and 6.9 times more likely to be treated in an alcoholic treatment centre. Compared to white Alaskans, Native Alaskans are also 1.9 times more likely to die by suicide, 3.1 times more likely to die by homicide, 10.5 times more likely to die from alcoholism, and 2.2 times more likely to die in an accident (Phillips and Inui, 1986: 126). Griffiths et al. (1995) found similar results in their research among the Inuit of Baffin Island. Research on American Indians, crime, and alcohol use, reveals that alcohol is implicated in 75 per cent of all fatal accidents, 80 per cent of all suicides, and 90 per cent of all homicides in the Indian population. Grobsmith also noted that serious crimes such as rape, homicide, and suicide occur with much more frequency in the Indian population. Indians have the highest crime rate in the United States, and the majority of these crimes are alcohol-related and perpetrated in a context where 'alcoholism is becoming a passed-down tradition, as courts are now seeing fifth generation addiction' (Grobsmith, 1989: 286–7).

Although the presence of alcohol in Aboriginal offending and victimization is well documented in U.S. research, a recent report on American Indian Police points out that when looking for more appropriate police and other responses to crime on reserves too little attention has been paid to the devastating presence of alcohol in communities (Greenfeld and Smith, 1999). However, in many Canadian Aboriginal reserves with by-law-making powers, problems caused by alcohol are taken seriously enough to result in the creation of 'dry' reserves. For example, when examining data on Aboriginal and non-Aboriginal homicides from a community perspective in Ontario, Doob et al., observed that 'because of the problems that alcohol has created, some communities have passed enforceable by-laws prohibiting the possession or use of alcohol. Even those reserves that have such by-laws and are not normally accessible by road have not, in fact, been invariably alcohol free' (1994: 45–6).

Tatz believes that alcohol is a symptom of a larger crisis of social breakdown in Aboriginal communities in Australia – a view of Aboriginal people in Canada shared by Doob et al. Support for this view was put forward as early as 1942 by Hayner, when he stressed the importance of tribal social disorganization as an explanation for crime among American Indians (quoted in Green, 1995: 100). Lee has also explored the link between culture conflict, social control mechanisms, and crime in Alaska native villages, and argues that indigenous culture in Alaska, like many indigenous cultures around the world, has been subordinated to Western systems: 'the relationship between the state and its agents of control to rural Alaska and its native residents remains strikingly colonial and native groups have experienced social inequity and deprivation often associated with colonialism (Lee, 1995: 179).

In their research into sexual abuse among American Indian families, Carter and Parker found that '[i]n many American Indian communities, the extended family has broken down and traditional child-rearing practices no longer operate' (Carter and Parker, 1991: 111).

Because most authors consider cultural change the major cause of alcoholism, suicide, mental illness, and violent death, Phillips and Inui set out to explore the specific social changes that are associated with maladjustment (1986: 131–5). In the past fifty years there has been dramatic outmigration of Native Alaskans from small villages to town and cities, and white Alaskans are now the dominant group. Philips and Inui found that alcohol-related disorders accounted for the greatest proportion of diagnostic variability between Native and white Alaskan offenders, and that higher rates of 'mental illness' in the native Alaskan population may be largely due to the higher frequencies of alcohol- related disorders. Alcohol abuse was also associated with violent behaviour, but it *did not appear* to be closely associated with higher levels of *acculturation*. There was, for example, no clear relationship between ethnic density of Native communities and the rate of arrest or the rate of referral. Compared to offenders from communities with less than 75 per cent Native Alaskans, offenders who resided in communities with 75 per cent or more Native Alaskans had committed an excess of violent crimes, were more likely to use alcohol or drugs at the time of the crime, and had a more common diagnosis of alcohol-related disorder. Violence and substance abuse were not, therefore, necessarily disproportionately associated with a high degree of contact with whites.

In understanding the issue of the over-representation of Aboriginal people in the Canadian criminal justice system, most commentators would appear to subscribe to the theory of acculturation and culture conflict. However, as discussed in chapter 2, the now well-established finding of regional variation in the levels of over-representation would lead us away from blindly embracing this approach. There is little reason to believe that Aboriginal people in Canada were differentially exposed to colonization, or that the impact and processes of acculturation vary so dramatically by region. But whatever the cause, the effect of alcohol abuse on Aboriginal crime and disorder is profound. For example, in their analysis of race and the Canadian criminal justice system, Roberts and Doob observed that the social situations leading up to the homicides are different from those of non-Aboriginals (1994: 14). The main difference is that so few of the Aboriginal homicides are premeditated and may occur during bouts of drinking when anger, fights and various other forms of interpersonal disputes erupt. In her research in James Bay, Quebec, La Prairie and Leguerrier (1991) found that long-standing disputes and tensions between community and family members, never acknowledged when people were sober, often erupted into violence when people were drinking. The Doob et al. research in Ontario revealed significant differences in Aboriginal and non-Aboriginal homicides. More Aboriginal than non-Aboriginal homicides occurred when the victim and suspect were socializing together, both had been drinking, and a fight, or a person seeking revenge, was involved (Doob et al., 1994: 52).

The question these findings beg is how and why this use and reliance on alcohol persists in communities and among offenders. In research on Aboriginal drinkers in Australia who quit without help, Brody discovered that social ties often posed major difficulties for those trying to give up alcohol (1993: 408–9). This same factor was identified in earlier research by Grobsmith. In her interviews with American Indian inmates in Nebraska, Grobsmith found that 100 per cent of the inmates had a substance abuse problem and alcohol was introduced to them mainly by relatives and friends. Parental abuse problems also played a major role in introducing inmates to alcohol and drugs at an early age. Getting drunk was considered acceptable recreational behaviour and overwhelmingly accepted by communities as normal behaviour (Grobsmith, 1989: 292–5). One explanation for the community and family acceptance of alcohol-related behaviour is provided by Brody (1993) who first noted that family kinship, obligations, and long associations are often cited as one of the fundamental strengths of Aboriginal people. Drinking with people enables public demonstrations of generosity and relatedness through the physical act of buying and sharing alcohol. The camaraderie of the drinking group also cements ties. However, this could also work against Aboriginals trying to give up alcohol. Giving up drinking not only involves dealing with the craving for alcohol but coping with changes to social interactions, lack of support from friends and drinking companions, and the resulting isolation.

The power of family and community ties was also found by Carter and Parker in their exploration of the reporting of sexual abuse incidents in American Indian families. The authors cite earlier work by Michael Dorris, who found that non-disclosure to the outsider of incidents involving drinking was the norm. Dorris quoted one interviewee who said: 'Family is important even if you come from a drinking family. Family is number one. And people think you're helping them if you don't tell the cops that they're drinking. You don't want to get them in trouble. You kind of cover up and hide for them. Because they're family. That's what families do' (Dorris, quoted in Carter and Parker, 1991: 112).

Traditional Indian values of non-interference and non-assertiveness, fear of public authorities and prosecution, and shame were other reasons cited for the non-reporting of sexual incest. However, the length of time women who were aware of incest in families waited to report the incident varied by the identity of the perpetrator. For example, stepfathers and other cohabiting adults were more likely to be reported earlier than fathers or siblings (Carter and Parker, 1991).

(ii) Who Are the Victims: Locating the Primary in Restorative Justice in Aboriginal Communities

The 'Offences against the Person' category of crime is a distinguishing character-istic of Aboriginal crime (Evans et al., 1998); within this category, family violence and sexual abuse constitute a large proportion of interpersonal offences, and females are the primary victims. In a comparative survey of offenders conducted in 1996, 10 per cent of all offences committed by Aboriginals were for a serious assault as compared to 2 per cent for non-Aboriginals. In addition, 20 per cent of Aboriginal offences were for sexual assault as compared to 12 per cent of non-Aboriginal offences (Johnson, 1997). This phenomenon appears to cross international lines. Carter and Parker's research on sexual abuse in Ameri-can Indian Families found that the risk for child incest significantly increases in geographically isolated communities. However, the authors also quote an earlier government document that states that 'approximately 80 per cent of American Indian families in urban areas now have a history of family violence including incest, sexual abuse and battering' (Carter and Parker, 1991). In a fact sheet on violence and victimization among Aboriginal Canadians, the National Crime Prevention Centre found that victims of sexual assault are mainly female, whereas males comprise the majority of homicide victims, and 80 per cent of Aboriginal women in Ontario were victims of violence (NCPC, 2000: 1–3). Various other studies have estimated that between 75 and 90 per cent of women in certain northern communities are abused, and that some 40 per cent of children in northern communities had been physically abused by a family member (B.C. Institute Against Family Violence, 2001).

The Griffiths et al. research on crime, law, and justice in thirteen Inuit communities in Baffin Island suggested that official statistics do not capture the extent of violence against Inuit women because abuse is not often brought to the attention of the police. This is supported in the interviews McGillivray and Comaskey conducted with Aboriginal female victims in Manitoba, wherein one woman remarked: 'For the first thirty-five times I got beat up, I never contacted the police, I think it was about that many times at least' (McGillvray and Comaskey, 1999: 118). McGillivray and Comaskey claim that this is the average number of times a woman is assaulted before she reports the violence. The RCMP in Baffin Island believed the reported spousal abuse cases were the 'tip of the iceberg' and that for every one reported, five or ten go unreported (Griffiths et al., 1995: 56).

The majority of inner city Aboriginal women interviewed in a study of Aboriginal people in the cores of two eastern and two western cities reported a person victimization. Unlike males, who were more frequently victimized by other males (relatives, friends, or strangers) ten times as many females were victimized by spouses, partners, and boyfriends. One woman said: 'I've been beaten up about 20 times – 18 times by my old man and a couple of times by a friend. I always had some kind of mark or bruise on me. Once I had a broken eardrum. I never went to the police for any of them' (La Prairie, 1994: 423).

More females than males also reported six or more victimizations. The majority of all male and females respondents reported childhood abuse and, while violent and severe victimizations were significantly higher for males, sexual abuse was higher for females. Child victims of family violence, and particularly of severe violence, reported more unstable family life, more moving around during childhood, and earlier involvement as offenders in the criminal justice system. Type of upbringing, parental drinking and severity of drinking, paternal unemployment, instability, and mobility were factors that predicted family violence.

Victims without access to any services and resources face bleak prospects. In commenting on the difficulties facing female victims, especially those in more remote areas, Moyer has pointed out that: 'Research studies on rural and northern women who are victims of domestic violence repeatedly comment on their isolation, lack of anonymity if they request police or other services, lack of support from the community (except, sometimes, for family members), and the lack of information and of services available in the community from emergency shelters to counselling to practical assistance in living arrangements and finances when the victim leaves the family home' (2000: 11).

This reality also crosses international lines. The report of the Aboriginal and Torres Strait Islander Women's Task Force on Violence found that women who live in more remote areas of Australia and are beaten or raped have no place to go or to find refuge. Women living in urban areas have a greater likelihood of finding some place of separation and safety (programs, shelter, refuges); women who reside in remote areas and who are violently victimized rarely have similar options. Geography places these women in positions of serious disadvantage (Daly, 2000a: 4).

In the final analysis, it is clear that restorative justice projects in First Nations will be forced to deal with offences that are serious, violent, and interpersonal in nature, if they wish to respond to the primary forms of victimization and 'heal and restore' the majority of victims and offenders. Most proponents of restorative initiatives will agree that these processes are not well-suited to cases of this type and magnitude. For example, while the courts appear united in the belief that sentencing circles ought not to deal with cases involving serious crimes against the person, Spiteri has documented a number of spousal assaults among the reported cases in which sentence was determined by a circle. Many of these cases fall within the legal threshold for circles set by Stuart in *Moses*, insofar as they carry a possible sentence of imprisonment of less than two years, but this standard is problematic for a number of reasons. The short prison terms that follow conviction in such offences may indicate that violence against women is viewed as less important than many - possibly most - other forms of victimization. As well, while most courts are aware of the complexities intrinsic to these cases, such as the possible presence of battered wife syndrome or the larger community opinion or climate around such acts, they have proven remarkably ineffective in reducing spousal abuse. These realities, which render the handling of such cases in the mainstream system deeply problematic, are unlikely to be alleviated in a community setting where political, social, and family tensions abound, and where there may well be a conspicuous lack of the programs or supports required to respond effectively to spousal assault. Moreover, while the 'under two years rule' was intended to limit circles to less serious matters, among Spiteri's cases was a charge of arson, which suggests that the rule may not be followed by community justice committees and programs (Spiteri, 2000).

At least in part, the tendency of community justice projects to ignore the legal standards, requirements, and safeguards contained within the dominant criminal justice system may be attributed to the trend in communities to focus on tradition as both the essential justification for alternative processes and the panacea for a wide range of social ills. The climate of 'traditional cultural revivalism' that informs many restorative justice programs advocates those programs as a means for avoiding the dominant system, and thus any inclusion of, or attention to, its standards and safeguards can easily degenerate into inherently political debates over their propriety within 'traditional dispute resolution.' If restorative justice programs are part of self-government, accepting some aspects of the system from which the program offers escape may be seen to compromise the autonomy of the restorative initiative. This brings us to a final, sticky issue that must be addressed before we can proceed to a detailed critique of particular forms of Aboriginal restorative justice: how traditional is restorative justice?

(iii) Locating 'Tradition' in Restorative Justice: Where Is It, and Does It Really Matter?

There are two parts to the belief that restorative justice reflects Aboriginal tradition. The first is that tradition as it was practised among Aboriginal people prior to European contact remains a central part of modern Aboriginal commu-nity life and is thus well known and understood by Aboriginal people. Second, the principles now articulated in and through restorative justice principles and practices were a customary and common part of traditional responses to viola-tions of local norms or serious crimes. O'Malley and others question the belief held by white officials that 'tradition' exists in a form clearly identifiable and agreed upon by Aboriginal people (O'Malley, n.d.). Dispossession, contacts with government officials, missionaries, trading centres, and the more contemporary forces of mass communication, education, relocation, and migration have pro-foundly interrupted and changed social and cultural life. McDonnell argues that 'all native societies, regardless of their traditional heritage, have long since been drawn into a complex history of involvement with the state ... within each Native Canadian community there are radical divergencies in education, occu-pation, religious affiliation, political involvement and so forth. This means that there are also quite different views on (and knowledge of), what passes for "our traditions"' (1995: 466–7). But, at the same time, O'Malley, like Dickson-Gilmore and others, suggests that the rhetoric of restoring tradition is a key feature of the development and selling of programs designed to deal with problems in postcolonial settings (O'Malley, n.d.: 5).

In exploring the intrusion of English law into the lives of indigenous people in the Canadian west to 1860, historian Russell Smandych cites the case of a Saulteaux Indian who was placed on trial at Red River in 1845 for the murder of a Sioux in an act of revenge for killing his father a year earlier, and convicted in the General Quarterly Court of Assiniboia. Smandych (1997) finds the trial and conviction in an English court noteworthy because, until that time, indig-enous people were left alone to settle matters as they would; this 'hands-off' approach is documented in the statements made by several historians. Europeans who arrived in western Canada adopted the practice of not interfering with 'crimes committed by Indians against other Indians' as well as 'the practice of sometimes accepting the use of traditional - often - "blood-for-blood" - Aboriginal methods of dispute-settlement themselves.'

Archaeologist Norman Hallendy (1994) describes another 'traditionally' adjudicated incident before the advent of 'white man's justice,' documenting the system of justice that once prevailed on southwest Baffin Island. The case reported to Hallendy by an Inuit Elder was that of a murder that took place in August 1924 and involved the death of one hunter at the hands of another. The Great Council, comprised of the 'Bosses' of the fifty camps along the coast, who came together only in times of importance for discussion and considered action, met to determine the fate of the accused. They gathered in a remote region of Baffin Island, in a place encircled by upright stones which was considered a special place for important deliberation, and ascribed the status of a parliament.

The interesting aspect of the traditional 'trial' that ensued in terms of restorative justice was that the accused fully expected to be killed and was resigned to dying. However, his life was spared on the condition that should he ever again be involved in another person's death in any way, at any time, his own death would swiftly follow. For him this fate meant 'my time to die is not yet come – my life is fated to continue' (Hallendy, 1994: 8). He remained physically in, but always apart from, the community, and, whether in the presence of friends or strangers, would always be vulnerable to retribution. The decision prescribed a standard of conduct to be followed for the rest of the accused's life, but it does not appear to have reintegrated him or provided for his forgiveness by other members of the victim's family or the community.

Among the Inuit, ignoring a problem, shaming, and social and physical ostracism were some of the informal responses to conflict and violations of social norms. More formal responses included song duels, fist fights, and wrestling matches. Regardless of the approach adopted or deemed necessary, the main objective of Inuit social control was the maintenance of peace and order (Tomaszewski, 1995). McDonnell's (1992) description of research on customary practices and the objectives of social control among the Cree of James Bay, Quebec, is similar to Tomaszewski's review of Inuit social control. McDonnell and other anthropologists have documented the physical movement of individuals and groups away from conflict and problems in hunting/gathering societies.

In his research on sentencing circles in six Saskatchewan and Manitoba communities, Green discusses traditional methods of social control and dispute resolution. He writes: 'Little, if any, autohistorical documentation exists respecting Cree and Ojibway culture prior to European contact. Given this shortage of evidence, written material on traditional dispute resolution practices of Aboriginal people represents interpretations by non-Aboriginals based on personal observations or discussions by Elders. The dynamic nature of culture must be recognized in analyzing "traditional" dispute resolution practices. Practices recognized and adopted within a culture depend significantly on current reality' (Green, 1998: 24–5).

Two of the main propositions contained in the recent *Gladue* and *Wells* Supreme Court of Canada decisions, and challenged by Stenning and Roberts in their article on the sentencing of Aboriginal offenders, are, first, their conclusion that 'most traditional Aboriginal approaches to sentencing place a primary emphasis on the goal of restorative justice,' and second, that 'there is an Aboriginal emphasis upon healing and restoration of both the victim and the offender' (Stenning and Roberts, 2001: 154). Stenning and Roberts argue that the proposition that most 'traditional Aboriginal approaches place a primary emphasis on the goal of restorative justice' implies that such an emphasis does not exist within the traditions of other ethnic or cultural groups in Canada. They also question the contemporary relevance of this proposition, arguing that 'the social, political and cultural situation of most Aboriginal people today is quite different from what it was even fifty years ago' (Stenning and Roberts, 2001: 162).

But while the Supreme Court of Canada decisions may be new, the sentiment and beliefs about the 'traditionality' of Aboriginal justice are not. In 1991, the Cawsey Inquiry was unequivocal in setting out what it believed were the differences in Aboriginal and non-Aboriginal 'world-views' (Cawsey, 1991), and it located justice and dispute resolution in terms that were consistent with the contemporary principles of restorative justice. In the Aboriginal world-view, justice and dispute resolution facilitate the restorative process, and restitution and reconciliation are used as a means of restoration. Offenders take an active role in the restorative process, and remorse, repentance, and forgiveness are important factors in reintegration (Cawsey, 1991: 6–7). This phraseology mirrors exactly the language of restorative justice that emerged a full decade later, and which was later reinforced and supported in the justice work of the Royal Commission on Aboriginal Peoples (Canada, 1996). Academic papers now commonly equate restorative justice with Aboriginal traditions, and sharply contrast the Aboriginal (restorative) and non-Aboriginal (retributive) approaches to justice (Griffiths, 1996; Neilsen, 1995; Ross, 2001). Rarely, if ever, is this contrast, or the 'tradition' of restorative justice in Aboriginal society, challenged by other academics, government bureaucrats, and/or criminal justice system officials.

Research by Dickson-Gilmore on the development of separate legal systems for the Mohawk reveals how current realities and the adaptation of traditional practices to these realities – the 'restoring of tradition' – have been key features in the development and selling of programs (Dickson-Gilmore, 1992; see also O'Malley, n.d.; Green 1998). Despite the more obvious ironies about the use of 'tradition,' the approach clearly finds favour in government, notwithstanding emerging concerns and criticisms among some academics and a number of Aboriginal people. For example, much of the rationale and impetus for the adoption of the Family Group Conferencing restorative justice approach for youth offenders in New Zealand was rooted in the perception of government officials and others that conferencing has strong roots in Maori tradition – Maori youth comprise a large percentage of young offenders in that country (Maxwell and Morris, 1994). Since the initial use of FGC in New Zealand in 1989, its Maori 'roots' have become conventional wisdom and, when exploring the indigenous 'traditions' of restorative justice, the New Zealand model is often cited (Cove, 2001; Blagg, 1996; Daly, 2000b). However, as Daly notes, these accepted beliefs can have other spin-offs. She argues that the belief that conferencing reflects Maori practices of dispute resolution, misleading in itself, has also led to the belief that conferencing is an 'indigenous' practice.

Academic commentary in New Zealand on the value of conferencing for Maori youth has 'range[d] from hesitantly positive or lukewarm to strongly critical' (Daly, 2000b). In Australia, Harry Blagg falls into the strongly critical camp. Because of their power over Aboriginal youth and their potentially inappropriate use of shame, Blagg is particularly critical of Australian conferences that use police as facilitators. But beyond these concerns, Blagg argues that there are inherent features of Australian Aboriginal culture and social life that would raise problems in conferences. For example, Aboriginal people may not live within the kind of imagined community that conferences require, most especially in regard to conflict and disorder management. A majority of Maori people may not operate within a shaming paradigm of social control. Like many historic Aboriginal peoples in Canada, these communities may operate more through avoidance mechanisms and language turns that deflect rather than promote confrontation. As well, Family Group Conferences appear to rely on a model of the family which is nuclear and grounded in parental authority (however one might choose to define this); however, insofar as Aboriginal society separates biological parenthood from child socialization, the child's biological parents may have little authority in relation to issues of law infraction and not feel either responsible or, in some cases, shameful, when the child commits a breach of law. There may also be significant culture differences among and between groups. Blagg notes that among Aborigines in Australia there is no fixed, hierarchically structured tribalism as there is in New Zealand among the Maori. Instead, age, kinship, and gender may be the critical ordering principles in the processes of control, and more 'corporate' groups like Community Councils (or by inference, conference circles) that shift focus from these principles to those of parental and family authority run the risk of weakening existing practices of maintaining order (O'Malley, n.d.: 17).

(iv) Examining the Context: How Appropriate Is Restorative Justice?

New approaches to Aboriginal crime and Aboriginal offenders have most frequently been rationalized on the basis of the belief that the mainstream criminal justice system is not equipped to understand and, therefore, to respond adequately and fairly to these offences and/or to this group of offenders (Roach and Rudin, 2000; Green, 1995; Stuart, 1996; Ross, 1992). There is also the belief that 'the circumstances of Aboriginal offenders are unique in comparison with those of non-Aboriginal offenders' (*R. v. Wells*), and, therefore, that these individuals require a different response from that accorded non-Aboriginal offenders. Collectively, this situation has fed into, and encouraged, the belief that the most appropriate response involves restorative justice practices (Neilson, 1995; Griffiths, 1996; Ross, 1996; Canada, 1996). However, contemporary Aboriginal communities have undergone considerable change over the past several decades and some of these changes are reflected in the type and volume of crime and disorder that now plague them. The earlier discussion in this chapter concerning the characteristics of crime and disorder among Aboriginal people provides some insights into the difficult challenges facing Aboriginal communities in implementing restorative justice programs. Despite the widespread belief that restorative justice has emerged from indigenous societies, it is not at all clear that the contemporary versions of these societies will be able to meet the challenge that operationalizing local restorative justice systems requires. Nor is it clear that modern Aboriginal communities are more able than non-indigenous/non-Aboriginal societies to adopt and practise restorative justice.

There are at least three problems that render restorative justice in contemporary communities difficult to achieve. These are distinct from, but framed by, the nature of offences, the characteristics of offenders and victims, and the geographic and emotional isolation of victims. The first problem is the long-standing and often entrenched divisions and tensions among individuals, families, and group. Even where a particular crime or incident may be dealt with in a satisfactory manner in a restorative justice forum, a history of strain and tension among families, other community members, and/or victims and offenders, may make it difficult, if not impossible, to retain that level of satisfaction over time. In this context it is often hard to 'uncouple' the event and the perpetrator, which Braithwaite and Mugford (1994) suggest is a condition for the successful reintegration of the offender.

The second issue is the increasingly non-communal nature of contemporary Aboriginal communities. Despite other changes, Aboriginal communities remain based upon and defined by kin and extended family or clan networks. While these networks once played a strong role in crime and disorder prevention, and acted in a supportive role to other adjudicators of conflict in communities, today these relationships may work against successful conflict resolution. Many communities have internalized Western views of 'objectivity' in justice that do not fit well in small communities where internal power relations and patterns of authority have been rendered asymmetrical and problematic over time. It is difficult to harness these relationships and achieve any perception at all of the fairness and legitimacy of community justice. Finally, there is the problem of the amount and normalization of violence in these communities. Violence cuts across socio-economic and geographic lines and is seen most readily in high levels of family violence and sexual abuse. Because family violence and sexual abuse are such significant elements of crime in these communities, it is difficult to imagine how a restorative justice project could exclude these offences. Any community justice project implemented to 'restore relationships' and 'reduce crime' that does not address the most common type of offences committed in the community will have difficulty reaching these objectives. But even where these offences are included, a desire among offenders, victims, and community members to restore or rebuild these relationships, when there are so many other factors at play, cannot be assumed Family violence and sexual assault generally present particular moral dilemmas for restorative justice. Many advocates, especially women and women's groups, have argued that restorative justice is an inappropriate response to family and sexual assaults.[2] Others, however, argue that there is a place for restorative justice in domestic violence because the use of the criminal justice system is, by itself, too narrow and confining for women who do not want their partners charged and/or incarcerated. Still others maintain that restorative justice is inappropriate because of power differentials either between victim and offender or within communities, and because of the difficulty of ensuring the safety of victims.

McGillivray and Comaskey (1999) argue that diverting those who have violated intimate relations of trust raises a number of problems. The voice of the victim may be more obscure than in the existing, mainstream system of justice because there is no prosecutor to represent her interests. At the root of the problem is the power imbalance created by intimate violence. The authors quote Hillary Astor, who argues that mediation – potentially part of any diversion program and characteristic of circle sentencing – is undesirable in intimate violence because 'violence creates an extreme power imbalance between the parties, because the parties do not have the capacity to mediate and because mediation does not provide for the needs of the person who has been the target of violence' (Astor, quoted in McGillvray & Comaskey, 1999: 151).

When McGillivray and Comaskey solicited the views of Aboriginal women on the criminal justice system diversion of their abusive partners, respondents expressed overwhelming support for punishment, but they also supported effective treatment programs. Respondents believed that sentencing was too lenient and that plea bargaining was a cause of lenient sentences because the facts presented to the judge were distorted (McGillvray and Comaskey, 1999: 117–19). Although respondents wanted effective treatment programs, they wanted treatment combined with, or incorporated into, a jail term, longer jail terms that would incorporate long-term treatment, and programs that forced abusers to confront their denial and deal with personal problems (McGillvray & Comaskey, 1999: 122). These preferences are clearly outside the realm of restorative justice.

In a recent paper on victims and the criminal justice system, Rupert Ross (2001) asks if there is a possible disconnect between the way victims and courts define their crimes. He questions how we should respond to victimization and how offenders may be held more accountable to their victims and the damage caused by them. Victims want to make certain offenders understand exactly how the victimization has affected their capacity for healthy relationships. In this approach, Ross moves sharply away from the 'forgiveness' principle inherent in restorative justice, and argues that to make an innocent victim 'forgive' the offender places a unwarranted burden on the victim and is a perversion of justice (2001: 6). He claims that the 'most successful encounters [he has] seen are victim-centered processes running parallel to the prosecution process' (Ross, 2001: 7). Restorative processes that are too 'agreement-directed' are unlikely to meet the needs of victims, owing to their focus on outcomes and the reality that, in many communities, restorative practices are administered by unskilled people or people whose main interests are reaching agreements and/or achieving agreement.

In her research on youth justice conferences in the Australian Capital Territory (ACT) and south Australia, Daly found support for concerns of potential revictimization of women in conferences. In the conferences she observed Daly judged seven of the twenty-eight victims to have been treated with disrespect, or to have been emotionally distraught, as a result of the conference. She also found conferences to be gendered events. While few offenders were female, women comprised 52 per cent of offender's supporters and more mothers than fathers were present at conferences. Interestingly, this trend shifted only in the context of supervising the completion of agreements; here, more men than women participated in the process, suggesting that the gendered nature of conferences persisted beyond the actual conference process and perpetuated the limited power granted to women through this forum (Daly, 2001: 14–15).

It would seem that if restorative justice is to be used for victims of sexual assault and adult victims of family and domestic violence, a number of changes will have to occur. Daly believes it is essential to move away from the lines of demarcation that are almost always drawn between restorative justice and retributive justice (Daly, 2000a). She suggests that the widely accepted contrast between Aboriginal justice (restorative) and non-Aboriginal justice (retributive) is too simplistic. Instead, she argues that we must seriously engage questions surrounding whether restorative justice can deliver a better or more effective kind of justice in diverse communities, especially those structured by socio-economic and political inequalities, and with age, gender, and racial-ethnic divisions. Daly argues that restorative justice contains emotional and psychological elements of both retributive and rehabilitative justice, and is just as capable of exacerbating divisions and inequality – as a result, we must be as cautious in our use of restorative processes as we are in our use of mainstream, retributive ones (Daly, 2001: 1). In questioning the appropriateness of restorative justice approaches like family group conferences for Aboriginal young people, Daly is concerned that 'sameness of treatment' can result in the expectation that outcomes for the most heavily marginalized members should and would be the same as those for its more conventional members, when clearly they cannot be so. She concludes that restorative justice principles and practices have the *potential* to deliver a better kind of justice than presently exists, but differing cultural sensibilities and relations of inequality must be addressed before this can happen. In short, and in contradiction to the apparent positions of too many commentators, the greater 'humane-ness' of the restorative justice process cannot be automatically assumed.

In her own observations of family conferences, Daly saw retribution, reparation, and reintegration. However, the general opinion about restorative processes in Canada, reinforced in the recent Supreme Court of Canada decisions of *Gladue* and *Wells*, runs counter to the argument that Daly and other feminist writers make about victims of sexual and 'gendered' assaults. This conflict is especially apparent in the argument that: 'if, say, poverty and a history of discrimination played a part in a young man turning to violence, our failing to punish him, or our punishing him lightly, ends up further hurting the people who were already hurt by his violence. It has been insufficiently appreciated that well-meaning compassion toward offenders can, in and of itself, do damage. Kindness toward the criminal can be an act of cruelty towards his victims and the larger community' (Hampton quoted in Daly, 2000a: 9).

The case for how victims are harmed when offenders are treated too easily or their acts are not condemned in an appropriate manner is compelling (Daly, 2000a). While acknowledging the difficulty of using restorative justice for sexual assaults, Daly, like Hampton, concludes that 'restorative justice must ultimately be concerned first with vindicating the harms suffered by victims (via retribution and reparation) and ... second with rehabilitating offenders ...' (Daly, 2000a: 20). Daly believes that in the final analysis 'one can neither fully endorse nor disparage restorative justice approaches in responding to sexualized violence or other gendered harms' (2000a: 20).

The status of victims in relation to the use of restorative justice appears to converge on the issue of where in the process the emphasis should be placed. Ross argues that the state should order offenders to participate in processes with victims in those cases where the victim believes that making contact with the offender will promote her recovery and rehabilitation. At the same time, Daly and other feminist writers express concerns about the limits of a restorative process that does not directly confront the problem of retribution, or that does not explicitly vindicate victims (Daly, 2000a: 9). However, both Ross and Daly agree that restorative justice practices may allow a more free-ranging discussion about the harm done, the injury suffered, and other aspects of the victimization than would be possible in a courtroom. While arguing the need to treat serious crimes seriously, Daly also believes it is critical for a justice system to identify more and less serious forms of sexual assault and other gendered harms, and to act accordingly. These distinctions will have to be confronted if restorative justice is to become an appropriate response for Aboriginal communities, wherein such offences promise to constitute a significant percentage of the caseload to be managed by community restorative justice processes.

While the matrix of victim and offender constitute one challenge facing communities, the ability of the community to provide effective and appropriate contexts for shaming and reintegration is another. Braithwaite and Mugford (1994) set out the 'conditions' for successful reintegration ceremonies: reducing recidivism and reintegrating offenders into a wider web of community ties and support, and giving victims a voice. While this subject will be explored in greater detail in the concluding chapter, it is clear that some of the conditions necessary for successful reintegration of offenders (and victims) may be problematic in Aboriginal communities, particularly communities which are geographically bounded and isolated. For example, 'uncoupling' the event and the perpetrator is difficult when the event may be part of a much longer history of tension between the two parties and/or their extended families. Similarly, the condition that 'co-ordinators must identify with all the private parties' can be difficult to meet in communities where knowledge and familiarity among people are intense; where putting a stranger into the facilitator role may be the only way to achieve the goal. The condition that denunciation must be by and in the name of the victim (and that the victim should be present) is probably among the most difficult to meet in these communities. As will be seen, evaluations of local justice projects in Aboriginal communities, albeit limited in number and often in approach, have repeatedly identified the difficulties facing victims. These range from coercion to participate, to issues of power differentials and community repercussions, through to the finding that local justice is more concerned with offenders and their needs than with victims.

Retributive justice and restorative justice are probably less far apart in many of their goals and objectives (e.g., maintaining order and social control) than advocates of either might like to suggest. We see this in both historical and contemporary terms in light of the fact that the goals of justice have changed little, even while practices have changed quite dramatically. However, belief in the differences persists and often finds voice in perceptions of the cultural 'fit' of restorative justice to Aboriginal communities and the Aboriginal world-view. It is difficult to understand the persistence of this belief in restorative justice as tradition. As O'Malley argues, '[t]here are enormous problems associated with the identification of the nature and content of "tradition" among a people already subjected to considerable cultural and social disruption' (O'Malley, n.d.: 9) Given its reintegrative functions, it is also difficult to imagine how restorative justice is a better fit in communities with high levels of social problems and crime and disorder than in those which manifest lower levels.

Yet there are a range of realities characterizing contemporary communities that may be more important to understand and address than whether restorative justice is 'traditional.' These include the difficult nature of much disorder and dispute in Aboriginal communities, and the characteristics of victims and offenders in those disputes. As well, it is crucial to appreciate and be realistic about the human and other resources available to support restorative justice, and its potential to meet the needs of victims, offenders, and communities. Those working in and with communities to develop and implement restorative justice programs must address some of the fundamental objectives of a justice system, which may be more consistent across cultures than is generally assumed. That is, the contrast may be one of means, rather than ends, and acceptance of this fact may provide the location for a better, shared understanding of community needs and program form and content. Even a quick glance at the historical record tells us that there were a broad range of responses to crime and disorder across Aboriginal nations, only a few of which are amenable to incorporation in a modern restorative justice program; indeed, the possibility must be entertained that, in some cultural contexts, 'traditional alternatives' may not be good ones to address contemporary crime and conflict.

This chapter has raised a number of issues that should inform the development and implementation of community restorative justice projects in Aboriginal communities, but which often appear to be conspicuously absent in the majority of restorative initiatives, including sentencing circles, conferencing, and healing circles. As we move into a deeper analysis of these project forms, it becomes apparent that the bulk of restorative justice practice in the Aboriginal context in Canada remains in the realm of a 'social experiment,' an experiment that may have serious implications for communities and justice.

CHAPTER 6

Testing the 'Magic': Sentencing Circles in Aboriginal Community Restorative Justice

> Many informal community processes have far greater potential to constructively change attitudes, build, rebuild relationships, promote mutual respect for different values, empower parties to resolve differences, and generally improve the well-being of everyone affected by crime, or by any conflict.
>
> (Stuart, 1997: 208)

> The alternative approach to the existing sentencing process was welcomed by many. It was seen by the judge and the chair of the [Inuit Justice] Task Force as a step in making the justice system more accountable to Inuit. The author's observations during the first sentencing circle in Nunavik suggest that it is unclear how that accountability is to be achieved.
>
> (Crnkovich, 1996: 169)

As observed in the introduction to this book, the circle has long been viewed as a symbol of importance and empowerment among many First Nations. As such, it is perhaps fitting that the most well-known and, at present, most entrenched of restorative justice initiatives within Canada – sentencing circles and healing circles – would be fashioned after this central cultural symbol. As informed by the circle, these initiatives assert the power of its central attributes, namely, balance, equality, and a holistic approach to life and the conflicts which are an expected and normal part of that life. Within the circle, we are told, inequalities between professionals and 'regular people' are broken down, as is the common reticence that impedes the sharing of information about conflict which is so necessary to its resolution and the healing of those affected by it. This apparent passing of the power to do justice from the state to the community through the vehicle of the circle is as much a part of the healing of the community as is the circle to those in conflict.

While the circle is important within many Aboriginal cultures, in the realm of restorative justice it has two primary incarnations – the circle as a place for taking responsibility for conflict and disorder, and the circle as a place for healing. While some commentators stress that the circle is always a place of healing, it is important to recognize that as categories of community projects, the sentencing circle is a thing apart from the healing circle. As will be seen, the sentencing circle is essentially an adaptation of one portion of the Canadian criminal trial process. That is, the sentencing circle is most commonly the place or process wherein an offender who has pleaded guilty (although this is not necessarily a firm requirement in all contexts) may participate with his or her community in the determination of a 'fit' sentence to follow from the acceptance of responsibility and demonstration of remorse deemed implicit in the guilty plea. It is difficult to define precisely the common elements that define a sentencing circle because 'there is no single model. Each community adapts Circle Sentencing [sic] to fit their particular circumstances' (Stuart, 1995: 2) While there is undoubtedly benefit in such flexibility, it has also caused more than a few brows to raise among those who prefer a degree of consistency and predictability across and within the criminal sentencing process.

Sentencing circles can be contrasted with healing circles, with which they may work in tandem, as in the case of the Community Holistic Circles Healing Program (the CHCH). Healing circles, while argued to share sentencing circles' focus on communication and the taking of responsibility for conflict by those who create it and their larger communities, are essentially therapeutic processes that meld traditional and modern approaches to 'healing' perpetrators and victims of crime. Healing circles will be discussed in chapter 7.

Consistent with the assumption that the circle is a pan-Indian cultural concept that crosses geographic, linguistic, and national boundaries are a series of concomitant ideas about the circle as a definitive element of the projects it informs. Perhaps the most basic of these ideas is that a circle-based restorative justice project is also, by implication if not by necessity, a community and an Aboriginal construct that is somehow better-suited than the dominant system to resolving conflict and 'restoring' victims, offenders, and their communities. Insofar as they speak to an ideal, such assumptions carry little risk. However, when the ideal is assumed to be the reality, it can obscure efforts to document those aspects of the circle tradition that may not apply to all communities, or function to the benefit of all parties.

(i) Sentencing Circles as a Modern Expression of Aboriginal Culture: Pan-Indianism and the Challenge of Erosion of Tradition

... there it is again, that goddamned circle, as if we thought in circles, judged things on the merit of their circularity ... yet I feel compelled to incorporate something circular ... because if it's linear then that proves that I'm a ghost and that native culture really has vanished ... (Dumont quoted in Anderson, 1998)

The idea of the sentencing circle is deceptively simple. Based on an assumption that much of the trouble with current sentencing processes is structural, the circle concept assumes that it is possible to achieve profound revisions in perspective and power relations by rearranging the physical structure of the courtroom. Thus, once a sentencing circle is agreed to be an appropriate process for determining sentence, the judge and counsel will exchange their formal positions for 'comfortable places' in a circle of seating occupied by the parties to the conflict, their communities of care, and interested community members. Here, according to the court in the 'definitive circle case,' *R. v. Moses*, the usual order of things in sentencing is fundamentally altered: 'By arranging the court in circle without desks or tables, with all participants facing each other, with equal access and equal exposure to each other, the dynamics of the decision-making process [are] profoundly changed ... The circle significantly breaks down the dominance that traditional courtrooms accord lawyers and judges. In a circle, the ability to contribute, the importance and credibility of any input is not defined by seating arrangements. The audience is changed' ([1992] Y.J. No. 50; p. 6).

While the shift in seating arrangements is a relatively straightforward under-taking, as with most simple changes, a number of devils pop up in the details. These range from broad philosophical questions surrounding the origins and pan-Indianism attributed to circles, through a number of sticky legal realities and power relations implicit in the sentencing process that transcend its physical structure, to a lack of evaluation of circles made worse by the grand promises they make to an often vulnerable and dependent population.

Let us look first to the origins of circles. Popular wisdom asserts that the sentencing circle is rooted in ancient Aboriginal traditions of dispute resolution which were either lost or undermined as a consequence of colonialism. In this regard, the creation of a sentencing circle in a community constitutes a number of important steps on the road to recovery from colonialism. Implementing a circle is at once an act of cultural reclamation through the resurrection of a lost tradition and an act of self-governance – a claim to a right to do justice for one's own people. While these are all positive steps for Aboriginal communities, many of which are struggling and rebuilding, there is a danger that their impacts may be more illusory than real. If those illusions facilitate empowerment and an activism in the direction of real change, they may be a good thing, if only for a while. The danger is that once the first-blush of circles erodes, participants are likely to be unclear about the nature of the power gained, its positive conse-quences, and the costs paid for them.

The illusions begin at the very foundation of circles. There is a quiet questioning emerging from many quarters about just how 'traditional' or Aboriginal the circle sentencing concept truly is, and an increasing volume of protest around assumptions that it is a pan-Indian one. While many cultures embrace the circle as a central cultural symbol, it is by no means ubiquitous – Iroquois people, for example, do not appear to have any particular cultural reference point for the circle and, were they to consider redrafting the physical setting of a sentencing hearing, would probably be more at home with a seating arrangement that replicates the clan-based structure that traditionally framed deliberations of governance matters 'over the fire.' Nor would it appear that the circle is apposite for Inuit communities, whose early experiences with sentencing circles have been seen by some observers as problematic in both practical and cultural terms. In the context of Nunavik, Crnkovich (1995) points out that sentencing circles are attempting to incorporate what are identified as Aboriginal traditions and values, but that the sentencing circle itself is not a traditional practice of Aboriginal peoples in Canada.

Crnkovich's statements are compelling, and she is among the very few commentators who have been prepared to challenge the sacred cow of 'traditionalism' in restorative justice in general, and sentencing circles in particular. As suggested in the previous chapter, sentencing circles may not be 'traditional' for many of the communities who are implementing or considering implementing them, and the assumption of 'pan-Indianism' made most often by outsiders and influential others promoting circles as options for communities is as problematic as the basic obfuscation and reduction of cultural differences and national identities implicit in the idea of pan-Indianism itself. Pan-Indianism has had clear value as a unifying force impelling joint activism. The difficulty resides in the strength of this concept: pan-Indianism obscures specific cultural differences to create a common identity that can unite members of very different cultural groups and nations into a force to challenge shared social and political problems. While it might be instrumental in impelling the state to work with communities on justice reform writ large, pan-Indianism is of less value in defining the details of that reform at the level of individual communities. By its very nature, it must obscure those individual and community cultures central to defining a relevant and sustainable justice project. Pan-Indianism, then, must be understood as one means to achieve the broad goal of Aboriginal justice reform, not as a mechanism to define the individual end of community justice projects. Insofar as the circle is an important cultural symbol and value for *some* First Nations, a sentencing circle will have *some* 'fit' in those communities, but this must not be taken to mean that it will achieve a similar fit in other communities.

The attraction of pan-Indianism resides largely in its utility as a mechanism for 'identity reclamation' among First Nations hard-hit by colonial processes; it responds to the very real and very tragic erosion of culture and identity which was a central goal of the policies of 'civilization' and 'assimilation.' This erosion may explain the tendency for some communities to gravitate towards sentencing circles, especially when they are proposed by influential outsiders such as judges, as means to include the people in processes that have previously excluded them. In the absence of traditional knowledge that might inform a local justice initiative, communities committed to positive change face the not insubstantial challenge of finding the 'raw cultural materials' from which to create a justice project consonant with their identity and traditions. In such a situation, the attraction of a sentencing circle is obvious and compelling: not only does the circle promise to fill the holes in traditional culture left by colonialism, the promise is made by powerful and influential outsiders – again, usually judges – who are offering through the sentencing circle a type and degree of inclusion and participation long-denied to the community, which they are told will fix much (if not all) of what ails the community. In such a context, the degree to which a sentencing circle fits with local culture becomes secondary; like pan-Indianism, sentencing circles are embraced as a means to an end. Despite their creation by outsiders and their somewhat obscure roots in indigenous culture, they provide a way to be 'traditional.' As stressed by Anderson: 'the point ... is that Aboriginal communities in general have suffered an erosion of traditional values and beliefs that served as mechanisms for dealing with disruptive and injurious behaviour. And with this erosion, traditional knowledge has increasingly diminished as well – most Aboriginals in Canada have little or no knowledge of their own traditions' (1998: 316).

The challenge is a multifaceted one. There can be little doubt of the veracity of Anderson's statement – a significant number of Aboriginal communities have lost much traditional knowledge owing to the same historical processes and policies that undermined their political and economic structures, fostering dependency through strategic underdevelopment. The irony is not lost that these historical processes are responsible not only for much of the social dysfunction and conflict which now moves communities to seek some manner of restorative program, but also for the erosion of those cultural processes and practices that might have coped with at least some of that dysfunction. Needing these programs as part of a community reclamation process, the community lacks many of the traditional skills that might inform them, and thereby redress the high rates of conflict between their people and the criminal justice system, at least part of which is cultural in nature. Communities thus become open and vulnerable to the arrival of experts or influential outsiders who offer not only a program, but one which they state confidentially 'fits' with the community's long-lost culture.

In this context, the degree of the fit is almost irrelevant – if one has lost the knowledge to render a community justice program uniquely Huron or Cree, a sentencing circle can at least ensure that it is 'Indian.' In the long process of recovery from colonialism, that may be enough for now.

The problem here is not that there is something deeply wrong with '*Indian* restorative justice programs,' but that there may not be enough that is right about these programs to enable them to keep many of the promises of self-governance and community restoration made by restorative justice to Aboriginal people. In some measure, the requirement of Aboriginality in these programs is curious. It relies in large part upon the accuracy of the culture-clash arguments of over-representation critiqued in Part I, and upon what appears to be an overwhelming pressure created by these arguments that restorative justice programs in Aboriginal communities must be uniquely and definitively *Aboriginal*. After all, if the essence of the over-representation problem is the differing legal cultures of Aboriginals and non-Aboriginals, then logic would dictate that any proposed solution must be imbued with Aboriginal traits, traditions, and practices; reforms must be unequivocally Aboriginal in nature, lest they simply replicate the problems they were designed to rectify (and, in the case of indigenization, create a number of new ones). In this way the culture-clash perspective has created a strong pressure upon communities to create programs that have significant 'traditional' content – an element that can also affect success with obtaining state funding, which is increasingly seeking an 'Aboriginal angle' in community programs. This has fostered an almost untenable situation for communities of the type referred to by Anderson – if your community has lost much of its traditional knowledge, how might you go about fashioning a restorative justice program that is somehow uniquely yours? If the influential outsiders who come into your community to hold court or assist in the development of a justice project are equally in the dark, the attraction of such pan-Indian initiatives as sentencing circles is undoubtedly quite strong.

In the same measure that pan-Indian cultural models tend towards reductionist and instrumentalist views of the many different Aboriginal cultures, those influential outsiders who gravitate to and promote such models may well be suffering from yet another critical misunderstanding with regard to Aboriginal communities: the absence of a clear and robust traditional or ancient culture in a community does not equate with the absence of a unique and robust *community culture*, and the latter may be far more important to understand, accommodate, and possibly reform, through restorative justice projects. We will return to this issue in the third part of this book.

Sentencing circles admittedly embody some traditional cultural elements which are relevant to some communities, some of the time, but the mainstream justice system and many academics and commentators have assumed that they are sufficiently traditional and 'Indian' to work for all communities, all the time. Sentencing circles do not, and will not, 'fit' with all communities and cultures, and to assume that any one cultural construct can fit all is questionable. What is more, in some contexts, this approach may be seen as downright pejorative. Again, the focus on pan-Indian initiatives is probably a logical consequence of its linkages with the line of argument stressing that over-representation is a product of a clash between Aboriginal culture and the dominant or mainstream culture that defines the criminal justice process. While some version of this argument may be true, such explanations – and the solutions they encourage – tend to assume that the clash is between *two* cultures – a 'white' one and an 'Aboriginal' one, when in fact it is a clash of different degrees between a dominant culture and a range of different and distinct Aboriginal cultures. It is difficult to see how that clash can be ameliorated by privileging one Aboriginal culture or construct above all others within a single reform, which is then presented to all Aboriginal communities and cultures as *the* reform option. This is not to suggest that there are not other options, such as conferencing, advisory panels, or the independent development of a community-based project rooted in local traditions, open to communities who do not share the 'culture of the circle.' But, when faced with an outside authority figure offering a reform option which is not only explicitly presented as 'traditional,' but which is also said to enable empowerment through inclusion in a process that does not appear to lay claim to often extremely limited cultural or community resources, many communities will take it. In so doing, the community is thrust into a pan-Indian justice model that requires them both to participate in a reductionist view of their own culture and to accept a 'parachuted project' that may have little grounding, ownership, or engagement in the local community. Furthermore, as will be seen, the issue of claims to community resources, whether human or monetary, made by initiatives such as sentencing circles is also problematic, as they are often far grander than is readily apparent in the circle session, and depend upon levels of agency that may not be present in all communities.

Central to much of the preceding discussion is the matter of how sentencing circles find their way into communities. With the possible exception of the Yukon community of Kwanlin-Dun which, with Judge Barry Stuart, is credited along with the conception and implementation of sentencing circles, they are almost without exception reforms injected into communities by outsiders, whether experts or judges. This betrays yet another assumption about this reform, namely that it is a grassroots exercise in self-government. It is difficult to see how this could be so given that sentencing circles are very much a creation growing out of the existing justice system introduced within Aboriginal communities, for the most part by the judiciary serving these communities (Anderson, 1998). The comments of a participant in an early sentencing circle in Sandy Bay in the late 1980s are apt: '[We] were approached and asked if we would be willing to try out this new way of dealing with young offenders. I believe we were approached by the magistrate [provincial court judge] at that time, who was feeling frustrated ... he felt it would be more effective if people from the community took responsibility and showed that they were affected and cared about the people that got into trouble. That might be a better way' (Bay quoted in Green, 1998: 48).

Those who work with Aboriginal communities in project development appear to agree that community projects which are designed with and by communities, which have a clear and rational link to extant community problems, and which actively incorporate local culture and accommodate the resource realities of the community are more likely to be 'owned' by the community and – accepting that survival of community projects generally is a tall order – are in equal measure more likely to succeed and persist. Since the credibility and success of community justice projects and reforms are contingent upon their status as truly community creations, it is difficult to see how the acceptance of an externally defined and controlled project can enhance self-governance. Parachute programs are only ever that, and by their very existence as external creations may be said to carry assumptions of community incapacity and limited agency – assumptions which must then exist in an uneasy alliance with assumptions that, while a community cannot develop its own project, it is competent to sustain someone else's project. Sentencing circles lie very much within this difficult tension, and it is to communities that the navigation of that tension falls.

(ii) Sentencing Circles as Self-Government: Empowering Communities to Do Justice or Off-Loading Responsibilities to a Context of Limited Agency?

To those who would see sentencing circles as an exercise in self-government, the value of circles in this regard resides in the responsibility assumed by the community for conflict and its resolution (an interesting view, given that state policy fostered the social conditions underlying much of the conflict, responsibility for which is now to be 'appropriately' offloaded to communities – but that is a matter for later consideration). That is, in most cases the circle will lead to a community-based disposition, the administration of which falls to family and friends within the offender's 'community of care.' Assuming that the latter can sustain the commitment made in the circle and, more importantly, has at its disposal the community programs and supports required to make most sentences real, community-based dispositions can be a powerful rehabilitative tool for offenders and communities. However, as noted earlier, too often those communities in most need of justice projects are also those in most need generally, and thus lacking in the very sorts of qualities and agency necessary to sustain a community justice initiative. While those communities in most need are also the least equipped to sustain the very programs that make circle sentences work, the judiciary seems relatively unconcerned about leaving the execution of sentences to them. The issue here is not the commitment and ability of community members, which are often remarkably strong and persistent, but whether these capable persons see their capabilities undermined by the absence of community programs and structures that are integral to the smooth functioning and effective administration of the justice project and the dispositions it creates.

When 'enlightened judges' offer a sentencing circle to a community without inquiring seriously into the capability of the communities and families to share the offender's responsibility for the sentence, a crucial piece of the picture is lost. Judges may end up accepting a sentencing recommendation which, taken outside the 'magic of the circle,' may simply not be sustainable. For example, in the *Moses* case, much of the three-part sentence ordered by the judge placed a considerable responsibility on the family of the offender. 'The first part commence[d] Philip's rehabilitation by immediately calling upon his family to reintegrate him back into their family and lifestyle' (*R. v. Moses*: 25). This requirement involved a commitment by the family to ensure that one of their members remained *at all times* with the offender on the family trapline, but it is unclear what else this 'reintegration' may have involved. The family is given responsibility for the offender and his rehabilitation, but very little direction as to how one might make this happen – beyond the direction to always accompany the offender and keep alcohol out of the home. The lack of direction is in itself deeply problematic, but it is made that much more so by the reality that, for many offenders, their families and 'communities of care' are often a very large part of the problem for the offender – evidence the 'viciously destructive childhood' and 'abuse and neglect' noted by the judge in *Moses* (3). In these circumstances, requiring the family to provide the solution may be unrealistic. Even if they have gone a long measure towards their own healing, the baggage and relational patterns in the home and family may undermine the most positive of intentions. In short, many families of offenders may be sufficiently fragile themselves that asking them to assume control over the fate of their most fragile and difficult members may not only be unfair, but place their own healing at risk. It may be difficult for those who made the undertakings in the circle to sustain their commitment as well as ensure the continued commitment of the entire family – possibly including members who were not present in the circle.

Furthermore, some may resent what they perceive as serving part of the sentence with and for an offender, and for an offence in which they believed they played no part; certainly, binding the innocent to the terms of a sentence which, in law, has no application to them is a legally questionable undertaking. While these issues may not arise in the immediate wake of a circle, when enthusiasm and commitment are high, they can become serious problems as time wears on, and commitments become more difficult to honour in the face of the demands of daily life.

The issues revolving around the responsibility faced by the family in many circle sentences are replicated at the level of the community, where questions of agency and resources are also important. If part of the circle's sentence is participation in some manner of therapeutic programming, it is incumbent upon those in the circle to be realistic about what programs exist in the community. In *Moses*, the third part of the sentence relied upon a commitment by the community to create the programs the offender needed to complete his sentence: 'The First Nation will develop a support program for Philip to upgrade life and employment skills, and provide continual counselling [sic] for substance abuse' (25). That such programming can and will be created seems a rather large leap of faith – did the judge enquire into the details of schooling, of the local job market, of whether there are appropriately trained counsellors in the community who have the time to see the offender on a 'continual' basis? The mainstream system, with its wealth of resources and personnel, cannot achieve or control these conditions, and yet there seems little reluctance to hand them off to small, often poor, and marginalized communities where such resources are desperately needed and conspicuously absent. If a successful sentence requires that such programming is in place and likely to remain so for the duration of the sentence, it is arguably incumbent upon the judge to ascertain that the structures are in place to ensure this is so. In *Moses*, the statement of sentence in this regard seems reminiscent of the practice of purchasing clothing in the size you want to wear, as opposed to the size you currently are. Promises of possibilities are not enough – there must be programming in place in the community that will fit the offender and the sentence at the time the circle transpires. Anything else is unrealistic, and depends upon a number of notoriously fickle factors, such as obtaining funding to develop and sustain the needed programs and the ability to attract trained personnel, in sufficient numbers to ensure all circle sentences are satisfied. The state, which appears to have embraced sentencing circles and restorative justice, must step in here, and provide the funding and support to enable First Nations to complete the task many of them have assumed willingly, in good faith – and often at the urging of representatives of that state.

What is perhaps most problematic about the circle sentence handed to Moses, his family, and their community is the almost non-existent attention paid to how they might respond to what may be the largest single factor behind Philip's difficulties: Foetal Alcohol Syndrome (FAS). While the judge made reference to the fact that '[s]ubstance abuse, criminal activities and the chronic failure to cope with the demands and discipline of a self-reliant existence are symptoms of Philip's struggle with the curse of fetal alcohol syndrome' (R. v. Moses: 20), no further reference is made to this matter anywhere in the decision. This is staggering, as it appears to the judge to lie at the root of the offender's problem, and is something which must therefore be central in the plans for rehabilitation. FAS is a medical problem, and one which requires significant skills, training, and commitment to manage – as demonstrated in chapter 2 of this work, it is also likely to lie at or near the roots of the criminality of approximately 70 per cent of the prison population. Insofar as the circle relies on volunteers to make its sentences work, and many communities lack the sort of structured, sustained, and specialist programs which can assist those with FAS to overcome the struggles they face, the challenges to circle sentences, and to the communities made responsible for them, cannot be underestimated. Here especially, communities must be provided with adequate and consistent program support and expertise.

As an act of self-governance, then, sentencing circles must rely on the presence of a sufficiently well-developed infrastructure to support offenders and their communities of care to meet the terms of a circle sentence – as will be seen, this is a significant obstacle facing most, if not all, community restorative justice projects. To reiterate, however, the problem is that in many communities this infrastructure is not in place – indeed, its absence is at once a central factor in the rates of conflict and disorder that render a justice project so necessary and an impediment to the success of that project. Communities caught in such a tension are understandably reluctant to wait until that infrastructure is in place to pursue sentencing circles or some other local justice initiative. At the same time, however, the initiative may have limited chances of success in the absence of even the most modest infrastructure characterizing most communities – even where programs appear to exist, they are subject to constantly imperilled funding, frequent changes in personnel, and a lack of evaluations which can ensure that the facilities offered are of the quality necessary to really make a difference. Judges who would present sentencing circles as an option for communities have an obligation to ensure that the community is equipped to accept that responsibility. This is not, as Stuart would seem to put it, a matter of heart. The sheer persistence of many Aboriginal communities in the face of colonialism and underdevelopment is proof positive of the tenacity and heart of these communities. It is rather a matter of a legal system which is prepared to take the time to ensure that it is not setting a community up for failure with a circle sentence, and a state committed to providing sufficient resources and support to create the infrastructure which is a prerequisite to its success. It benefits communities little simply to declare that 'First Nation's [sic] have the best knowledge and ability to prevent and resolve the long list of tragedies plaguing their communities' (R. v. Moses: 22); judges involved with sentencing circles have a moral obligation to ensure that this knowledge and ability are evidenced in a solid infrastructure of sufficient and successful community programs which can support circle sentences and those serving them.

The qualifications on sentencing circles as a form of empowerment and self-government are not limited to those created by gaps in community agency and resources, but extend to those implicit in the legal realities and the power relations contained within circles. The latter are evident in the nature of the limitations on the sentencing process in the criminal law and the fact that, while the sentencing circle may contribute to an appearance of power-sharing, this contribution may be more illusory than real. While the value of community participation in the sentencing process through consultation and sharing in the circle should not be discounted, lay members of the circle must understand that their contribution is not necessarily definitive of the sentence. The community may assist in shaping a sentence, and will ultimately be largely responsible for ensuring that those sentenced meet its terms, but it must never be assumed that this assistance equates with the power to make the actual decision about sentence. This latter task will always fall to the judge. As observed by McEachern C.J. in the *Johns* case: 'The public must be made to understand that the court retains both authority and jurisdiction to impose whatever sentence the judge, rather than the circle, decides or recommends in any particular case. In other words, the circle, representing the community of the accused in the entire process, and the prosecutor, representing the larger public in the court proceedings, may assist and advise the judge, but the judge and the judge alone must decide what sentence should be imposed' (quoted in McNamara, 2000: 216).

In this statement the judge was speaking not only to a general 'public,' but probably also to the individual and particular community publics served by sentencing circles. That the ultimate decision must, in law, always remain with the judge is well-established, and this fact constitutes a significant challenge to the view of sentencing circles as promoting self-government or empowerment on the part of a First Nation. This is not to deny that participation in a circle may increase a sense of pride and accomplishment in some community members, and that this may be important to achieving real self-governance over the long term. But early commentators and proponents of circle sentencing tended to claim that the movement would have remarkable transformative effects for communities. Circles were said to build communities and empower their members (Stuart, 1996; Donlevy, 1994; Arnot, 1994) by granting responsibility for conflict and its resolution within their communities. They were presented and embraced by communities as exercises in self-government. While we face an almost total lack of any evaluation that might indicate the degree to which this potential has been realized, if at all, it is perhaps more unsettling that these promises were made in the first place. To promise empowerment through a reform that leaves the basic distribution of power untouched, wherein the judge retains the power of decision making, is at best overly optimistic, at worst misleading. Some community members may feel somewhat empowered by participation in the circle, or by having their recommendations accepted and reified in a sentence, but this is something quite apart and quite distinct from the much broader and more meaningful empowerment consonant with self-government. The issue is not that sentencing circles cannot have empowering impacts, but rather that it is unlikely that those impacts will be of the quality and quantity suggested by circle advocates who speak of self-government. Communities may be signing on to a program of reform that offers much less than they may have been led to believe, and in which the promised 'empowerment' is attended by significant costs. These include costs associated with implementing a sentence and supporting an offender for whom there may be little in the way of program and therapeutic supports available locally. Sentencing circles may not be all they have been made out to be, and given the costs implicit in their implementation, communities should be made fully aware of what they are taking on when they agree to a circle sentencing.

Sentencing circles require the state and its legal system to surrender precious little power or authority while placing a very large and sometimes unwieldy responsibility on communities. Communities must trust the system sufficiently to share freely the information on which the circle depends and prospers, and trust the judge to use that information in good faith and in a way consistent with the intention and integrity with which it is given. As if this were not enough, the community must then also accept responsibility for the sentence and for seeing that sentence through – no mean task given the socio-economic base and limited infrastructure of Aboriginal communities. To the cynical, this looks rather like a classic case of system offloading; not only is the community required through the circle to buy into its processes and participate in its sometimes rather problematic work, they must also bear the human and monetary costs associated with taking responsibility for 'healing' offenders and victims. The appearance of offloading is heightened by the multiple references by circle advocates to the effect that sentencing circles not only achieve more relevant dispositions, but achieve them at a much lower cost than mainstream structures (Stuart, 1996: 202;

R. v. Moses: 15). Given the promises made by circles and the impediments to their realization in many communities, one wonders whether those advocates define 'costs' as including anything other than the purely monetary.

The possibility that sentencing circles are relying upon, and sentencing offenders to, programs that are either non-existent or of questionable efficacy or functionality is troubling. And in the most common form of the solutions proposed to address this problem, sentencing circles act as little more than referral bodies to non-community-based programs. Some of those working in the field in Aboriginal justice projects have expressed concern over the possibility that circles are merely an 'hiccup' in the existing order of things, whereby an Aboriginal offender is briefly taken out of the mainstream system and placed within the putatively more appropriate community and cultural context of the circle, only to be returned to that system owing to a lack of adequate community programs or resources. If this is in fact the case – and once again the evaluations necessary to confirm it are absent – an entirely new set of potential problems materialize. Building upon the questionable empowerment and self-government issues, the new problems implicit in this observation from the field reinforce the possibility that sentencing circles may constitute little more than a mechanism of apology for a system that changes very little. If circles are tending to refer Aboriginal offenders out of the community to programs which may well have been the destination for these offenders had they been sentenced in a non-circle context, the question is begged of precisely what it is that circles do differently, and the possibility that they are means of co-opting communities becomes more likely. Greater scrutiny of, and transparency around, sentencing circles may be in order.

The lack of options in many communities places those involved in circles in a difficult, possibly untenable position: they must either accept offenders into the community in the absence of programs and hope that their essentially untrained families and communities of care can provide the 'healing' required, or refer those offenders to outside programs which, while they may have some Aboriginal, if not local community, content, deny the offender the community-based sanctions and healing which are central to the promise of restorative justice generally and sentencing circles in particular. Neither of these choices seems particularly attractive, and they lead us to question whether sentencing circles really do offer a superior alternative to mainstream justice. How can sentencing circles make 'real differences' (Stuart, 1996: 1) in the absence of local infrastructure requisite to simply making those sentences possible?

Returning to the subject of the monetary costs, it is important to recognize that not all judges involved in circles agree with Stuart's claim that they reduce the expense associated with the sentencing process. Thus Judge Lilles of the

Yukon Territorial Court, in direct contradiction to Stuart, acknowledges that 'sentencing circles are more time consuming and therefore more expensive than processing offenders through the formal court system. Unlike other restorative processes, it is a court hearing and therefore requires the involvement of a judge along with support staff' (Lilles, 2002).

If, as observed by Stuart, a poorly planned circle can 'take more than two hours to complete' (1996: 208), this would certainly seem to involve a much more protracted process than is the case with a mainstream sentencing process, which often lasts only a few minutes. And yet, while there are certainly more 'billable hours' for court personnel involved with circles, these would seem to be relatively minor costs if circle sentences can lead to more informed, relevant, and workable sentences for offenders. The much larger part of these costs resides in the price that may be paid by victims and offenders and their communities of care, insofar as the former's participation in the circle and a resulting sentence is complex and sometimes problematic, and the latter must bear the costs associated with ensuring the terms of the sentence are carried out. There may be further costs to the larger community as well, which must now use its limited human resources to implement a sentence that might otherwise have been provided by the dominant system. What may seem to outsiders to be much lower economic costs of sentence implementation may prove far from such for the community that must meet those costs, as well as the human and emotional ones associated with the difficult task of 'doing justice.'

As a form of self-government, sentencing circles may be overrated both in terms of cost-savings and empowerment. What is probably definitive about the ability of circles to achieve these ends are the idiosyncrasies of individual judges and individual communities. A community with significant human and monetary resources may achieve much through a sentencing circle, although admittedly these achievements may simply constitute enhancements of high, pre-existing levels of agency and self-government. This will also undoubtedly impact on the variety and degree of costs associated with a circle, which are also likely to be a function of the nature of the judge presiding over the circle. If the judge is truly engaged in meaningful consultation, the circle will probably be that much more rewarding for all involved. As Lilles of the Yukon Territorial Court acknowledges: 'the weight given to circle deliberations will determine whether the community is indeed a full partner. On one hand, the judge may view the circle's deliberations as merely advisory. The other view is to adopt the recommendation of the circle as long as it falls within the scope of a fit and proper sentence ... Unless the judge is prepared to concede substantial decision-making authority, there will be little motivation for the community to participate' (Lilles, 2002: 6).

The essence of the issue here would seem to depend upon how individual judges define 'consultation,' a factor which affects not only the community's view of the process, but the degree of consistency across circles in different communities. Thus we see that in a circle in Nunavik, the legal authority of the judge constituted a significant challenge not only to the integrity of the circle, but also to the promises it makes regarding community empowerment and self-governance:

> [The j]udge ... attempted to clarify his role and the roles of the other participants. He explained that everyone in the circle was 'on the same level' and 'equal.' However, some confusion was caused when, after stressing this equality, he explained that he was 'not obliged to follow advice' given by circled members ... Referring to the group's work as 'advice' while stressing the equality of everyone in the circle presents a mixed message. Raising questions about how 'equal' the members really are is likely to reinforce skepticism about the ability of circle sentencing to provide the community with a real opportunity to share in the sentencing responsibility, since true power appeared to be reserved to the judge and everyone else to be a mere advisor. For the more cynical, it leaves room to speculate about whether the court was truly willing to explore real alternatives to the traditional sentencing procedure. (Crnkovich, 1996: 165–6)

Insofar as the ultimate power to define sentence remains at all times with the judge, it is difficult to envisage how altering the interior design of courtrooms and the dress and decorum of the actors can somehow challenge that fundamental reality. Indeed, there is little reason to assume that participants in a circle have many illusions about where the power resides, regardless of where the powerful sit.[1]

(iii) Circumventing the Legal Niceties: Circles, Sentencing Disparities, and the Issue of Fairness

The potential for variability across circles, and therefore possibly across the sentences they define and impose, has proven to be a matter of serious debate and concern among those involved with or thinking about sentencing circles. Variability raises the issue of differential treatment of offenders and, more importantly for the courts, the possibility of disparity across sentences for offenders convicted of similar offences perpetrated in similar circumstances. Disparity in the dominant system has long been critiqued as a problem, and something to be avoided as a simple matter of fairness – in essence, those who 'do the same crime, should do the same time.' In the realm of sentencing circles, however, the problem of disparity is transformed into a significant benefit. As framed by

Stuart, 'there should be more, not fewer differences in sentence' (*R. v. Moses*: 8), as this permits sentences and sanctions to fit the offender, if not the offence; going further, Stuart opines that this freedom to vary is the 'principal value of Circle Sentencing [which] lies in its flexibility to bend to the vision of each community' (1995: 2), and encourage the 'magic of gathering people together in a circle' (1996: 208). On this view, the imposition of guidelines to create uniformity across circles and, by implication, potentially less disparity across the sentences they fashion, would undermine the ability of communities to craft processes consistent with individual community cultures, and in accordance with the nature of a given conflict, the parties involved, and the issues raised. Circles, in short, must be left unfettered to vary as need dictates, and insofar as the circle process must be permitted to vary, so too should the sentences they define: 'In at least two significant ways, the circle will accentuate differences in sentences for the same crime. The circle, by enhancing community participation, generates a richer range of sentencing options. Secondly, the circle by improving the quality and quantity of information provides the ability to refine and focus the use of sentencing options to meet the particular needs in each case' (*R. v. Moses*: 8).

As circles were created to attend to differences between communities writ large (that is, between 'the' Aboriginal and 'the' non-Aboriginal), the point would seem to have some merit. It is countered, however, by those who support uniformity both as an administrative convenience and a legal necessity. In a cogently argued critique of sentencing circles, Roberts and La Prairie have raised compelling arguments urging caution in the ready acceptance of disparity. It is their position that consistency across sentencing is a legal requirement, and one which may have implications for the integrity of the administration of justice, given that 'equity of treatment also lies at the heart of public conceptions of fair sentencing' (Roberts and La Prairie, 1996: 75). While there is good reason to be sceptical about taking too seriously the popularity contest that is public opinion (especially in regard to Aboriginal issues, where it has been revealed too often as, at best, myopic, and at worst, pejorative), the key is *which* public's opinion really matters. In the realm of Aboriginal justice reform, the public opinion of consequence is not so much that captured in non-Aboriginal opinion polls, but the often untapped public opinion in Aboriginal communities – hence the crucial issue of community consultation in the development of justice projects, an issue we will return to in Part III.

As a matter of law, the sentencing provisions (s. 718) of the Criminal Code certainly stress that sentences for similar offences committed in similar circumstances should be similar in nature. At the same time, however, the Code directs judges to consider all sanctions other than imprisonment that are appropriate under the circumstances when sentencing Aboriginal offenders. This might be taken to suggest that judges should be looking for consistency across sentences for similar offences committed in similar circumstances by *Aboriginal offenders*, insofar as section 718(2)(e) directs judges to give especial consideration to the issue of reducing over-representation in sentencing. Thus the consideration here is less one of disparities in sentence across offences committed by *offenders generally*, than of disparity across sentences for offences committed by *Aboriginal offenders*. The problem is that, while this may require us to reconfigure our understanding and analysis of disparity, it does little to overcome the fundamental problem with disparity in the minds of the public – whether Aboriginal or non-Aboriginal, is disparity *fair*?

Fairness is no small issue for First Nations people, as it is something which even the most cursory historical study quickly reveals has long been absent in the relationship between their communities and the state, fiduciary obligations notwithstanding. There are, of course, numerous examples of the lack of fairness in the administration of justice to Aboriginal people, including the obvious examples of Donald Marshall, Jr, or Helen Betty Osborne – examples which have become the touchstones for evidencing the failure of the Canadian criminal justice system to provide justice to Aboriginal people. The absence of fairness and justice implicit in the relationship between the Canadian system and First Nations is vexing and the negative implications it has for relations between Aboriginal and non-Aboriginal Canadians must not be underestimated. This situation must be remedied and the preferred remedy appears to be restorative justice initiatives such as sentencing circles. Whether this remedy will work, however, remains deeply uncertain. Sentencing circles see disparity as central to a community-based, rehabilitative, and restorative approach. As asserted by Stuart, disparity in sentence is a positive and necessary result of the circle process, insofar as this 'provides the ability to refine and refocus the use of sentencing options to meet the particular needs of each case' (*R. v. Moses*: 8). It is the reasons for the disparities that matter, not the disparities themselves – it is apparently okay to be 'unfair,' as long as you are unfair for the right reasons – and the implicit assumption in Stuart's reasoning seems to be that Aboriginal communities will accept and favour disparities in sentence which are of their own making, through the vehicle of the circle.

The questions that threaten to undermine that assumption are, quite simply, how are we to define disparity in this context and across whom should disparity be measured and matter? Traditionally, when disparity in sentence is raised, it is largely in the context of whether offenders are receiving similar sentences for similar offences; if we accept that section 718(2)(e) now directs us to consider Aboriginal offenders as a separate category for purposes of sentence, discussion about disparity in relation to sentencing circles might logically become a discussion about variations in sentence across Aboriginal offenders convicted of similar offences. Are Aboriginal offenders and their communities likely to be more forgiving of disparity across Aboriginal offenders than is the non-Aboriginal community? In addition, given the nature of sentencing circles, an argument can be made that disparity must be defined differently. That is, disparity in the courts is largely a matter of judicial discretion, and thus where it is looked upon unfavourably, it is largely deemed to be the judge's error. Disparity that comes out of a sentencing circle is a creation of the circle, and thus at least appears to be 'approved' by the community of the circle and, by implication, the victim. Insofar as we tend to link the seriousness of the sentence with the seriousness of the victimization, concerns over disparity of sentence might be expected to impact strongly on victims and their communities of care.

In the realm of sentencing circles, then, the issue of disparity has at least two aspects. First, where there is significant disparity in sentences meted out to Aboriginal and non-Aboriginal offenders convicted of similar offences perpetrated in similar circumstances, by a sentencing circle and a judge respectively, what are the implications for perceptions of fairness on the part of communities? Second, what is indicated in the assumption on the part of proponents of sentencing circles that the Aboriginal public is more forgiving of disparity across Aboriginal offenders, and what are the implications of this assumption for Aboriginal victims and their communities of care? The first aspect speaks to the question raised in the opening pages of this book concerning whether, in the frantic rush to find effective reforms to Aboriginal over-representation, we have embraced restorative measures – and especially sentencing circles – which have not been proven to offer a better or more viable quality of justice to First Nations. It is possible to weigh the matter by considering the nature of the cases deemed suited to a sentencing circle process, and the sentences they have generated. This will also permit analysis of the assumption that the Aboriginal public is more forgiving of the disparity expected in sentencing circles, reserving a broader examination for later in the text.

In *Moses*, Mr Justice Stuart stressed that, as a general rule, the circle should limit its activities to 'cases where the primary objective is rehabilitation,' and that cases carrying the possibility of 'jail sentences in excess of two years' may not be appropriate for the circle sentencing (*R. v. Moses*: 10). Since this decision in 1992, the courts of appeal in particular have increasingly moved towards a more detailed and specific set of guidelines for determining case suitability for sentencing circles. Consistently, these higher courts have taken the position that, while there is a clear need for 'rules, or, alternatively, well-publicized guidelines for circle sentencing,' this is a task for the lower courts and those experts who might assist and advise them (McNamara, 2000). To date, the most well-received set of guidelines are those contained in the decision of Fafard J. of the Saskatchewan Provincial Court in *R. v. Joseyounen*. In that case, Fafard outlined a series of seven criteria which ought to direct the minds of those considering the use of a sentencing circle: (*R. v. Joseyounen*, 1995: 442–6):

1. The accused must agree to be referred to a sentencing circle;
2. The accused must have deep roots in the community in which the circle is held and from which the participants are drawn;
3. There are Elders or respected non-political community leaders willing to participate;
4. The victim is willing to participate and has been subjected to no coercion or pressure in so agreeing;
5. The court should try to determine beforehand, as best it can if the victim is subject to battered women's syndrome. If she is, then she should have counselling and be accompanied by a support team in the circle;
6. Disputed facts have been resolved in advance;
7. The case is one in which a court would be willing to take a calculated risk and depart from the usual range of sentencing.

The guidelines established in *Joseyounen* reflect a number of important shifts from the relatively uncomplicated and somewhat romantic view of community articulated in *Moses* in particular, as they appear to embody a much more complex understanding of the nature and implications of 'community' in circle sentencing. For example, while *Moses* and other discussions of circles focus on the many benefits implicit in community members coming together in a restorative setting to aid their peers who are experiencing conflict, there is a conspicuous absence of concern about who enters the circle and why. Like all communities, Aboriginal communities do not lack for internal political tensions, factionalism, and the usual sorts of machinations that arise whenever people are thrown together in small – and in many cases – dysfunctional units and expected to simply get on with life. When these are overlain with the politics and complicated relational patterns and tensions within families, the potential for problems to arise in apparently cooperative endeavours is not small. *Moses* expresses concern over the motivations of offenders, stressing that they must come to the circle for the right reasons and with the proper attitude, but does not seem to perceive that offenders are not the only circle participants whose motivations require scrutiny. *Joseyounen* appears to recognize this oversight, urging those judges implementing circles to scrutinize participants for their politics and involvement in the community; thus we see a direction that 'Elders' and 'political leaders' who would join a circle should be 'respected' and 'non-political' (*R. v. Joseyounen*, 1995: 442).

The challenge, of course, resides in the nature of the court and sentencing processes that provide the larger context for sentencing circles. In a rural setting where a circle sentencing is one part of a circuit court process, judges and court personnel enter the community only infrequently and then with clearly defined and over-large agendas. This tends to limit their knowledge of community dynamics to those which are readily explicit in the conflicts before the court, or which are communicated to them by community members who have some relationship with court personnel. Faced with limited direct experience of the community, and informed in many cases by a few influential or elite persons who may have agendas of their own, judges are not necessarily in the position to control for the many tensions or injustices that may elude the inexperienced eye.

The issue of community dynamics is very much intertwined with what manner of conflict and which parties come into a circle, and the nature and degree of justice they may find there. In the small but growing research and commentary questioning the impact of communities on circles, there are increasing questions of whether 'the community can be an appropriate vehicle for equitable, effective and efficient change' (Clairmont, 1996: 129). As argued above, many Aboriginal communities are, thanks to the colonial process, characterized by dysfunctional power structures and social relationships, and unless these are fully understood and carefully controlled for, the potential for them to be replicated within the circle is significant: 'Care must be taken to ensure that family and kinship networks and the community power hierarchy do not compromise the administration of justice. As in any community, there is a danger of a tyranny of community in which certain individuals and groups of residents, particularly those who are members of vulnerable groups, find themselves at the mercy of those in positions of power and influence' (Griffiths and Hamilton, 1996: 187–8).

There can be little doubt that hierarchy, a quality stressed by many Aboriginal communities as absent from their traditional political cultures, has found its way into their midst and has in too many instances assumed a dysfunctional and destructive form. Those who suffer its effects are numerous, and include not only those who are perceived as different, but also and especially women and children. As will be seen in Part III, 'difference' is a sticky issue in many First Nation communities, and a common stumbling block in the development of a justice project is determining who will 'qualify' for the project's services. Tensions around whether resident 'whites' or those of mixed ancestry, or from other nations or communities, should be able to participate in a circle or other type of project are often powerful and divisive. Since any of these people, as residents in the community, may find themselves involved in conflicts with 'real members,' establishing restrictive terms of access to a project may be counterproductive for conflict resolution.

The concern that community justice projects like sentencing circles may simply revictimize the less powerful members of communities is important. *Jouseyounen* directs judges to attempt to ensure that the victim has not been coerced and, if the case involves domestic abuse, whether the victim may be suffering from battered women's syndrome, and to attempt to control this through counselling and support in the circle (*R. v. Joseyounen*, 1995: 442), but these directives do not seem to have effectively penetrated local justice structures in many communities. In a recent review of two Aboriginal justice projects in the Northwest Territories and southern Alberta, Ryan and Calliou caution that, while sexual and domestic abuse cases are not especially uncommon in the north, '[n]o Dogrib man has ever been convicted of sexual assault by a Dogrib jury. In Wha Ti, even sexual assaults against female children have not resulted in convictions' (Ryan and Calliou, 2002: 10).

Other commentators make similar observations, echoing concerns about community perceptions of, and reluctance to deal with, sexual abuse, and adding to these a well-documented reluctance to respond effectively to domestic abuse as well. According to Ryan and Calliou, a large part of the problem is that, in too many communities, 'abuse of women is seen as normative' (2002: 9) – that is, Zellerer informs, such abuse is not seen as a 'crime' (1999: 346). In some northern communities, women risk 'social ostracism' when they report abuse and pursue redress from 'a community that does not want to hear about it or believes it is the victim's responsibility to put up with abuse' (Zellerer, 1999: 349). Here especially we are confronted with the limitations of community justice. Sentencing circles cannot address cases of abuse that do not come to the attention of the court, nor can they provide justice for all parties if shared community norms about injustice do not include physical and sexual abuse of women and children. Indeed, circles may do much to entrench those attitudes. If judges are, as Lilles (2002) observes, bound to respect the content of circle consultations in their sentencing decisions, or risk the alienation of the community from the circle process, how might they condemn socially dysfunctional norms without estranging those who hold them?

There is, of course, a converse reality that impacts on the freedom of choice of victims in Aboriginal communities. Where a sentencing circle is deemed by the community and its elites to be an exercise in self-government, those who would reject a circle as their preferred means of redressing their victimization may find it very difficult to do so. Rejecting the community process is seen as rejecting the community and its self-governance agenda, and few victims are likely to be prepared to accept the social and political consequences of this potentially unpopular choice. Once again, then, victim consent becomes unclear, and judges may not be in a position to recognize the controversies involved in a victim's choice to participate, any more than they are able clearly to see or challenge the intrusion of subtle but significant dysfunctional power relations into the circle. In the same fashion, it may not be apparent that the presence of some 'communities of care' in a circle serves to entrench a dysfunctional normative position, rather than to create an open, honest place of healing. There is little reason to assume that, for example, a Dogrib sentencing circle would react differently from a Dogrib jury, and the consequences for the victim in a circle could be that much worse given her participation, and thus implicit complicity, in its processes and outcome.

What are the implications of sentencing circles for fairness? If we assume that the dominant system deals well with the abuse cases which, it appears, constitute a majority of the cases sentenced through circles, then the requirement constraining any judge to ensure a sentence is 'fit' may offer some comfort to victims – that is, sentences must be reasonable and relatively consistent with those imposed in similar cases. Recalling our earlier discussions of the Criminal Code provisions, one would assume, for example, that sentences for Aboriginal men convicted of sexual assaults committed under similar circumstances would need to be similar, and to have some consonance with more general sentencing trends in regard to such offences. The challenge is determining exactly what this means in the realm of sentencing circles, and whether what circles may deem a fit sentence bears any relation to determinations made by mainstream sentencing processes, or to the perceptions of victims.

In Part III, we will address the issues of fairness and disparity writ large, pursuing the question of 'fitness' and the possibility that sentencing circles in particular, and restorative justice in general, risk diminishing Aboriginal victims' experiences in the name of 'healing' and 'restoration.' Early indications suggest a strong need for caution on these issues. For example, in a collection of reported decisions of sentencing circles between 1990 and 1999, Spiteri (2000) reveals that of the seventeen cases found, the majority involved serious or very serious offences, including sexual assault, arson, and impaired driving causing death. The severity of these offences (and the fact that the majority were dealt with through suspended sentences or probation) raises questions about fairness to victims and to communities. We will also entertain the controversial issue of whether similar offences involving non-Aboriginal parties would be permitted to be processed through a restorative project or followed by a sentence to be served in the community. These are crucial issues, as they speak to the possibility that in restorative justice, Aboriginal victims in particular may find themselves once again participating in a two-tiered justice system. This time, however, their experience is made that much more poignant by the fact that their revictimization is at the hands of their own people.

CHAPTER 7

'Taking Responsibility': Conferencing and Forums in Canadian Aboriginal Communities

No single event can possibly achieve permanent and lasting change however dramatic the impact and however emotional and real the feelings are that are generated at the time.

(Maxwell and Morris, 1994: 42)

In order to change societies, it would seem that sentencing circle or family group conferencing participants and participation would have to move from being a model of society to a model for society. The capacity of sentencing circles or family group conferences to achieve this goal remains unknown.

(La Prairie, 1995: 88)

The current landscape of community restorative justice in First Nations in Canada is defined primarily by a triad of restorative initiatives comprised of sentencing circles, discussed in the previous chapter, 'family group conferencing,' also known as 'community conferencing' or 'forums,' and 'healing circles.' While these three program approaches dominate the community justice terrain, beyond their shared space as 'restorative practices' and a common vulnerability to the same sorts of pressures and tensions implicit in a community context, they manifest important distinctions in their structure and focus. For example, while sentencing circles focus in large measure on the offender (notwithstanding the participation of the victim in some, if not all, circles), conferences or forums claim to direct their focus to the 'event' – that is, to the conflict rather than those who participate within it. Healing circles, as exemplified by the program at Hollow Water, are distanced from both sentencing circles and forums by a number of factors, including their emphasis on healing not only the offender but all parties to a victimization. Hollow Water's Community Holistic Healing

Circles are further set apart by the apparent fact that this program appears to be a truly local, grassroots effort by the community to respond to the very high rates of abuse and dysfunction characterizing their families, as opposed to a 'parachute program' developed externally and imposed on the community by outside elites. These roots, claimed but not realized in many community restorative justice projects, are important, as they may well render Hollow Water the closest thing to a true *community* justice project yet seen. As such, the potential to learn from their experience is great.

This chapter will describe and discuss community conferencing approaches as well as that found in healing circles. As will be seen, these projects encounter many of the same problems that challenge sentencing circles, including the realities of the community that inform the program and the limitations of justice structures to ameliorate the much larger social and economic problems that define and encourage conflict in Aboriginal communities. Our discussions here provide an excellent base from which to move to the consideration of the future of restorative justice among First Nations found in Part III, insofar as the current situation suggests that efficacious community justice may be as much a matter of being open to developing a wide variety of programs for a range of different communities and cultures, as of understanding the continuum of social, political, and economic challenges faced by First Nations communities in Canada.

(i) Talking about Conflict: Conferencing and Forums in First Nations in Canada

That Family Group Conferencing should have received the prominence it has in discussions of restorative justice is interesting, since conferences were not originally conceived within a restorative justice paradigm or in pursuit of restorative objectives (Cove, 1997: 30). They emerged instead as one part of a larger response by the government of New Zealand to the profound and accelerating rates of youth in conflict with the law or in need of social services programming or care. This response transpired within a larger social context characterized by what Tauri has referred to as the 'radicalization of Maori land and identity politics' (1999: 2) which informed a sense that not only were dominant social service and justice structures 'viewed negatively by Maori "clients"' (1999: 2), they also failed to ameliorate the problems facing many New Zealand families, Maori or non-Maori. The coincidence of these factors inspired a number of changes in the way the government of New Zealand did business, including the incorporation of Maori philosophies and phraseology in the state bureaucracy and, more importantly for purposes here, into legislation intended to address the compelling challenges facing New Zealand's indigenous communities in particular.

The *Children, Young Persons and Their Families Act* of 1989 was the culmination of earlier, largely non-productive efforts to deal effectively with children and youth who were either in need of care to secure them from abusive personal or family environments, or who were actively in, or at risk of, conflict with the criminal law (Hassall, 1996: 18). Earlier legislation had focused on formal legal responses to dealing with youth in crisis or conflict, placing the primary responsibility for child welfare on the courts, police, and child protection services. Families or 'communities of care,' commonly perceived as the bigger part of the problem for troubled youth, were not involved in state responses to these children, beyond being recipients themselves of social service attentions and ameliorative attempts. The assumption that families, as those most closely involved with youth, might be involved in crafting solutions to a youth's problems was not part of the social service or justice picture.

The 1989 Act challenged these assumptions, and drew upon Maori approaches to family and conflict resolution which saw individual actions as inseparable from the actor, who was in turn not severable from his or her family, both immediate and extended (Hassall, 1996: 18). Actions and actors were not perceived as distinct from the larger group, and thus responsibility for actions extended beyond the individual to the family. In this new legislative approach the courts, police, and child protection services were to step back from their point position in dealing with youth and play a secondary role behind families, who assumed the responsibilities which had once fallen to these formal bodies. In coming together with social services or justice officials to respond to youth in conflict or crisis, the family itself was to be 'restored' or 'healed.' Thus the Act saw redemption in responsibilizing families – focusing on the positive contributions the family could make to resolving a youth's problems would repair both child and kin, and limit the need for state intrusions into this intimately personal realm.

The mechanism through which this transformation of youth and family was to occur was the 'Family Group Conference' (FCG). These conferences had much in common with the victim–offender reconciliation programs which, by the juncture of the passage of the *Children, Young Persons and Their Families Act*, had been in place in Canada for over a decade, and were relatively well-established and researched. In the New Zealand context, however, the reconciliation effort would involve a much larger group than the offender and victim. As they developed in the wake of the Act, FGCs are comprised of the youth responsible for the conflict or victimization, his or her family and community of care, normally consisting of supportive individuals invited to the conference by the family, as well as the victim, his or her support group, a representative of the police, and a mediator or manager for the conference (Morris and Maxwell, 1998: 3). The manager, commonly referred to as a 'youth justice coordinator,' is an employee of the Department of Social Welfare; a social worker and, in some cases, a lawyer, is often present at the conference (Morris and Maxwell, 1998).

Family Group Conferences are directed to a range of objectives beyond simply diverting a youthful offender out of the formal court system. Consistent with a focus on the offence or act that links the offender and the victim, the conference must address the needs and interests of both parties in crafting an efficacious response to that act. Thus for the victim, the conference not only provides a means through which the impact of the offence can be communicated, whether directly or through a spokesperson, it is also a source of a material or other compensation for the harms created by the offence. For the offender, the conference can provide insights into the consequences of his or her choices for others, whether the victim(s) or the communities of care which surround both them and the offender.

These goals are shaped by a number of assumptions which are central to Family Group Conferencing approaches and shared by such restorative models as sentencing circles. Thus for example, conferences eschew the formality of dominant processes, embracing the emotional dimension of conflict and its resolution, and returning control over those processes to the parties and the community. The latter is construed narrowly and sparingly, however; within the conferencing approach 'community' is comprised only of those with specific relationships to the offender(s) and victim(s), and this community is presumed to have some responsibility for the conflict and its resolution. Thus the conference provides a forum for victims and their families to express resentment or anger, while at the same time imposing an obligation to articulate their needs and participate in fashioning a response that will meet those needs. Offenders are expected to explain their behaviour, to respect the input of the victim, and to endeavour to repair the 'symbolic and emotional damage' caused by their actions through the making of apologies and restitution, whatever form these might assume. In so doing, they may earn reintegration into the larger community, and the victim and his or her support group are expected to support and embrace that reintegration. To the degree that victimization has a marginalizing and isolating impact on victims, participation in the conference is also intended to return them to the fold. Oversight of these activities is expected to reside with justice project officials who, as more formal participants and facilitators, ensure that the rights of all parties are respected, and that the basic rules of the process, most notably those of 'community decency and civility,' are respected. In fulfilling this capacity, officials are expected to take a secondary role to other conference participants (La Prairie, 1995: 9–10). Morris and Maxwell describe a Family Group Conference as follows:

> The family group conference is a meeting between those entitled to attend, in a relatively informal setting. The room is usually arranged with comfortable chairs in a circle. When all are present, the meeting may open with a prayer or blessing, depending on the customs of those involved. The youth justice coordinator then welcomes the participants, introduces each of them, and describes the purpose of the meeting. What happens next can vary, but usually the police representative reads out a summary of the offense. The young person is asked if he or she agrees that this is what happened and any variation is noted. If he or she does not agree, the meeting progresses no further and the police may consider referring the case to a Youth Court for a hearing. Assuming the young person agrees, the victim, or a spokesperson for the victim, is then usually asked to describe what the events meant for them. Next, a general discussion of the offense and the circumstances underlying it occurs ... Once everybody has discussed what the offending has meant and options for making good the damage, the professionals and the victim leave the family and the young person to meet privately to discuss what plans and recommendation they wish to make to repair the damage and to prevent reoffending ... When the family are ready, the others return and the meeting is reconvened ... this is the point at which the young person and the family apologize to the victim. A spokesperson for the family outlines what they propose and all discuss the proposal. Once there is agreement among all present, the details are formally recorded and the conference concludes ... (Morris and Maxwell in La Prairie, 1995: 4)

FGCs, then, resemble sentencing circles in that they require an admission of responsibility by the offender, which then triggers their removal into a process which is less formal and intended to provide a non-carceral response that builds up parties and their communities of care through communication, apology, and an undertaking to make restitution and 'reform' offenders. The actual process by which this happens, however, manifests important differences from sentencing circles, in that FGCs reside outside the dominant system, and do not consistently hand the authority for the resolution over to a system-based official such as a judge.

While, in its original incarnation, FGCs prioritize the involvement of family and attempt to downplay the role of professionals, this trend is not apparent in FGCs in other jurisdictions. In Australia, for example, conferences were originally established in New South Wales in Wagga Wagga, and in contrast to New Zealand, were very much a function of the police (La Prairie, 1995: 13). Both here and in Canberra, the Australian Capital Territory, conferences are still coordinated by police officials and held at the local police station, which is seen as lending a 'certain gravity to the proceedings' (La Prairie, 1995: 13). In this model, the police act as facilitators between the victim and offender, who are accompanied by persons supportive of them who may or may not be family members. Increasingly, other states and territories of Australia have moved to the use of trained non-police facilitators in conferences. Notwithstanding such distinctions, however, conferences generally share an orientation that focuses on the offence, the harms it has imposed, and the negotiation and development of a resolution that repairs those harms as much as possible, thereby restoring the often overlapping communities of victim and offender.

The conference process centres on the provision of an opportunity for victims and offenders to 'tell their stories'; to this end, the offender opens the process by presenting his or her view of the events, following which the facilitator will lead a period of questioning directed to ensuring the wrongful act and its harms are acknowledged. Questioning is not limited to the facilitator, and other conference participants are free and encouraged to interject with their own questions and queries. The victim is then given the opportunity to speak, and the facilitator will attempt to ensure that the victim can communicate the nature and magnitude of the harm caused by the offence, and the range of needs and interests they feel must be addressed in a resolution. If a resolution is achieved by the close of the conference, its terms will be formalized and a program of follow-up will be struck; if no resolution is possible, the case can be returned to the courts (La Prairie, 1995: 14). Participants may also simply decide to reconvene another day.

Conferences are as likely to deal with very serious offences as are sentencing circles. An important distinction in this regard between these two processes, however, is that, as described in the previous chapter, emergent (and apparently largely ignored) guidelines for sentencing circles confirm that these are not appropriate for offences carrying a possible sentence of two years or more in jail. Why conferences should not be fettered in this way is unclear, although it may be that the more directive structure and considerable pre-forum preparation performed by facilitators makes them a more certain and predictable context for dealing with more serious offences. Whether this supposition holds through to the outcomes is questionable, however, and given the inadequate evaluation of these two models, we really do not know whether conferences are, in fact, more effective in meeting their goals than sentencing circles.

For some commentators, the perceived effectiveness of police-based conferences as a means of conflict resolution is limited by the deep involvement of police who, for the predominantly Aboriginal clients of FGCs, represent symbols of non-Aboriginal authority, oppression and, too often, injustice. This reality, it is argued, detracts from the shared journey that is conferencing, and results in resolutions which are of uncertain ownership by the youth and family. This would seem to be a concern that could be applied equally in the Antipodes and Canada, and yet, insofar as it falls within that larger category of criticisms that assert Aboriginal over-representation is a function of racial discrimination within the system, its veracity as a factor impeding conferencing is yet to be determined conclusively. Moore, in his evaluation of conferencing at Wagga Wagga, dismisses this view, asserting that the assumption that police cannot play a meaningful role in conflict resolution simply *because they are police* is a good example of the 'disturbing clichés' which have featured in debates around conferencing. While Moore's point is well taken, it is worth remembering that these negative clichés are outnumbered by the positive ones which support, without question or critical scrutiny, the grand claims of community and restorative justice. It is hoped that as research on, and evaluation of, restorative projects accumulates, we will be able to abandon clichés all together.

Whether the police can successfully manage the transformation of their external image as agents of law enforcement to facilitators of dispute resolution is unclear, and this is a matter of importance for Aboriginal restorative justice programs in Canada, where the most well-known and well-developed conferencing model is that of the Royal Canadian Mounted Police's 'Community Justice Forums' (CJFs). Strongly reminiscent of FGCs in Australia, these forums involve similar processes of communication and facilitation, but are less likely to enlist police facilities as their primary venue or to offer officers as facilitators. CJFs tend to be held in a non-police setting and to use trained personnel other than police as facilitators. The latter is facilitated by the RCMP's apparently strong commitment to community education as an important and integral aspect of their process. Central to their forum project is the training of community people in facilitation and mediation, and the education of local band police, social service personnel, and band council representatives in the conferencing process.

Cases are referred to forums by police and Crown counsel, and both offenders and victims are considered essential to the process. Only those cases in which the offender has accepted responsibility for his or her actions, and which are deemed to be appropriate for a forum by the facilitator, are eligible for diversion. As well, offender participation must be fully voluntary – something that may be difficult to gauge given the alternatives available to most offenders at the time a conference is presented to them as a viable option.

While Community Justice Forums are not the sole articulation of conferencing in Canada at this juncture, as noted by Immarigeon, there are few formal programs operating here that enlist the principles or procedures associated with

New Zealand's Family Group Conferences (Immarigeon, 1996: 167). The Canadian conferencing scene is characterized by major pilot projects that include the use of family group conferences at three sites in Newfoundland and Labrador, all of which focus on conferencing of child protection and family violence cases, and in Manitoba for juvenile offending involving Aboriginal youth (Immarigeon, 1996: 168). Canadian interest in restorative justice and family group conferences is demonstrated by the fact that there are now frameworks for their use in several provinces.

Of particular interest here is the Aboriginal youth justice pilot project in Winnipeg, Manitoba, which involved tracking the use of family group conferences as means for developing sentence recommendations for Aboriginal youth who had been found guilty of an offence, and for whom a predisposition report had been ordered. The pilot project involved eight such youth, and the goal of the FGC was to compile an 'action plan' of recommendations for responding to the offence and the offender; that plan would then replace the requested presentence report to the court (Longclaws et al., 1996: 195). Insofar as the FGC was, for all practical purposes, part of the sentencing process, their use was less an act of diversion than a brief 'blip' in the standard legal process for dealing with young offenders. In this regard, then, the FGC in Winnipeg was similar to a sentencing circle as it formed one part of a more formal process, albeit one which transpired to one side of that process.

The FGCs which formed the basis of the pilot project involved both male and female youth, ranging from thirteen to seventeen years of age. The offences they had committed included robbery, assault, possession of a weapon, and theft over a thousand dollars, and all but one participant had a previous record of conflict with the law. While initial convening and subsequent facilitation of the conference was the responsibility of an Aboriginal graduate student, upon determining that the offenders and their families were interested in participating in a conference, it fell to the families to invite immediate and extended family members to join the conference. Additional non-family participants mentioned by the youths were contacted by the convenor, who was also responsible for ensuring that the victim was informed of, and invited to, the conference. The venue of the conference appears to have been determined either by circumstance or by the offender and his or her family, such that the conferences were split between institutional settings like the Manitoba Youth Centre, where the youth had been denied bail, or in one case, the home of relatives of the offender. While it is obvious that youth in custody will have little latitude to determine the location of an FGC, where there is no such constraint, leaving the determination of the location to the offender seems an odd choice. It seems questionable whether victims could be expected to be comfortable with a process held in such a clearly non-neutral space as an offender's home or that of an immediate family member. It is also unclear whether conferencing in a prison is any more neutral or potentially less problematic for the victim and his or her community of care – or, for that matter, for the offender. These concerns appear to have been borne out in the conduct of the conferences: only two of the sixteen victims who were invited to participate in an FGC agreed to attend, the remainder limiting their input to the inclusion of their victim impact statement in the conference. While the authors of the report on the pilot project suggest that the victims' general reluctance had more to do with timing and inconvenience than anything else, it is interesting to observe that so few chose to attend.

Victims were not the only reluctant participants in the Winnipeg FGC pilot project: a number of system practitioners did not appear either. For example, the authors note that while 'Aboriginal agency social workers were helpful to the process and showed a willingness to bring all possible resources to the sharing circle,' non-Aboriginal social services personnel were inflexible and, apparently, unhelpful in facilitating the FGC process (Longclaws et al., 1996: 200). As well, although all the lawyers involved in the youths' cases were informed of the conferencing process and invited to attend, 'none showed up,' asserting that legal aid would not compensate them for the three to four hours consumed by the conferences, nor, given their workloads, could they afford that time. For their part, the police indicated that they did not wish to participate in the process while 'charges were still before the court' (Longclaws et al., 1996: 200). While what lay behind the apparent split in support of the FGC between Aboriginal and 'mainstream' social workers is unclear, providing compensation for professionals who attend conferences – including those organizing and facilitating the process – and ensuring a better understanding of the nature of the process itself and its relationship to the dominant system may solve the problem. To the degree that earlier concerns about the possible negative impact of police on the conferencing process and the free flow of information are accepted, their reluctance to be involved may, however, not be a problem. The same might be said of the lawyers, who might well be uncomfortable with the nature of the disclosures made by their clients in the FGC process.

Once in session, the FGCs adopted a conferencing process that evidenced some deviation from the standard practice as established in the New Zealand model, primarily in the latter portion of the conference. The early part of the process centred upon the opportunity of the parties to tell their stories, and thereby convey the nature of the impact the offending had upon the victim, his or her family, and the family of the offender, leading to a later discussion of recommendations that might be made to the court. Following this exchange of views, however, the family of the youth appears to have met separately from the larger group and, with the aid and direction of a social worker from an Aboriginal agency, come to a consensus on an action plan they felt would satisfy the court; they were also given the opportunity to meet privately to reach this agreement (Longclaws et al., 1996: 202). This shift in standard conferencing patterns appears to encourage imbalance between victim and offender in the process. Although the majority of victims chose to participate only through a paper contribution, it is unlikely that the two who chose to be present at the conference were not affected in some way by their apparent exclusion from final discussions on the action plan. Insofar as it does not appear that any provision was made to return the final agreement to the larger group for their discussion and approval, it is difficult to see how the FGC as a whole could claim ownership of the outcome. To the degree that healing requires some measure of such ownership, it is difficult to see such conferences as unqualified successes.

Failure to return the recommendations to the entire FGC for a final discussion and approval would seem an important oversight, and had such a reconsideration been part of the process, it is possible that the FGC's action plans would have been better received by the court.[1] As it was, upon the presentation to the bench of the proposed sentences agreed to by the family within the FGC, 'the court largely ignored the families' recommendations' (Longclaws et al., 1996: 204). While this reluctance may have had something to do with the flaws in the Winnipeg FGC project, the authors of the report do not appear to accept this possibility; instead, they argue that 'neither defence lawyers nor prosecutors emphasized or advocated for the family group conferences' recommendations to be included in the courts' orders and the judges never strayed far from the lawyers' recommendations ... Attention, therefore, needs to be given to presenting the plans in a manner that ensures that they receive greater acceptance' (Longclaws et al., 1996: 205).

While there is certainly little to be lost in perfecting the process of presentation of an FGC's report to the court, it may also be ventured that, had the process been constructed in a manner that ensured greater support from victims and criminal justice professionals, as well as neutrality in location and process, the court may have been more amenable. The apparently consistent reluctance of victims and professionals to participate in the Winnipeg FGC is deserving of greater investigation, and serves as a reminder that, while the courts generally appear to be supportive of restorative measures such as conferences and circles, that support may be withheld if there are difficulties with the process that may be perceived as impairing the balance and communication within the process and ownership of the outcome.

Concerns about family group conferences extend beyond those implicit in descriptions of the process such as that of the Winnipeg pilot project, and which are echoed in assessments of FGCs in other contexts (for example, Cove, 1997). For example, while the researchers involved with the Winnipeg project observed that, in their experience, even 'disorganized' family groups were able to participate successfully in an FGC, and 'to come to a consensus and develop reasonable plans for dealing with their young offenders' (Longclaws et al., 1996), other commentators do not share this experience. In his study on the Wagga Wagga model, Waters (1993) cautions that conferences, which rely so heavily for their success on the health and agency of the family group, may not be able to transcend those larger social forces that threaten families, such as unemployment and poverty, and the breakdown of family supports that so often characterize the backgrounds of youth in conflict with the law. The challenges faced by families more generally have also created the distinct possibility that, for many youth – and especially for those from 'disorganized' backgrounds and who experience conflict with the law – their families may not be the most important influence in their lives. A family group conference is unlikely to succeed if it proceeds from an assumption that family is foremost in the youth's life (La Prairie, 1995: 18), or that it possesses the moral sway necessary to reintegrative shaming processes. Indeed, it would seem important for those convening FGCs to explore the possibility that not only is the family not the most important participant in the process, it may in fact comprise a major part of the youth's problems. And while a conference may assist in ameliorating some of those problems by bringing troubled youths and families together and empowering them to resolve a shared challenge, this may be asking more of the FGC and its participants than is fair in the majority of circumstances. There is also the more fundamental difficulty of ensuring that members of disordered or dysfunctional family units can be relied upon to attend a conference, and the implications for the youth if this putatively vital component of his or her 'community of care' does not follow through on an agreement to attend. In such a situation, a conference is likely to make the youth's situation worse rather than improve it, and convenors and community justice workers must give careful consideration to including the family. In such circumstances, the convenor's time may be better spent attempting to determine who might replace or qualify the family in the FGC. Clearly, the reliance on some measure of functional community of care in conferences may constitute a significant stumbling block for some offenders, and where such a community does not exist, a conference simply may not be an appropriate mechanism for responding to acts of conflict and disorder (La Prairie, 1995).

The challenge of defining the appropriate community of care is not the only one facing FGCs; those responsible for the process must also be the subject of scrutiny. Where a conference model is adopted in a community and local persons are trained to convene and facilitate the process, careful attention must be paid to

whether the facilitator has the confidence of the parties and the larger community. This is equally a factor in conferences that involve police to the degree
evidenced in the police-based model of Wagga Wagga. Here we encounter not
only the sticky issue of the perceived legitimacy of the police as 'peacemakers,'
but also the additional complication of the blurring of the line between policing
and social work – something which reports into Aboriginal policing in particular suggest is problematic for police, if less so for those they police (see, e.g.,
Brodeur, 1991). Furthermore, as indicated in the Winnipeg pilot project, there is
a danger that requiring the significant involvement of criminal justice professionals will either mean that these individuals do not participate, owing to time
constraints and demanding schedules, or that the conference will be subjected to
delays similar to those experienced in the dominant system as professionals try to
find mutually convenient dates in their calendars in which to attend conferences.

Proponents of FGCs and forums argue that these processes are a better 'fit'
with Aboriginal communities, as they more closely approximate the cultural
values and interests of these groups. This aspect of conferences is certainly
apparent in the New Zealand context, and it is no less so in programs such as the
Winnipeg pilot project or the remarkable number of 'informal' modified
conferencing models under way in many Aboriginal communities. And yet, there
is good reason to query precisely what it is we are talking about when we refer
to the cultural fit of conferencing – are we referring to the larger historic and
traditional culture of the indigenous group, or the modern community culture
that informs current patterns of community life and which may bear only
limited resemblance to that larger, earlier cultural form? According to critics of
conferencing such as Tauri, not only does conferencing not replicate traditional
Maori processes of conflict resolution, but FGCs have 'failed in those areas that
supposedly distinguish it as a Maori inspired justice forum' (Tauri, 1999). In his
view, family group conferences offer at best a new and improved form of
indigenization, and at worst an elaborate diversion of Maori from true juridical
self-determination through the theft of Maori traditions and concepts that might
be better used by Maori to craft their own truly Maori justice process (Tauri,
1999). While others are not so extreme in their criticisms, Robertson is exem-
plary of those scholars who, conducting and reviewing evaluations of FGCs,
note that the most consistent evidence of the incorporation of an other-cultural
component to the process is the inclusion of 'culturally-appropriate people' in
the FCG, leading him to remark that 'it can be legitimately asked whether or not
such strategies transcend tokenism' (1996: 61). If, in fact, FGCs and forums are
not able to document a clear and relevant cultural pedigree, then it seems logical
to question whether these are likely to be any more effective in conflict
resolution and amelioration of disproportionate rates of incarceration of Ab-

original people than is any legal structure which is not culturally relevant and informed.

The crux of the conferencing issue in relation to its 'Aboriginality' is found in the nature of the processes that lie at the heart not only of FGCs, but of sentencing and healing circles as well. As noted earlier in this work, a great deal has been made of assumptions that culture is not only the cause of much of Aboriginal peoples' conflict with the dominant system, but it must also be the central focus of efforts to resolve that conflict. While this seems a reasonable concept, what has tended to happen with program development is that communities, faced with an erosion of knowledge of their traditional dispute resolution practices, are forced to buy into pan-Indian approaches like sentencing circles or accept other-cultural approaches such as the FGC. There is no more reason to assume that a Maori-inspired justice structure will carry much greater relevance for Aboriginal communities in Canada than will a non-Aboriginal system, than there is to assume a good fit of a general 'Indian approach' in all communities. The latter issue is perhaps more compelling than the former, insofar as the other-cultural approach seems a simple extension of classic culture-clash arguments. The problem with the pan-Indian approach is that it may well conflict with other aspects of local cultures which remain more robust. For example, conferencing and circles both rely heavily on facilitated communication between the parties involved in or touched by conflict. That is, their success is dependent on people coming together in an open forum to discuss what are often very difficult personal situations and problems. Experience with facilitation and mediation generally quickly disabuses one of the notion that such communication is an easy thing for a party or a facilitator. However, when the basic difficulties are overlain with a persistent cultural value of reticence, the challenges facing conferences and circles become clear.

The Cree of Northern Quebec, for example, have long held as a central cultural attribute an imperative of non-confrontation which, when combined with strong cultural imperatives against embarrassing others or disclosing 'family business' outside the immediate household, create significant barriers to the communication at the core of conferencing and circles. Much of what transpires in these forums requires Crees to actively contradict cultural values and imperatives which, despite many other changes in their way of life and culture, remain alive and well and are definitive aspects of their modern community life. The rather ironic result is that, in order to participate in a 'traditional justice project,' Crees must conduct themselves in ways which are inherently non-Cree. That is, they must bring together the people most important to them to engage in a facilitated 'confrontation' over matters which they have long been taught not to discuss at all.

While the challenge implicit in this conundrum is far from small, it can be overcome, albeit with considerable dedication and effort by community members. Thus in one James Bay Cree community, a 'quasi-conferencing approach' has been adopted in a local justice project which has been under way for nearly four years. Here, Crees trained in facilitation conduct circles comprised of individuals in conflict and their communities of care, many of whom find their way to the circle conference through requests by family members for a conference or, less frequently, by police through the vehicle of pre-charge diversion. The circle conference process is overseen by a justice coordinator who, with the pool of facilitators, decides on the suitability of the case to the circle process, organizes and convenes circles, and liaises with police, school, and social service personnel in the community. While the project has had modest success, implementation of the conferencing approach has not been easy and the project's long-term prospects are uncertain. They remain qualified by such factors as the alien nature of the conferencing process, which intimidates many community members notwithstanding facilitation of that process by 'one of their own,' the unwillingness of either federal or provincial governments to provide adequate or sustained funding support, and the difficulty of ensuring follow-up of agreements made in circle conferences. While these may not be problems unique to the Cree Project, the probability of its success is probably no greater or less than that of the majority of Aboriginal community justice projects. It would appear that, to some degree at least, it may be possible for community culture to overcome the challenges of the pan-Indian nature of most restorative justice models; however, it is imperative that those who work in or with communities in the creation of restorative justice projects understand that a pan-Indian approach may be quite a bit less than that term implies, and the necessity for adjustment and alterations in practice must be appreciated. As we will discuss in the next part, it is here that the importance of community consultation prior to and during project implementation is thrown into relief.

There can be little doubt that family group conferences and forums are attractive on a number of levels and to a range of parties. To those in the criminal justice and social services, the effort to engage and enhance family and community accountability for those in conflict with the law is undoubtedly welcome, insofar as it broadens the realm of responsibility for 'fixing' the problem while at the same time retaining the social and justice workers' role in crisis and conflict resolution. For many practitioners, then, FGCs and forums offer an alternative to the unquestionably frustrating and limited official responses implicit in old approaches, without the unpleasant requirement of downsizing. At the level of the state, these approaches fit well within larger government agendas of financial retrenchment and 'responsible citizenship' (Hassall, 1996). Cast as opening the system to informal, alternative, and 'traditional' processes, FCGs and forums shift responsibility for conflict from the system to families, a devolution that not only promises some cost savings, but also resonates with a growing conservatism that relies upon the voluntary sector and presses personal responsibility for a range of family and social problems. In the realm of Aboriginal community justice, however, attention must be paid not only to the levels of agency characterizing families and communities, but also to the fact that FGCs and forums are the products of another cultural context and, as such, may require a good deal of alteration to provide a good fit. In the absence of sustainable funding and a steady and abundant supply of volunteers to implement them, these restorative approaches face a considerable handicap.

(ii) Healing Circles and Community Justice: Hollow Water and the Community Holistic Circle Healing Program

> At the most basic level, when Aboriginal people speak of community healing they suggest that there are many individuals within their communities who must heal themselves before they will be capable of contributing to the many tasks that lie ahead. They talk of finding ways to help support those who must heal deep wounds. (Lane et al., 2002: 18)

It is in the realm of Aboriginal healing projects that one encounters in its most profound form the focus on culture as both the explanation and cure for over-representation and the range of larger social, historic, and economic pressures that feed into conflict with the law. In part, this focus may be seen as an inevitable consequence of the fact that the origins of the modern healing movement are found in community efforts to combat substance abuse – a community pathology which has long been understood as a response to the historic marginalization of Aboriginal peoples. Most of the earliest programs, which stretch back just over two decades to the early 1980s, targeted alcoholism as a means of ameliorating much of the dysfunction characterizing families and communities (Lane et al., 2002: 10). In so doing, those developing and administering these programs discovered a much more compelling problem, namely, that the substance abuse that was sundering their communities was largely attributable to a much wider series of tensions and problems, many of which were deeply embedded in their communities and their peoples' psyches. Alcohol, long thought to be 'the problem,' was really only a symptom of living within societies suffering a range of ills. As these incipient efforts began to yield positive results in responding to substance abuse, '[a]boriginal healing programs sprang up across the country addressing such issues as addictions, sexual abuse, parenting, family violence, depression, suicide, anger and rage and eventually the residential school syndrome, (Lane et al., 2002: 11).

These programs adopted a range of forms, ranging from residential treatment settings, through one-on-one therapeutic counselling models, personal growth workshops, and retreats through such traditional practices as sweat lodges, healing ceremonies, fasting, prayers, and traditional teachings (Lane et al., 2002: 11). As community workers became more convinced of the importance of the latter in responding to the many challenges facing those who accessed their programming, a clear shift away from non-Aboriginal therapeutic approaches and the 'medical model' ensued. Programs increasingly looked to culture and, perhaps more importantly, traditional spirituality, to guide their treatment initiatives.

The 'culture as treatment' paradigm (Lane et al., 2002: 22) is thus a prominent feature of most, if not all, of the more than a thousand ongoing Aboriginal Healing programs on reserves (Lane et al., 2002: 10). Many programs will refer in their descriptions to being or incorporating 'traditional' responses, 'culturally relevant' interventions, and activities that reflect and support cultural traditions. Sometimes culture can refer to meetings and other justice forums that are held in an Aboriginal language; some can open with prayers and the use of sweetgrass. Traditional lore is also sometimes used to encourage offenders to change their behaviour and Elders often advise on the cultural components of projects. However, Clairmont notes that 'there is some question to the substance of the native distinctiveness that characterizes these initiatives' and that there is often 'some ambivalence among community and panel members concerning the relevance and appropriateness of traditional values and especially native spirituality' (1994a: 26). Obonsawin and Irwin (1992) also question tradition as an acceptable ingredient in community justice projects, given the vast changes in communities since traditional times. However, 'healing' and attendant traditional and cultural activities have become a central part of mainstream restorative justice and New Age ideology.

There are a range of Aboriginal cultures across Canada, and considerable diversity in what is deemed to comprise 'healing' and thus those therapeutic or curative efforts which stem logically from different healing forms. Notwithstanding this variety, Lane et al. found in their national canvass of healing programs that all such approaches tended towards a shared set of foundational elements. Among these are a set of core principles that include a belief that healing comes from within, and that it is not possible to heal individuals and communities separately and independent of each other (2002: 12). Any attempt to restore and rebuild individuals from within which fails to assess and address those larger, external community factors that encourage dysfunctional behaviours is doomed to failure. This view dovetails with a larger, common agreement that healing work generally involves: 'overcoming the legacy of past oppression ... [through] the transformation of inner lives, as well as family and community relationships and the social and environmental conditions within which people live. *In other words, healing means moving beyond hurt, pain, disease and dysfunction to establishing new patterns of living that produce sustainable well-being*' (Lane et al., 2002: 12, emphasis in original).

This perspective is seen to manifest approaches to practice that set healing programs well apart from non-Aboriginal or mainstream therapeutic models. Thus, as discovered by Lane et al., those who develop and implement healing programs accept the efficacy and viability of traditional healing methods, and focus upon the spiritual and emotional elements of behaviour. Healing programs embrace nurturing and endeavour to create a trusting and caring context for participants. This tends to translate into non-confrontational and largely unstructured processes. As with restorative justice programming more generally, there is an imperative of apology throughout which, in healing programs, is articulated through an emphasis on participants' needs to ask for forgiveness from those who have been wronged or hurt through their behaviour. This imperative is viewed as a fundamental prerequisite to healing. These attributes of healing programs are contrasted with mainstream models, which are seen to be inappropriate for responding to the needs of Aboriginal peoples insofar as these models tend to focus on cognitive-behavioural approaches which are highly structured and goal-oriented, and which eschew apology and nurturing in favour of confrontational and challenging styles of treatment delivery. According to Lane et al., these 'polarities' express a tension which is common and constant, and which pits professional, Western models against grassroots, indigenous ones (2002: 23).

While the tension identified by Lane and his colleagues is probably somewhat less extreme than described, there can be little doubt that mainstream therapeutic efforts to respond effectively and efficaciously to the needs of Aboriginal communities, like their justice counterparts, have met with limited success. In the same fashion that the criminal justice system simply removes offenders from communities to institutions, with no benefit to either the individual or the community, social service workers have developed a habit of sending community members with alcohol or drug abuse problems 'outside' to residential treatment programs. In neither case have the results been positive,[2] especially when substance abuse feeds into patterns of conflict with the law such that, in too many cases, the 'residential treatment program' is a prison. Recognizing these realities, the community of Hollow Water[3] in the early 1980s initiated its own alcohol treatment efforts, only to discover that the effective redress of the rampant substance abuse in the community required a much more broad-based community healing effort to deal with the epidemic of sexual abuse that was both a large catalyst for, and consequence of, alcoholism. Following an initial disclosure of abuse by one member of the community in 1986, a small group of individuals mobilized in response to the disclosure. The result of their efforts is the Community Holistic Circle Healing (CHCH) program.

The Community Holistic Circle Healing program is a process-oriented approach that draws upon the fundamental principles of Anishnawbe spirituality, the 'Seven Sacred Teachings,'[4] in the implementation of a thirteen-step program for healing those caught in cycles of abuse and conflict. Within those seven teachings reside concepts that may be seen to coincide with the ideals often expressed as central to restorative justice. For example, the teaching of 'courage' as a sacred concept involves facing responsibility for actions taken, seeking forgiveness, and apologizing to those who have been harmed. Within the teaching of 'honesty' is the direction to be honest with to 'your self, your family, and your people,' while the teaching of love encourages an absence of judgment through the seeking of a deeper understanding of others and their behaviours (Couture et al., 2001: 28). These are clearly concepts seen throughout the 'healing movement,' and are very much those intended to exemplify restorative practices.

As they inform the thirteen-steps program of CHCH, the teachings are said to encourage honesty in the process, both in the acceptance of an initial disclosure and in the continued support of victims and victimizers. Thus we see in the initial phase the clearly structured response to disclosure (step 1), which involves mobilizing a CHCH assessment team under the direction of a coordinator, who directs the process and works with RCMP support to conduct the investigation into the disclosure. The team as a whole is responsible for ensuring that all phases of the thirteen-steps model are completed in proper sequence, and with full follow-up. Step 2 of the process focuses on 'protecting the child/victim,' a task that involves coordination of a number of social services agencies, including Child and Family Services, and ensuring the victim is secure in a safe setting with allies and access to counselling and/ or medical services, if needed. Once the child is safe, the team moves to step 3, 'confronting the victimizer,' and it is here that the CHCH has encountered its first criticisms. Consistent with the belief held by the CHCH program workers that 'the major focus of sexual abuse needs to be shifted to include the victimizer,' and that victimizers must also have an ally on the team and support in the community, some commentators both within the communities served by CHCH and outside those venues express concerns that the healing process is too 'victimizer-centered' (Couture et al., 2001: 1). While there is certainly a case to be made for this perception, insofar as the thirteen steps appear to focus to a great extent on the perpetrator of abuse, as will be seen, the advocates for CHCH state strongly that this focus has made the program stunningly effective in addressing the needs of, and thereby 'rehabilitating' and 'healing,' victimizers. We will return to the question of CHCH's success in a moment.

Steps 4 through 5 focus on providing information and support to the family and community of care of the parties to a conflict or abuse situation. Thus Step 4 concentrates on supporting the spouse of the victimizer, while Step 5 focuses on the family or families of the parties. This is an especially crucial matter, given that 'in many cases the family of the victim and the victimizer will be one and the same. In most cases they will be from the same community. In all cases the pain brought about by a disclosure will have a rippling effect throughout the community and many people, in both immediate and extended family/ies [sic] will be affected' (Couture et al., 2001: 93).

The sixth step is the first point of conspicuous involvement of the 'outside' legal system, as it is at this juncture that the team will meet with the RCMP and the Crown prosecutor to decide how best to proceed with the case at hand. The goal is to reach this step within four days of the disclosure, or when the first five steps have been completed, whichever is first. At this meeting, all the known facts will be presented, and the group will generally be presented with three possibilities for proceeding. Where it is determined that the facts do not support the allegation, the victim will be returned to the family and 'the family worked with until it is back into balance' (Couture et al., 2001: 94). Where the facts are deemed sufficient, but the case is seen as too serious or requires resources that exceed those available in the community, it will be passed over to justice officials to be processed through the criminal court structure. Where the allegation appears substantiated and within the ability and agency of the community to respond, the victimizer will be presented with a choice of proceeding within the CHCH processes. If he or she selects this latter option, a 'Healing Contract' that specifies the victimizer's responsibilities in the process will be drawn up and presented to that person. Here again we see grounds for the concerns that victims are secondary to the CHCH process, insofar as there does not appear to be any provision at this point to consult the victim to determine his or her view of the best process for responding to the offence. While an argument may be made that, since the team includes an ally of the victim, and one might assume police and Crown counsel will also be oriented towards the victim, the interests and needs of the victim are very much part of this determination, it is curious that the victim should be so conspicuously absent from this crucial point of decision making. This would seem to set a rather dubious precedent for the seeking of balance between all those affected by abuse and participating in the healing circle process.

If the victimizer chooses to participate in the CHCH program, the seventh step requires him or her to admit to the actions in question and accept responsibility for their impacts. Central to this step is the provision of a 'voluntary statement' by the victimizer to the RCMP that discloses in full the victimizer's total involvement with all victims – including those other than the individual whose disclosure has initiated the CHCH process. The pressure behind this statement resides in the fact that, should the victimizer not fully avow all abuse experiences and the CHCH team become aware of this, the case will automatically revert to the formal court process. While this disclosure is undoubtedly an important part of the healing process, it may also be seen as a dangerous departure from the victimizer's due process rights. Not only does this individual have to admit guilt to the immediate offence to gain entry to the program, a practice which disturbs many commentators, but he or she is further required to self-implicate for any number of other, currently undetected offences. Again, while this is certainly important for community protection, it is clearly also a bonus for criminal justice officials, who will possess a much fuller record from which to proceed should the offender recidivate in the future. In requiring full disclosure of all incidents by the abuser, moreover, the right of the victim *not to report* is usurped. This seems especially problematic given that, for many victims of abuse, the reassertion of some measure of control over their lives and choices is a central part of healing. How great is the potential for victims to heal if the choice to disclose their abusive situations is taken away by the very person responsible for the loss of control implicit in the abuse itself? Here, again, the spectre of too great a focus on the victimizer arises, to the apparent disadvantage of the victim.

Steps 9 through 10 involve preparing all parties, including the victimizer (step 8), the victim (step 9), and the families (step 10) transpires. Generally, this preparation consists of explaining what is going to happen in the healing circle and what is expected of all participants. While the victimizer must be readied to face his or her accuser and the families, the CHCH team will also work with the victim, who 'must be prepared to the point where he/she/they are at least willing to TRY to forgive the victimizer for what has happened' (Couture et al., 2001: 95, emphasis in original). Once all the parties are ready and assembled, step 11, 'The Special Gathering,' takes place. This step is comprised of ten separate steps that combine in a healing circle process wherein all parties are given an opportunity to speak, express their emotions and needs, and participate in the finalization and acceptance of the Healing Contract struck with the victimizer in Step 6. This contract will address three primary themes, including some degree of restorative punishment – that is, such consequencing must 'enhance the community as well as the victimizer's self-esteem,' and will usually involve some manner of community service work (Couture et al., 2001: 99). There must also be measures to ensure protection against further victimization and treatment for the victimizer, most commonly in the form of individual counselling. Once this contract is accepted by the circle, the victimizer will make a public apology to the victim(s?) and the group, and acknowledge acceptance of the terms of the contract and the understanding that, should he or she fail to keep the contract, their case will be returned to the courts for formal processing. A closing ceremony is performed, and the actual Healing Circle is concluded. It is followed by the implementation of the Healing Contract in the community, which comprises Step 12 and is generally assumed by CHCH staff to require no less than two, and probably five, years to complete. Completion of the contract leads to a 'Cleansing Ceremony' in step 13, an important aspect of which is the formal reintegration of the victimizer, and which is also intended to 'honor the victimizer for completing the healing contract/process' (Couture et al., 2001: 100).[5]

In comparison to other community restorative processes discussed to this point, there is little question that the CHCH process is much more structured and characterized by considerable pre-circle work and planning. It is certainly the most mature and well-accepted of any healing program in Canada, as well as the most researched. Two evaluations, however, both of which are formative in nature, establish that, while the program appears to be 'successful,' it is not without problems. For example, in her evaluation of Hollow Water, Lajeunesse (1996) found that, while community members were generally supportive of the principles that informed the Community Holistic Circle Healing Program, they had limited knowledge about the specifics of the program and only a small percentage of community members had participated. At the same time, the deep involvement of the community in the delivery of CHCH services was seen as both its greatest strength and a source of problems. The healing process mobilized community members to deal with the widespread sexual abuse characterizing their community, but insofar as the community is composed of families, and families maintained different levels of power and rivalries within the community, there is a danger that decisions made in the circle may have, or appear to have, more to do with family-based alliances and animosities than with the needs of a given case. Thus while the CHCH encourages families and communities of care to participate and become involved in the healing process, in so doing families were given considerable power to determine outcomes and, in some cases, to act on larger political and social tensions which, ideally, had no place in that process.

Another finding by Lajeunesse reveals the complexity inherent in the involvement of communities of care in healing circles. Despite the community-driven nature of the process, and the significant involvement of victim and offender support groups, neither victim nor offender groups felt they had much support from the community. This finding begs the question of whether there is a distinction between the support a community gives to a program, and the support it is prepared to give to those who participate in it. There may be significant overlap between the two, but it is also important to recognize that, while a community may support a program because that program is seen as an important institution, whether in terms of community development generally, or as a specific exercise in the direction of self-determination or self-government, that support may not translate into a similar support for those in need of the community's processes. While the CHCH program itself speaks to significant levels of community agency, and attracts considerable acclaim for Hollow Water as a 'successful community enterprise' and an example to other communities, it also reveals the depth of the problems facing the community. It is one thing to be known for institution building; it is quite another to be known for the reasons that necessitated that institution.

A more recent evaluation sheds some light on the success of the CHCH through the conduct of a much-broader based evaluation than that implied by its title: 'A Cost-Benefit Analysis of Hollow Water's Community Holistic Circle Healing Process' (Couture et al., 2001: 6–7). On the view that a proper evaluation requires the provision of a context for understanding the data, the evaluation by Couture et al. engaged analysis of overall community health and well-being, and assessed the CHCH program within that larger context. The resulting evaluation is remarkably reticent on what might be deemed the more negative aspects of the CHCH model, which, in two short paragraphs in the opening chapter, are limited to three problems, including the excessive victimizer-orientation noted above. Couture et al. also observe that some community members expressed a concern that the view of Anishnawbe tradition articulated in the Hollow Water healing process was not shared by all members of the community; however, since the program was deemed 'traditional' and part of an activist agenda by some community members to take responsibility for local problems locally, victims sometimes felt pressured to participate in the CHCH when they would have much preferred taking their problem to the dominant criminal justice system (2001: 1). Notwithstanding these weaknesses, the evaluation states strongly that: 'Significant changes have occurred. Community members indicated that on a scale of 0 (being the no [sic] health or wellness) to 10 (being the fullness of life) that the community was at 0 in 1984–1986. Substantial movement toward health and wellness has occurred. Most of the members in the community view themselves to have moved slightly more than halfway on the scale toward health and wellness (Couture et al., 2001: v).

This success seems to be mirrored in the victimizers who participate in the program as well. Couture et al. report that of the 107 offenders participating in the program since its inception, only two have recidivated – a remarkable degree of success indeed – even though Lajeunesse was unable to find recidivism data for her evaluation. No similar information is presented in the evaluation in regard to the impact of the CHCH processes on victims' lives. Notwithstanding that omission – and the persistent overemphasis on victimizers at the expense of victims it suggests – it is important to acknowledge that the CHCH's reported rate of success with offenders is nothing short of spectacular. It eclipses that of standard criminal justice system processing, which estimates recidivism among sexual offenders (the bulk of Hollow Water's clientele) at approximately 13 per cent higher than that experienced by CHCH participants (Couture et al., 2001). While these figures are remarkable, it is important to qualify their enthusiastic reception with an understanding of how the cost-benefit evaluation tabulated recidivism rates. Given the confidentiality issues implicit in the nature of the caseload and offences managed by CHCH, the evaluators: 'included a step-by-step explanation of the time, costs, and benefits of using the 13-step process in its information gathering. The results of one offender were then multiplied by the number of offences as reported in statistics from Hollow Water. The low recidivism rate for the number of offenders sentenced to the CHCH process was then validated through the Correctional Service of Canada's computerized Offender Management System (OMS)' (Couture et al., 2001: 7).

Assessing the success of a program by multiplying the success of a single participant by the total number of participants is somewhat unorthodox, and it is difficult to state with certainty what, if anything, this tells us about the CHCH's true success rates. The problems with this approach are made worse by the fact that the OMS suffers from a fundamental flaw that is especially problematic with regard to the tracking of abusers. That is, the OMS will only report recidivism *where this is detected* and *the offender is apprehended and convicted* of a federal offence. Not only must the abuser be apprehended, he or she must also be charged, processed through the formal system (and thus not through the CHCH or a similar diversion or healing circle program), and convicted. Clearly, then, we must be extremely cautious about accepting at face value the claim of a 2 per cent reoffending rate. Caution is in order because, more than any other crime, sexual abuse of children, especially intrafamilial abuse, has a massive 'dark figure.' That is, for every act of abuse detected, and for which a victimizer is held legally accountable and convicted, there will be a significant number of others which are neither reported by victims nor admitted by offenders. And while the CHCH program demands full disclosure as a prerequisite to participation, it is difficult to accept without question the implicit claim that all those who participate do, in fact, make comprehensive statements. This is not a criticism of the circle or its power, nor can concerns over the accuracy of these success rates be easily dismissed as residing in the 'dominant society's inability to see and understand what they (CHCH) are doing, to discern how core healing principles are actualized and thus why CHCH ultimately is successful' (Couture et al., 2001: 15). It is not a matter of rejecting that 'the circle is the ... conveyor for healing energies,' nor is it a result of 'insensitivity' by outsiders (Couture et al., 2001: 15). Rather, a healthy scepticism must inform the reception of any program or approach that deals with such serious forms of exploitation and with highly vulnerable victims and families. The failure to ask such questions places at risk, as the CHCH has itself been said to place at risk, the needs, interests, and future of victims in favour of those who victimize.

The persistent question of recidivism is an important one, and one which certainly cuts to the core of the CHCH's success with victims and victimizers. And yet it has been argued that an appreciation of the healing impact of the program requires a much broader understanding of the communities central to the CHCH, the origins of the cases of abuse and conflict the program addresses, and the larger question of community healing. Many commentators suggest strongly that the benefits of the CHCH extend far beyond the work done with the immediate parties to abuse or conflict. In this light, the 2001 cost-benefit evaluation asserts that the community as a whole has been profoundly changed by the rise of the CHCH program, largely because the CHCH staff 'recognise that community development is crucial' (Couture et al., 2001: 17) and that such development occurs only through a multifaceted approach to healing that looks to the support and nurturing of all families, and to the creation of a healthy, able, and empowering community. As framed by one outside observer of the program, 'The real advantage of the Hollow Water Program is that it is holistic in the sense of integrating treatment of the offender and the victim, their families and the whole community' (Marshall, 1990).

Insofar as the CHCH considers the larger social, economic, historical, and political contexts and pressures that feed into patterns of conflict and disorder in communities, this initiative moves well beyond other restorative programs and may well have much greater chances of succeeding at the level of community – notwithstanding its uncertain record of success with offenders. The challenge, of course, is that such a broad-based, holistic approach to community healing requires remarkable dedication from CHCH staff; it also requires significant resources. As with all community programs, worker burn-out is a serious risk, as most community justice programs tend to draw upon a small core of highly motivated, capable individuals whose time and resources are often stretched across a range of other programs. Although the CHCH has reportedly not yet experienced staff burn-out, it is difficult not to see this as a distinct possibility in the not-too-distant future, especially given the expansion plans presented by staff to Lane et al. in the 2001 CHCH evaluation (Couture et al., 2001: 17, 26).

This evaluation also speaks to the limited resources and funding that currently flow to the CHCH, and which are reportedly threatened by the success claimed by the program. As reports of abuse diminish – a trend which is taken as indicative of the success of the CHCH, without recognizing that victim concerns or reluctance to come forward may also be at work – the 2001 evaluation suggests that the state may be looking to cut the costs associated with the program. While this fear does not seem to have been realized in the wake of the report, it is not only monetary resources that are placed in jeopardy when programs are seen to succeed. Too often as well, those staff members who constitute the core of the program find themselves increasingly in demand as speakers at conferences or to government agencies, and become less able to dedicate themselves fully to maintaining the program. It is also the case that, as scrutiny of these rather rare success stories in justice intensifies, cracks in the veneer appear that may obscure the program's claim to success – the issue of recidivism rates in the wake of CHCH healing processes and the dark figure behind official rates of sexual offences in particular are good examples of such questions.

For all these caveats, it seems clear that, unlike many community restorative justice programs in First Nations, the CHCH program is a true community initiative, and one that reflects considerable agency and commitment among a critical cohort of people of the Hollow Water Community. Whether the experience of program building here can be replicated in other contexts remains to be seen, however, given the distinctions which characterize the Anishnawbe who reside in Hollow Water. Educational rates in this community exceed those of other Aboriginal communities, as well as those of the non-Aboriginal community of Manitoba, and yet in many other respects Hollow Water is little different from the majority of Aboriginal communities. It has long suffered from high unemployment and outward migration, although the CHCH's advertised success and the increasing sense of security in the community have ameliorated these problems to some degree. It is also a population dominated by youth. Over half of Hollow Water's population is under the age of twenty, and since it is largely the young – and males – who commit the bulk of crimes, Hollow Water faces an intensifying challenge over the next decade. Whether it can respond to the challenge successfully will depend upon the degree to which the CHCH can continue to sustain those qualities which, as will be seen in the final part of this work, are necessary to successful and sustainable community restorative justice programs. It is to a consideration of those attributes that we turn in the final section of this work.

PART THREE

Completing the Circle and Advancing the Dialogue

This final part of the book brings us full circle. In the opening part, we addressed the question of community, both as a geographic reality and a creation of social relationships, history, and struggle. We considered different definitions of what it means to be a community, and the implications of those definitions for the development, implementation and, by implication, success of community justice projects. Central to these definitions was not only who constitutes the community for purposes of program jurisdiction and administration, but also whether the smaller communities of care – and communities of conflict – that define that larger entity and, in turn, inform and make necessary community justice projects, are such that they also undermine and challenge those projects, and indeed, the very communities themselves. As the research and experience discussed to this point suggest, the tests facing community justice projects, many of which are inherent within communities themselves, constitute the most compelling challenges to the viability, sustainability, and success of these projects.

In the first part we also looked to what appear to be the primary motivations behind the community restorative justice movement within Aboriginal communities, focusing on the excessive conflict and disorder that characterize too many of these communities and which, combined with the over-representation of Aboriginal people in the Canadian system, have mobilized many communities to search for alternatives. The question which arose here is one of the dominant themes of this book: whether the problems that have led to current patterns of conflict and over-representation can be remedied by alterations in the way criminal justice is managed by both the state and First Nations. Looking to the explanations of over-representation and the largely unsuccessful ameliorative efforts which they have inspired, it seems increasingly apparent that the need for community justice is less that promised by an alternative criminal process than that which is consistent with much larger change in the direction of social justice. Our critique of institutional reforms in chapter 3 reinforces the apparent veracity of our belief that social justice, rather than criminal justice, may be the proper locus of reform. The impotence of institutional initiatives in both stemming the continuing tide of over-representation and reducing conflict in communities is now readily apparent, and reinforces perceptions that these phenomenon may be beyond the narrow focus of the criminal law to correct. We may need to look beyond the system to interrupt the debilitating and dysfunctional cycle currently characterizing relations between Aboriginal communities and the criminal system. There is little question that the marked inability of system-based reforms to reduce over-representation and address the social realities and forces that appear to underpin and flow from it has provided a strong impetus towards restorative justice in Aboriginal communities.

Part II was occupied largely with defining and critiquing the theory and practice of restorative justice in Aboriginal communities, focusing on the history of restorative programming and providing direct analyses of the dominant initiatives. To this end, chapter 5 contained a detailed analysis of the nature of the challenges facing restorative initiatives in communities, raising questions about the 'imperative of tradition' in restorative justice projects, as well as the difficult and highly personal nature of the disputes these projects must manage. Chapters 6 and 7 then outlined and analysed the 'holy trinity' of Aboriginal community justice in Canada: sentencing circles, conferencing/forums, and healing circles. It is clear from these discussions that the apparent enthusiasm generated among communities and outside governments for the establishment of these projects is not matched by a similar zeal for evaluation. Thus, after nearly two decades of restorative justice activity, we remain largely in the dark about whether our efforts are accomplishing what we originally set out to achieve.

This brings us to the question of precisely what it is that we do know about this great experiment of restorative justice, and the implications of the gaps in our knowledge for projects, individuals, and communities. This final part of the book narrows our focus to an examination of the limited extant evaluations of restorative projects in Aboriginal communities, and attempts to impose a firm grasp on what we can say with some measure of certainty about the community restorative justice movement in the Aboriginal context. Questions about the susceptibility of Aboriginal communities to the passion and politics of restorative justice, and the roots of this susceptibility, are also raised. We enquire whether this vulnerability might emerge from the fact that, too often, communities immobilized by the nature and extent of their social problems and accustomed to the imposition of external 'solutions' by influential outsiders and experts have embraced restorative processes because their delivery does not alter this precedent. From the perspective of those outsiders, the rapid infusion of restorative practices into communities may have to do with the fact that Aboriginal people, cultures, and communities are particularly vulnerable to being romanticized, and in that sense are perceived as a natural 'fit' with restorative justice. Insofar as a link with the distant past can often provide a legitimacy that is absent from such popular movements as restorative justice, there may also be an instrumentalist element in the rush by outsiders to associate restorative principles with Aboriginal cultures and traditions. The danger, however, is that cultures and communities may be exploited in that rush, which also threatens to trample over individuals' rights, whether those individuals are parties to conflict who seek restorative responses, or the volunteers and community justice workers who administer them.

The larger realities of communities must be addressed in attempting to understand not only what we expect and demand of restorative justice, but how a collective community response to the high rates of violence and victimization has come about. If the latter have prompted the collective responses that dovetail so nicely with restorative principles, the question becomes how and by whom have these been organized and how have they been linked to restorative justice. Given the character of many Aboriginal communities, we wonder whether restorative justice has the potential to go beyond the superficiality of crime and disorder and mediate/influence the new power groupings that have emerged in contemporary communities. Is restorative justice able to influence other community decision-making processes in more democratic directions? In that event, what conditions encourage or discourage this influence? Finally, and perhaps most importantly, given the intrusiveness of many restorative processes and outcomes, where is the accountability which must inform programs and communities?

For many Aboriginal groups and communities in Canada, the decision to adopt or identify with restorative justice is closely aligned with self-government. It expresses, in part, the desire of Aboriginal people, and Aboriginal politicians in particular, to build self-governing institutions around something that stands in stark contrast to the system employed by mainstream society. The cherished ideal of Aboriginal self-government has placed culture and community at the forefront of justice as the legitimate means (and incorporating the appropriate tools) for assuming greater control over justice. There is a widespread belief among Aboriginal and many non-Aboriginal commentators on justice matters (Canada, 1996) that the state lacks the capacity to deliver justice to Aboriginal people and communities in a satisfactory and appropriate manner. Indeed, the common perception is that it has "forced Aboriginal dependence on dominant, adversarial and coercive, non-Aboriginal justice authorities, institutions and processes" (Depew, 1996: 22). There is good reason to suggest that a similar imposition of restorative options is doing little to unseat historic dependencies – in fact, it may only be shifting the direction of that dependency. In restorative justice, dependency is too often directed to 'experts' and consultants, who then redirect it to the community as a whole. And while that eventual redirection may seem a positive end that encourages self-government and self-determination, if the community is not ready or able to support the range of dependencies implicit in community justice, it is difficult to see how such redirection can restore individuals, relationships, or the community itself. This concern has at least two implications for those seeking to offer constructive, realistic assistance to communities through the development of restorative initiatives. First, attention must be directed to determining community agency; second, we must ensure that, before we work with communities to develop programs, we are clear about what we are creating and our desired goals. Perhaps most importantly, we must be certain that the structure – the means – are logically and rationally linked to those goals. To do this, we must be in possession of answers to some very basic questions about restorative justice, including, and most importantly, what do we know about restorative practices in Aboriginal communities, and how do we know it?

CHAPTER 8

The Bottom Line: What Do We Know, and How Do We Know It?

It is now well-established that evaluation of Aboriginal community restorative justice projects is unusual, even where it is held out as a condition for continued state funding. Where evaluation does occur, it too often avoids addressing some of the more troubling or sticky issues that can arise. Why this should be so is left unsaid. At some level, there is probably a certain reluctance on the part of the state to impose evaluation on programs that tend in the majority – but certainly not all – of cases to function on short-term, shoe-string budgets, with unclear or at least ambiguous levels of community support, and largely through the efforts of a small group of highly committed volunteers. It may be politically more than a little difficult to impose rigid evaluation measures on such initiatives, and there is undoubtedly a perception in some quarters that, owing to the location of restorative projects within communities and 'traditional culture,' such evaluation may place outsiders in the unenviable position of appearing to impose 'non-Aboriginal standards' on Aboriginal communities and, what is worse, to be appraising 'tradition.' While such political dynamics certainly pose difficulties, insofar as the relative lack of evaluation renders restorative justice an ungrounded theory, and the projects it informs 'experiments,' those of us who support such initiatives owe it to communities and their members to approach the project professionally and in a manner that respects and protects community interests, however individually divergent these might be. And as noted at the outset of this text, insofar as restorative justice has made big promises to communities which are in desperate need of their realization, and thus vulnerable to those who make them, the importance of evaluation is that much more significant.

This is not to suggest that evaluation has been entirely lacking; rather, what has transpired in this regard is a tendency to impose evaluations that are less structured and rigid in method than probably ought to be the case, given the nature and functions of restorative justice projects. Thus we see that, consistent with criminal justice practices more generally, evaluation of restorative justice processes tends to be limited to those which are embedded within a 'participatory' or 'action/advocacy' approach. While such approaches can provide significant insights, their application to the Aboriginal community restorative justice context has led only to limited outcomes and materials. The New Zealand and Australian community accountability or family group conference approaches have been, or are in the process of being, evaluated, and evaluation literature from the United States and elsewhere on mediation exists, but there has been virtually no systematic evaluation of sentencing circles or conferencing in Canada. While evaluation of healing circles, most notably Hollow Water, has been greater, the two public evaluations have been of limited value. Thus, despite the considerable interest in restorative justice – an interest fuelled in large measure by Aboriginal organizations and communities – there is no attendant body of research that reports on the processes of, or the degree to which, the goals and objectives of restorative justice are being met. As a result, we do not have clarity about what those goals and objectives ought to be, beyond vague statements of 'healing' and 'restoration,' nor do we have a sense of how the main players in restorative processes perceive those processes and their outcomes. This is especially true in the case of victims, who play such a critical role in restorative justice. It is particularly important to understand victim perceptions, experiences, and levels of satisfaction with its processes and outcomes, and yet we remain largely in the dark on this very important aspect of restorative programming.

In short, then, we have very little evaluative data upon which to draw to assess our success with community restorative initiatives in Aboriginal communities, and what data does exist is of very recent vintage. While some positive results are evident, particularly with regard to community satisfaction about exercising greater control over justice matters and responding to local problems locally, there have been a number of other less positive findings as well (La Prairie, 1998). In her survey of the extant evaluative data, La Prairie determined that the failure to consider and strategize around issues of community agency were recurring themes in a number of Aboriginal community justice projects. For example, in the programs whose evaluations were analysed, the potential efficacy of community justice projects was substantially undermined by the absence of an awareness of basic agency issues in personnel and processes. These projects consistently suffered from inadequate project development and training of project personnel, factors that fed into problems with the basic functioning of the project, which in turn damaged the credibility of both the restorative process and those administering it. Associated problems included a tendency for project workers to move too quickly with implementation, with the result that community members were often largely unaware of the project and thus neither had ownership of it or were prepared to support it. Moving too quickly also sometimes involved taking on very serious or complex conflicts and cases before the project, its personnel, or the community generally were ready, thereby risking further damage to the project's credibility. As well, La Prairie found that some projects were characterized by a troubling lack of accountability, both to their funding agencies and to the community as a whole; at the same time, most suffered from a lack of resources. This suggests that administration of these projects is problematic, and that greater attention to their functioning and funding is crucial (La Prairie, 1998). Finally, it is important to recognize that while many restorative justice projects are characterized by anecdotal reports of their 'success,' it is not clear what this means, nor is the impact of local programs on offender rehabilitation and crime rates obvious.

Most Aboriginal justice projects span community, offender, and victim matters, and the reason for this is simple. Victims and offenders are part of families and families are circles within other circles – relatives, community and government (Pennell and Burford, 1994). However, for purposes of examining the impact of justice reforms, we have arbitrarily decided to discuss each separately, largely because the results of evaluations can be quite different for offenders, victims, and communities. While the discussion of the previous two chapters has been primarily about specific restorative justice initiatives and Aboriginal communities, the evaluation findings presented here will include those from a wide range of Aboriginal justice projects because of the interrelatedness of issues, whether pre- or post-restorative justice. Some of the evaluation findings as they relate to Aboriginal communities, Aboriginal offenders, and Aboriginal victims are discussed in detail below.

(i) Justice Reforms and Aboriginal Communities

A number of community findings are common to projects, whether they are 'indigenized' or stand alone. Three such findings predominate the evaluation outcomes, and the first is the remarkable similarity of problems facing communities – it is clear that insofar as Aboriginal communities share similar problems, their attempts to ameliorate those problems are likewise similar. A second finding documents a general lack of knowledge and awareness on the part of community members of the operation and practices of the mainstream criminal justice system, notwithstanding the degree to which it intrudes into their lives. Finally, projects appear to be consistently unable to provide general knowledge and understanding about their form and functions to the communities they intend to service. While these are significant and substantial challenges, they rank as relatively distant seconds to what is perhaps the most common finding, namely, that regardless of the level of a community's knowledge of a project, there is a profound perception on the part of the people that there must be a clear and clean separation between political and justice processes.

La Prairie found precisely these concerns about controls expressed by community members in her research among the Cree in James Bay in (1991) (La Prairie and Leguerrier, 1991); among the Dene in LaLoche in 1997 (La Prairie, 1997); and in the Yukon in 1992 (La Prairie, 1992). Obonsawin and Irwin (1992) found that the main community concern about the Sandy Lake First Nation justice pilot project in northern Ontario was that the elected leadership should not involve itself in the judicial process. Thus, for example, we see that in this community there was a strongly expressed belief that employing a band councillor as the full-time project coordinator made the links between the political leadership and the justice system too strong.

Community members in the four community projects evaluated by Clairmont in 1994, particularly those in the smaller communities including Sandy Lake, also articulated concerns about how local elite exercised their power and the potential of this to lead to abuses of a local system. Clairmont describes the demise of a local Aboriginal justice project on Vancouver Island as a result of local interference in a case of serious sexual assault by a powerful and political community member. Such interventions, which may be seen in some cases to spring from the many cross-cutting ties informing conflict and its resolution in small community contexts, are illustrative of one of the fundamental tensions within community justice – the community focus is intended to render criminal justice and conflict resolution more intimate and relevant, but that same intimacy may allow unacceptable levels of bias to enter the process. This is especially so given the often well-entrenched, asymmetrical, and dysfunctional power relations found in many contemporary Aboriginal communities. While many influential outsiders and experts argue strongly for community involvement, that involvement may serve primarily to replicate and reinforce larger inequalities and tensions, thereby undermining the efforts of the project and the credibility of restorative measures. In response to these sorts of imbalances, some commentators on community Aboriginal justice have recommended that all power and/ or family groupings should be represented on justice panels, councils, or justice groups, in order to mediate the impact of power differentials in justice matters (Clairmont, 1994b). While this could go some distance in equalizing access to a circle or forum, it is important to recognize that the power relations apparent on the surface of communities are also often well-entrenched in the minds of community members. Ensuring that all groups are represented in a project and its processes may enable all viewpoints to be at least potentially included in a circle, but those facilitating restorative processes must be aware of tensions that may be imported into the process and work diligently to make the equality of access real and apparent. For restorative processes to 'work,' all parties must be able to access a genuine level of involvement and ownership of that process.

Returning to Clairmont's 1994 study, we see that although some concerns were expressed about various components of the projects, there was general community support for local control. In all four programs reviewed by Clairmont, respected community members had become involved as panel or council members, suggesting a good degree of ownership and credibility characterized the programs. A similar finding was reported by Obonsawin and Irwin in Sandy Lake, Ontario (1992), and by Bracken (1994) in the evaluation of the Dakota-Ojibway Probation Service. Three of the main strengths of the Sandy Lake project were the involvement of Elders; the increase in community control, responsibility, and participation; and the provision of an alternative to jail, thereby resulting in more community-based sentences (Obonsawin and Irwin, 1992: 62). Thus, both Clairmont and Obonsawin and Irwin found some signs of the 'institutionalization' of local justice through the actual implementation and operation of projects and their range of use. However, both also noted that, while communities may accept new initiatives that give communities greater control over justice, this does not necessarily translate into a good understanding of the projects. Thus for example in their evaluation of the Nishnawbe-Aski Legal Services Corporation, Campbell and Associates found good support for the multiservice legal model inherent in the corporation, and for the need for it to reflect Aboriginal culture (Campbell Research Associates, 1995). However, the researchers also reported concerns expressed by community members about the limited degree to which it was promoting institutional development within communities – something which may not have been prominent among the goals or purposes of the corporation.

Despite the promise that restorative processes are uniquely able to rebuild and restore communities, we have very little evidence to suggest that these or similar reforms are advancing either institutional or community development and, thereby, greater community autonomy. Again, Clairmont provides important insights here, informing that the changes created by the four programs he studied were both limited and very incremental. Notwithstanding this, he argues that 'presumably as they prove themselves and advance in the realization of their objectives, their mandate or jurisdiction will expand and more and more community members will be experienced in diverse aspects of justice decision-making and policy' (Clairmont, 1994a: 28). In the interim, however, indications in these communities were such that Clairmont was inspired to query whether the programs at issue are far less community-oriented and informed than it would appear. In his view, the manner in which the four community projects

functioned give rise to concerns that they are 'basically reproducing the approach of the larger society's justice system in relation to handling minor
offences by focussing upon individual offenders, largely ignoring victims' or
community's concerns, and without any well-conceived and specific rehabilitation or healing strategy' (Clairmont, 1994a: 29).

These concerns are not minor. In some Aboriginal communities, a central
criticism of the outside justice system is not simply its irrelevance to life as lived
in especially rural or isolated communities, but its impotence in reducing or
punishing acts of crime and disorder. In her work in James Bay, Dickson-Gilmore
reports that a common concern of Elders in one Cree community was that the
system was perceived to be 'too easy' on offenders. Because the criminal system
functioned outside this community – court was usually held an hour's drive
away in a neighbouring non-Cree community – and serious offenders 'disap-
peared' into southern institutions, there was a perception that offenders were not
punished appropriately or effectively. From this, one motivation for a community project was to ensure that offenders were 'really punished'; that is, they
would face sanctions and processes that forced them to confront their actions,
accusers, and victims, and to face consequences which mattered in the community. Here we revisit an argument raised earlier about the cultural nature of
justice, and the reality that restorative practices in Aboriginal communities
should not be measured against the larger criminal system and culture, but rather
on their own terms.

That being said, as noted earlier, community and cultural ownership of a more
relevant and informed justice process cannot be taken to mean that this process is
automatically a better one, or that the justice it dispenses is consistently more
relevant and, therefore, 'just' in the eyes of the community. In the Attawapiskat
and Sandy Lake First Nation pilot projects, the most troubling weaknesses
characterizing their processes concerned the uneven and, in some cases, unfair
application of 'community standards' to some very serious criminal acts. Most
notably, Elders were often perceived as too lenient, particularly with sexual abuse
cases, and they had difficulty handling serious charges. In some contexts, these
concerns related to the lack of training and to the uneven selection of the Elders.
However, community members and leaders also commented on the fact that
there was friction between the project personnel and the local council over the
exercise of local authority and control in these matters. The distance between
expectations for, and the reality of, local justice, were also identified as weaknesses not necessarily of the projects, but of the poor education of community
members about them (Obonsawin-Irwin, 1992: 63).

As will be recalled from the preceding chapter, in her evaluation of Hollow
Water, Lajeunesse found that while community members were generally sup-

portive of the principles that informed the Community Holistic Circle Healing Program, they had limited knowledge of the specifics of the program. At the same time, and consistent with emerging trends across restorative programs generally, the deep involvement of the community in the delivery of CHCH services was seen as both its greatest strength and a considerable liability. The strength lay in the ability of the 'healing' process to mobilize people to deal with sexual abuse problems in the community; the weakness lay in the constant danger that family-based alliances can become, or are perceived to become, a key factor in decision making. There was also the perception among many community members that greater care needed to be taken by program workers to safeguard the confidentiality of private information about individual cases – insofar as communities tend to be small and cross-cutting ties plentiful, breaches of confidence were too common and undermined the credibility of the process and of promises made in the circle (Lajeunesse, 1996).

Other community justice programs appear to manifest similar mixed results. Thus, for example, in their evaluation of the Justice Development Worker programs established to initiate the development of justice programs in communities through the use of a dedicated 'justice worker' and funded by the Aboriginal Justice Directorate (Department of Justice), Campbell and Associates found significant community ownership and decision-making benefits (Campbell Research Associates, 1995). The researchers also reported that these programs produced the additional benefit of unintended 'cross-cultural training,' insofar as they provided a context for Aboriginal and non-Aboriginal personnel to work together in improving the administration of justice. At the same time, however, these programs appear to have suffered from the same sorts of problems endemic to community initiatives, as the research documents that they were hampered by the challenges posed by the involvement of 'political' community members in the program, discussed above. In addition, these programs had limited impact on institutional or community development, as workers tended to an excess focus on simple service delivery, as opposed to tasks and services aimed at prevention and early intervention in problematic situations. Consistent with overall trends, there were also problems with community understanding of the role and functions of Justice Development Workers in the community, a situation which was unlikely to change markedly. The limited resources allocated to the program restricted the likelihood of an expansion of services that might include larger community education about the program.

The 1999 evaluation of the Community Justice Program of the Government of the Northwest Territories, Department of Justice, modelled after the Justice Development Worker program and implemented to stimulate the creation of local justice projects, revealed that people in communities generally did not understand the role of either the community justice specialists or the community justice committees (Campbell Research Associates, 1999). It was also discovered that the specialists themselves were not clear about what they should be doing and, because the specialists are part of a larger justice initiative in these communities in the Northwest Territories, this role confusion spread over into other justice areas – including the work of the thirty-one local community justice committees. Like local Aboriginal community justice initiatives elsewhere in the country, those in the Northwest Territories are attempting to address a wide range of concerns. These include ensuring there are adequate and appropriate levels of community accountability, which can constrain the misuse of power found in some justice projects, which undermine victims' rights. As well, the Northwest Territories initiatives were struggling to develop adequate administrative structures and strategies to address ongoing needs for staff training, as well as appropriate staffing, and for the establishment of policies and procedures, reporting and record-keeping central to accessible and coherent community programs. However, despite the lack of clarity about functions and other problems, most people interviewed in the eight community field work sites generally supported the need for these kinds of initiatives and identified the importance of exercising greater control over justice matters. But the evaluators also noted that although the focus of the evaluation was the Community Justice Program, respondents often pointed out that many of the justice-related problems that communities are attempting to address are rooted in social conditions well beyond the power of community justice projects to affect. These include alcohol abuse, family conflict, inadequate parenting skills, lack of recreational and other opportunities for youth, and unemployment (Campbell Research Associates, 1999).

The accountability of local projects to the communities they serve is another issue raised by community members in evaluations of these projects. This issue is often manifested in a lack of information in the community about what the project does, why it was established, and who is running it. These kinds of concerns were raised in the Hollow Water Program evaluations, as well as the Nishnawbe-Aski and Sandy Lake projects, suggesting that one of the most critical issues for projects – particularly in the development and implementation stages – is consultation and communication with communities. However, accountability of local justice projects to communities is an ongoing issue and it is unlikely that projects will survive in any robust form if this is not addressed and ensured. Accountability may be encouraged and made more likely through a process of community education, which results in greater knowledge about the project. Greater community engagement increases levels of local support. We will explore the issue of accountability in detail later in this part.

As we move into the urban setting, evaluating the impact of community justice becomes complicated by the fact that the concept of 'community' here may be quite different and more difficult to define. This is especially so in cities like Toronto, where the Aboriginal population is widely dispersed among the larger, non-Aboriginal one. In the evaluation of the Aboriginal Legal Services of Toronto's Community Council Program, in which Aboriginal offenders meeting certain eligibility criteria are diverted from court to a community panel, it became apparent that 'community' was quite broadly defined. Here, those who sit on the Community Council are recruited from the scattered and differentiated Aboriginal community, and in many cases the recruitment effort is aided and informed by nominations of potential members by Aboriginal agencies which operate across the city. For purposes of the Community Council Program, the 'community' clearly includes Aboriginal agencies. To the degree that these agencies are the bigger part of that community and council (which seems to be the case), it is not surprising that the evaluation was able to assert that the council returns a greater amount of responsibility to the Aboriginal community. A similar finding was revealed in the evaluation of the Thunder Bay Indian Friendship Centre Aboriginal Community Council Program, where many of the community council members and those interviewed are professionals working in a range of Aboriginal and other community agencies (Campbell Research Associates, 2000b).

(ii) Justice Reforms and Aboriginal Offenders

Evaluations of community restorative justice projects evince a remarkable consistency in the support and praise they elicit from offenders. For example, in the evaluations of the Attawapiskat and Sandy Lake justice pilot projects conducted in 1992 by Obansawin and Irwin, offenders and their families were generally satisfied with the process and the decisions. Subsequent evaluations of other local justice projects have found similar levels of satisfaction on the part of offenders. Bracken (1994) found that probationers communicated a general satisfaction with the service provided by the Dakota-Ojibway Probation Service, and the evaluation of the Hollow Water Community Holistic Circle Healing program revealed that victimizers were the most satisfied of all groups (i.e., community members, victims) and had received the most attention and service from it. The evaluator of the Hollow Water program concluded that one of the main explanations for the higher level of offender satisfaction was that so many of the processes included in the program involved the needs of the offender. However, there was also a perception among some community members (and among some members of the offenders' families) that offenders were not getting enough help from the program and were engaging in behaviour, such as drinking, that put them at risk to reoffend. Many of the offenders who were interviewed also showed a low degree of empathy for their victims and little awareness about their own risk to reoffend. Like victims, however, offenders did not feel a great deal of support from the community (Lajeunesse, 1996).

Clients of the Toronto Aboriginal Legal Services Community Council Project, interviewed as part of the implementation evaluation, viewed their diversion experience in a very favourable light. They considered the strength of the project to be that it was Aboriginal controlled and thus had a 'cultural understanding' of Aboriginal people, qualities that were seen to render it a 'true alternative.' As well, offenders praised the program as focusing less on them as offenders, and more upon the offence they had committed. In this way, the program was seen as contributing to offenders' ability to see and respond to the problems that caused the offence, among others (Moyer and Axon, 1993).

In the process evaluation of the Prince George Urban Aboriginal Justice Society program for diverting youth to a 'resolution circle,' the sentiments expressed by the participants were generally very positive. While the program claims to have made a difference in the lives of the youth there are no intermediate or long-term outcome data to support this claim. However, of the sixty-five referrals to the program, half (thirty-three) did not attend their circle, were not contactable, or were unsuitable. For the youth who participated, the rates for agreement completion were very high (Prince George Urban Aboriginal Justice Society, 2000). At least in part, these rates of completion may have been influenced by the possibility that the weakest individuals did not attend the program, resulting in a somewhat inflated rate of success.

Despite the length of time many programs have been in place, little data exist on the degree to which these alternative approaches have reduced reoffending or reintegrated offenders into family and community life. The original evaluators of the Hollow Water project were unable to collect follow-up data (Lajeunesse, 1996) and the more recent cost-benefit analysis discussed in the previous chapter does not include any reliable data on whether the program actually reduces reoffending (Couture et al., 2001). Unless reoffenders – if they are detected – are continuously diverted to the alternative project, which is unlikely in the case of sex offenders (the target group for the Hollow Water program), cost savings are unlikely to extend beyond the initial divertees. If reoffending is high this will not only affect the viability of the program, it will affect costs as well.

No follow-up recidivism data were generated from the Thunder Bay Community Council program at the time of their evaluation in 2000. However, the coordinator of the program felt that the program worked best for individuals who were already motivated and taking some action on their own to resolve their problems. In general, offenders who had participated in the alternative program were satisfied with the decision and conditions determined during the hearing with the council members, in part because they had the opportunity to contribute to the discussion and the decisions and felt that the realities of their lives were taken into account. All clients interviewed in the evaluation reported having some contact with the services and programs required by the terms of their conditions (Campbell Research Associates, 2000b).

In the evaluation of the Aboriginal Legal Services of Toronto Community Council Program, it was found that two-thirds of clients complied with their Community Council orders. While this seems a very good outcome, the program does not seem to have had as strong an impact upon recidivism rates. Thus the reviewers noted that almost the same number of individuals who had been convicted of offences in the two years prior to their involvement with the Toronto program had convictions registered against them following the program. There was an overall decrease of 8 per cent in criminal behaviour for the group as a whole, from 184 convictions pre-program to 170 post-program, and a further 11 per cent decrease in the average number of charges per client. Only 22 of the 106 clients were interviewed, but two-thirds reported an improvement in their living arrangements and a reduction in transiency, and half had been involved in education or training programs. Generally, offenders felt that the program was a more meaningful alternative for them than going through the mainstream system (Campbell Research Associates, 2000a).

(iii) Justice Reforms and Victims

Griffiths notes that one of the most critical issues confronting Aboriginal community justice relates to the role and rights of victims, particularly those who are the victims of violent crime and sexual abuse (Griffiths, 1996). Concerns have also been raised, frequently by Aboriginal women's groups, about the ability of community justice initiatives to protect individuals vulnerable to this kind of victimization. Support for these concerns is provided in the body of evaluation literature on local Aboriginal justice projects. For example, in their evaluations of Aboriginal justice projects, Lajuenesse (1996) and Clairmont (1994a) found lower levels of victim satisfaction as compared to levels of satisfaction of offenders and leadership. Obonsawin and Irwin, in their 1992 evaluations of the Attawapiskat and Sandy Lake justice pilot projects, found that the most serious concerns expressed about the projects were by victims and police (Obonsawin and Irwin, 1992). But concerns and support are often contradictory, as might be expected. Some victims in Bracken's (1994) evaluation of the Dakota-Ojibway Probation Service expressed concern about reserve-based justice while at the same time expressing a positive attitude about the greater accessibility of probation officers and their knowledge of Aboriginal culture and language. This suggests that what makes a program a 'success' may be complex and multifaceted, and may differ across different categories of offences and victims.

Evaluations of Family Group Conferences in particular have produced some interesting and often contradictory findings. For example, victim levels of satisfaction in FGCs conducted in New Zealand and Australia have been mixed. The experience of victims in restorative justice programs had not been very positive in the Maxwell and Morris evaluation (1993). Somewhat later, the RISE evaluation found that while victims usually had a better experience with a conference than did victims who went through court, sometimes a conference was a much worse experience than court (Sherman and Strang, 1997). However, on balance, the victims in RISE who participated in conferences were most often moderately satisfied with their experience, both in absolute terms and in comparison with victims whose cases were dealt with in court. In fact, the conference process was especially beneficial in reducing fear of offenders in cases of victims of violence. Strang (2000) found that conference victims were also much more satisfied with the amount of information they were given about the process and with the respectful treatment they received. However, it should be kept in mind that in these cases people lived in a large urban area and family violence offences were not included. As noted in previous chapters, in the Aboriginal context, most offences involve interpersonal violence, and most offenders and victims are related or familiar and live in the same small communities. In fact, most of the Aboriginal community offences involve some form of family violence, broadly defined.

FGCs are intended to focus on the offence or conflict, and by implication with relative equality on both offender and victim. This would seem to suggest, then, that a successful conference would be one in which both parties' participation in, and satisfaction with, the process, is emphasized. And yet, it appears that victims are remarkably consistent in their modest attendance at FGCs. This was seen clearly in the report of the Winnipeg pilot project, and it is apparent in much larger studies, such Morris and Maxwell's case studies of FGCs in New Zealand. In their words: 'our research (Morris and Maxwell, 1993) indicated that victims attended only about half of the family group conferences; the reasons for this were related primarily to poor practice: they were not invited, the time was unsuitable for them, or they were given inadequate notice of the family group conference and informed of them in good time' (Morris and Maxwell, 1998: 8).

In their view, the lack of participation of victims was not due to an absence of desire or interest on the part of the victim to meet with the offender – indeed, they assessed the number who expressed a clear unwillingness to participate at approximately 6 per cent — but rather to poor practice. Morris and Maxwell further assert that, on the basis of their research, that those victims who did attend found the conference to be a positive process: 'About 60 percent of the victims interviewed described the family group conference as helpful, positive, and rewarding. Generally, they said that they were effectively involved in the process and felt better as a result of participating' (1998: 8).

Specifically, they reported that victims who felt positively about the process were especially affected by the opportunity implicit in the FGC to influence the outcome of the conference, and to meet with the offender's family face-to-face to assess their attitude, gain an understanding of why the offence occurred (Morris and Maxwell, 1998: 9), and assess the likelihood of recurrance. While this positive benefit should not be discounted, it is important to qualify this endorsement. First, if victims were present in only about 50 per cent of the family group conferences held, and 60 per cent of those victims felt positively about the process, this means that only about one-third of all victims obtained benefits from the conference process. While this is not to be scoffed at, it certainly suggests a much more modest degree of success than popular discourse around FGCs would tend to associate with these processes. It is also an accomplishment which is not consistent across evaluations of restorative projects in general, and in Aboriginal communities in particular. According to La Prairie: 'evaluations of projects in Aboriginal communities suggest that while leaders, offenders and project personnel are usually very supportive of new community-based approaches, victims are usually the least satisfied group (Obansawin-Irwin Consulting Inc., 1992, 1992a; Clairmont, 1993, 1994). This finding is also reflected in the larger body of popular justice literature, especially in relation to mediation and alternative dispute resolution' (La Prairie, 1995: 18).

And while family group conferences tend to achieve higher levels of victim satisfaction than other approaches, those achievements seem highly vulnerable to issues of context and process. For example, the success of the Wagga Wagga program for victims is suggested by Moore and O'Connell (1994) as linked with the involvement of the police in the conference, and primarily with holding the conference at the police station. This is due at least in part to what appears to be the perception of some victims that workers in other programs act on behalf of offenders, a perception which is unlikely to be directed at police.

While there is significant optimism about conferencing — as there is across most restorative justice approaches — the limited state of the research does not offer much conclusive grounding for that optimism. At this point, it is reasonable only to say that, among restorative options which have been assessed for their 'success' (an ambiguous term at best), family group conferencing appears to offer clear but modest success for at least some participants, but that this is highly dependent on the process and context of the FGC. More research and evaluation is required, especially in regard to such questions as follow-up and fulfilment of conference agreements (Robertson, 1996).

Victims are also often concerned about possible repercussions if they testify in local forums, and even about being heard or their needs addressed when they do. Relevant here are the risks associated with sentencing circles, especially those dealing with family violence cases. The experience with circles in Nunavik, discussed in chapter 5, is again telling. As described and analysed in a case study by Crnkovich, the circle does little to reassure victims who may be intimidated by the circle process, its openness, and focus on the offender. This case revealed the reluctance of victims and participants to speak in the face of domination of circle discussions by high-profile members of the community, who seemed much more concerned about the offender (Crnkovich, 1996). Healing circles do not fare much better. The evaluation of the Hollow Water Community Holistic Circle healing program found that only 44 per cent of those who participated in a circle found it a positive experience and 33 per cent found it to be a negative one. The most important finding in this regard was that only 28 per cent of victims found sentencing circles a positive experience, as compared to 72 per cent of offenders (Lajeunesse, 1996). In fact, it is apparent from the evaluations of the CHCH program that victims were the group most dissatisfied with the program. Victims and their family members generally felt they had received less help than they needed and participated in fewer processes related to it than, for example, offenders. While they appreciated that the program gave them a place to report their victimization and to talk about it, they generally felt they needed more ongoing help than was provided by the program. More disturbing is the finding that a significant minority did not feel that the offender was appropriately dealt with by the CHCH process, a factor that undoubtedly affected victims' overall less positive experience of sentencing circles and the perception that they did not receive active support from the community (Lajeunesse, 1996). Similar concerns were uncovered in the Sandy Lake First Nation justice pilot project, wherein Obonsawin and Irwin (1992) encountered clear indications from victims that, while they were generally supportive of the concept of Elders in court, they had the most reservations about the type of sentences handed out and the lack of compensation provided to victims.

While victims of youth dealt with by the Prince George Urban Aboriginal Justice diversion program are mainly business or corporate victims, many of the personal victims refused to participate in or contact the program. Little information is available to explain this finding, but one victim expressed a level of discomfort with the program which was associated with being non-Aboriginal. Given that the wider community generally viewed the process as Aboriginal-focused, this is clearly a limitation of the program's public education component. However, insofar as the majority of Aboriginal crime involves Aboriginal victims, as an imperative for improvement of program services and delivery, education of the non-Aboriginal public may be secondary to the need to educate the Aboriginal community. Notwithstanding this, the Prince George program hopes that its general, continued public education will also touch the non-Aboriginal community, and thus encourage non-Aboriginal victims to see the value of the program (Prince George Urban Aboriginal Justice Society, 2000).

The victims interviewed during the evaluation of the Thunder Bay Indian Friendship Centre were among the most enthusiastic of all the justice programs reviewed. Victims in that program perceived that the decision regarding the client's conditions had been made by consensus and that the decisions had taken their own circumstances into account as well as those of the offenders. In general, victims were satisfied with the conditions that had been imposed in hearings. Only one victim was not sure whether the program helped the offender accept responsibility for his behaviour (Campbell Research Associates, 2000b).

An interesting addendum to the perceptions of community members, offenders, and victims is the perception of mainstream criminal justice and social service personnel to these projects. According to the Hollow Water evaluation only 34 per cent of the victims felt the community was supportive of them after going through the program. This appeared to be the result of the obvious lack of community understanding about the program. Those most supportive were project personnel and employees of outside criminal justice system agencies.[1] Similar levels of support characterize the views of non-Aboriginal system personnel in regard to community justice initiatives among Aboriginal peoples. For example, in a 1996 article in the *Lawyers Weekly*, entitled 'Sentencing circles gaining acceptance from lawyers,' the suggestion is made that 'hundreds of sentencing circles have been conducted in Saskatchewan and in several other provinces and in the north,' and that while Crowns may appeal their use under certain conditions, such as an offender being a danger to the community, by and large there is support for this approach (Foden, 1996: 14). Criminal justice personnel – Crowns, duty counsel, and police – all viewed the Community Council Project of the Aboriginal Legal Services of Toronto favourably. They particularly felt that diversion for many of the cases that involved factors like alcohol was very appropriate (Moyer and Axon, 1993). As well, the evaluation of the Thunder Bay Indian Friendship Community Council Program revealed that the program's relationship to the criminal justice system was very good. The Crown attorney was very positive in his assessment of the program and highly supportive of it. There was even widespread agreement among the external criminal justice agencies, funding agencies, and the community council members that the program was implemented as originally planned and met their expectations – even though outcome data were unavailable. This factor was key to the success of the project and may have resulted, in part, from the involvement of justice personnel from the initial, planning stage, and from clearly defined protocols between the mainstream system and the alternative project (Campbell Research Associates, 2000b). It is important to recognize, however, that the desperation of many system workers to find solutions to the long-standing and difficult problem of Aboriginal over-representation in the mainstream system may well contribute to the positive opinions that mainstream players hold of local projects. These perceptions may reflect a quiet sense of relief among dominant system personnel that they are no longer in the war alone, and therefore solely responsible for the many battles lost, rather than a genuine belief that Aboriginal programs will be more successful.

(iv) So, What Do We Know, and How Do We Know It?

The limited evaluation literature to date stresses the need for greater involvement of victims in most, if not all, programs evaluated, as well as a need to ensure that serious, dedicated pre-program preparation informs all programs and processes, and that one part of that preparation is public consultation and ongoing community education about the project. Likewise, it is crucial that those developing and implementing programs have a clear understanding of the program, of its processes and goals, and where each individual within fits within that process and what functions they must perform. There must be functions that link the program with both community and outside agencies upon whose supports and resources the success of the justice project depends. There must be provision for sufficient workers in a project to enable it to function smoothly. Workload and responsibilities must be shared over a sufficient number of workers to avoid undue pressures impinging on a few select individuals, who thereby become the essence of the project. The tendency for Aboriginal community justice programs to become the province of one or a few volunteers is all too common, and endangers both workers, who risk burn-out, and the project as a whole, which cannot function without these persons. Employing sufficient workers, however, requires sufficient resources, and the evaluations suggest strongly that, for the majority of community justice projects, funding is insufficient, short term, and uncertain. And while securing funding often means that community political bodies, such as band councils, must become involved to some degree with the project, they must also maintain a sufficient distance to limit the intrusion of politics into the administration and functioning of the project. This applies as well to the involvement of individuals who are, for any of a range of reasons, sources of controversy or highly politicized within the community. Care must be taken to ensure that those who run the justice project are themselves viewed as 'just.' The credibility of the project is linked to the credibility of its workers, as is the success of its processes. Clearly, then, successful community projects depend heavily on the human and other resources which are present in the community.

Although limited, the existing evaluation literature provides some useful and important insights into the kinds and levels of human and other resources that communities require for the promotion and maintenance of local justice, and the ways in which these local initiatives may or may not capture the attention and support of the wider community. In a commentary on the 'new' justice, La Prairie (1998) notes that despite the fact that communities have an increasing volume of social problems to deal with, and a relative lack of human and other resources to do so, interest in implementing and controlling local justice systems persists. However, even where a large multifaceted organization like the Nishnawbe-Aski Legal Services Corporation is implemented, it can still be haunted by the same resource, accountability, and citizen participation issues as are smaller programs. Linden and others emphasize the need for the involvement of local communities in defining problems, determining strategies, and implementing programs. They suggest that the most effective community programs are those that are decentralized, involve the participation of local people, and link their clients to other community institutions (Linden, n.d.). This is not sufficient to ensure success, however. As observed by Depew, the path to community justice is fraught with obstacles: 'The status of community infrastructures and other resources may also place limits and constraints on the design, implementation and further development of popular justice. The available social, political and economic resources in a community may or may not be adequate or appropriate to support and sustain certain types of popular justice structures and processes. Or, there may be difficulties encountered in organizing around existing resources, regardless of their adequacy or appropriateness – an issue that speaks to more general problems of social organization' (1996: 21).

The level of human and other resources in communities is essential not only to the success of projects, but to their very implementation. Community justice projects in Canada, Australia, and New Zealand employ community members in various positions of responsibility. Some roles are adjudicatory, and involve decision making about offenders, while others, such as those of sentencing panels, are advisory, and consist of providing judges with advice and input. The Gitsxan 'Unlocking Aboriginal Justice Program' and the Teslin Tlingt initiatives use clan members in a variety of justice roles. Others are involved in council formats or councils where decisions are made about community justice approaches, particularly crime prevention strategies. Because of the interrelatedness of problems and needs in communities and within Aboriginal populations, the justice strategies are often a part of a broader strategy focusing on health, employment, alcohol abuse, suicide, and similar social problems. Because of self-government interests, many hope that these local justice strategies will lead to greater community empowerment and institutional control. Most also have responsibility for ensuring that justice strategies and approaches are 'culturally relevant.' They may or may not involve Elders, but Elders usually have some role in the delivery of justice activities.

A recurring theme in field work on local justice projects, alluded to above, is that it is usually the same people in communities who become and remain involved in these projects, and these individuals often suffer 'burn-out' and considerable frustration. Mobilizing community members beyond a few individuals appears to be a difficult task. There are a number of reasons for this, both cultural and social. One explanation appears to reside in the fear of some community members that stepping out into the public domain may make them the subject and object of gossip (La Prairie, 1992; McDonnell, 1992; Depew, 1996); another is the concern about having to judge others or, worse still, being perceived by community members as 'judging others.' Concern has also been expressed about possible repercussions from other community members, particularly offenders and/or their families. Finally, there is the cultural prohibition against getting involved in other people's business. These are not minor concerns, and they may prove remarkably difficult to overcome, as they are very much a part of community and, in some contexts, traditional cultures. The literature suggests that local justice requires that participants have strong social and cultural bonds, socialization, and values, but it must also be recognized that some aspects of those cultures and values *may work to the detriment of the project* (La Prairie, 1998; McDonnell, 1992).

Community mobilization is neither straightforward nor easy. It is difficult to mobilize people who already hold negative perceptions of justice, especially as many of these perceptions have been perpetuated and reinforced through numerous inquiries into the relationship between Aboriginal people and the criminal justice system – none of which have led to real change. Furthermore, in the small, 'face-to-face' communities characteristic of many Aboriginal reserves in particular, concerns about what other people might think of volunteers, or of potential repercussions from involvement in justice projects, are not minor hurdles. For while many reserves may be characterized by economic marginality and dysfunctional power relations, as noted previously in this book, they are still 'home' to many Aboriginal people and a refuge from the often negative scrutiny and further marginalization experienced 'outside.' To risk this acceptance and security (however limited it might appear to outsiders), through participation in a project that may well be of uncertain origin and even more dubious future, is no small thing. These risks are enhanced by the fact that many of those whom outsiders would recruit to a justice project may already face considerable stress in their lives, which too often involve difficult family and extended family situations. If you are accustomed to being disempowered and marginalized and have had little opportunity to become involved in and adapt to a work situation such as that offered in local projects of this kind, there may well be little 'up side' to volunteerism.

There are also concerns about 'taking on too much' in communities with few human and other resources. People who are originally involved in projects also abandon them. While 'burn-out' is the most often cited reason for this, some of the evaluation literature reveals that projects often do not adequately determine which offenders and offences the community has the capacity to deal with (and which should remain with the mainstream criminal justice system), nor in a related vein, are these programs characterized by adequate mechanisms for selecting and assessing which offenders are suitable for local approaches. Similarly, many programs are unable to identify appropriate and feasible interventions, or to clearly identify the range of human and other resources in communities to support those interventions or the operation of the project as a whole. A lack of clear and attainable objectives often compromises the work of projects, as activities undergo constant flux and change. Projects can also be compromised by inconsistent and unsupportable 'picking and choosing' about what they do, and a failure to distinguish between what communities have resources to deal with, and what they prefer not to deal with, even where the resources are available. If, for example, the objective of local justice is self-government and the exercise of control over justice, this goal is unlikely to be met if every serious offence and offender – or every 'unpopular offence' – is sent to the mainstream justice system, or if the project only ever handles very minor offences. At the same time, not all communities desire control over serious offenders or offences, and still others are insufficiently developed, resourced, and supported to take them on. A reluctance to assume a full jurisdiction, which may be quite sensible in the face of high rates of conflict and limited program development and experience, may also function to weaken the project in the eyes of the community and the external agencies, including the criminal justice system. Thus some community programs find themselves caught in a classic catch-22: take on serious cases and risk failing, to the detriment of the justice project, or avoid those cases in favour of simpler, less controversial ones, possibly to the detriment of self-government. It is an unpleasant and largely unnecessary conundrum, created primarily by the imposition of external pressures on communities to conform to poorly informed and researched assumptions about how community justice should work and the goals to which it should be directed.

Community involvement in local justice projects often starts out strong, but will ebb over time (La Prairie, 1997). This appears to happen for a range of reasons, including the failure of most projects to keep the community informed about their activities and outcomes. Again, then, we see the importance of continual community education by projects which can keep the community *writ large* engaged and supportive of the justice initiative.

Projects also fall out of favour with communities where they suffer continued erosion to their credibility by the inability to clearly distinguish them from the local government, which can lead to allegations of local political interference or a sense that certain individuals – or, in many contexts, certain families – are controlling the process. In some cases projects fail not because the community fails to support them, but because they are internally unsupportable or unsustainable. Thus we see that some projects fail owing to personnel issues, such as a lack of adequate training or inadequate management or administration of the project, which tends to result in the project taking on cases that are inappropriate or for which resources are not available. Similarly, too many projects lack clear goals, which undermines the development of rational and reasonable means for achieving success. This raises again the crucial matter of ensuring that the project is sufficiently developed and resourced – whether in human or monetary terms – before it begins to take cases.

In her comments on the establishment of the Youth Justice Committees in Alberta, Neilson noted that some of the developmental issues related to a perceived lack of organizational legitimacy (Neilsen, 1995) and resistance to what she describes as the 'knowledge technology' of the committees, which included their right to exercise control, and a general failure to support the resource needs of the committees (Neilsen, 1995: 19–22). As one possible means by which to structure the development and implementation of projects, and thus avoid such challenges, Moyer and Axon suggest that the developmental phase for Aboriginal justice programs should involve three sub-phases: a needs-assessment phase, a project development phase, and a pre-implementation phase (1993: vi). They argue that the efficiency and cost-effectiveness of projects is often impaired by inadequate pre-implementation development, and that projects ought to reflect consensus, which can take some time to acquire and properly execute in relation to decision making about cases. In addition, many Aboriginal communities have had little or limited experience in exercising control over justice or other matters, and require sufficient time, resources, and guidance to develop an understanding of and commitment to the project.

While pre-program development is unquestionably important, it is also clear that those programs which achieve full implementation (sometimes in spite of an absence of pre-program development) can continue to face significant challenges even after many years of operation. Often these problems were evident early on, but not dealt with when first detected. For example, the Native Courtworker Program, a national program that has been in operation for over well over twenty-five years, continues to be hobbled in attaining its fullest articulation and success by unclear objectives and weaknesses in administration and management. The most recent reviews and recommendations for change in this program also urged greater clarification and standardization of activities, a need that remains outstanding. Despite these weaknesses, and in the complete absence of any evaluations that might confirm the magnitude of difficulties with the Native Courtworker Program or which measure its impacts against any objective criteria, it is widely deemed a 'success.'

For projects that have been in place for some time, one of the reasons for continued problems of legitimacy and credibility relates to the fact that little information about their processes or outcomes has been forthcoming. One such criminal justice alternative is circle sentencing. Although this approach has been in use for over ten years, little offender outcome or victim satisfaction data have been generated. This kind of information is useful not only for understanding how the approach works; evaluation data, especially if they are positive, can address concerns of critics. For example, a 1999 article in a Whitehorse newspaper, titled 'Offender discredits sentencing circle,' covered a Yukon case that presented sentencing circles in a very negative fashion. It dealt with an offender who had not observed the conditions imposed by the circle and who subsequently reoffended. Considerable criticism from the victim and community members was generated not only about the particular case, but about the use of sentencing circle more generally. As this incident illustrates, in the absence of other data to counter or contextualize it, an entire approach can be called into disrepute by one case (Steinbachs, 1999).

To date, justice 'partnerships' in the Aboriginal context have been limited to state and political/service organizations or community negotiations, and have primarily been about the scope and resourcing of local justice. While 'community,' with its connotation of homogeneity, consensus, and cultural relevance, remains the locus of Aboriginal justice activity in Canada, the exact nature and form of partnerships between Aboriginal governments (national, provincial/ territorial, and/or local) and Aboriginal communities (individual, groups, agencies) over justice matters has yet to be determined. Nor is there clarity about the relationship between the mainstream criminal justice and local Aboriginal community systems, although protocols for collaboration have been developed on an individual project basis. Perhaps a more informed discussion about what links and separates Aboriginal and non-Aboriginal communities, and what these connections may or may not mean for local justice, is needed. This may be especially so when the discourse around restorative justice assumes that secondary institutions (particularly those related to criminal justice) could be used to improve communities by replacing some of the responsibilities of primary institutions.

The notion that secondary institutions located within communities can be enlisted – or expanded – to improve those communities relies on two somewhat unstable assumptions, namely, that there is both a moral order in communities and the existence of institutions that have shaped it. New groupings and new standards have been created in Aboriginal communities in response to a range of intermingling pressures, such as historical processes, geographic isolation or urban concentrations, community governing structures, and contemporary realities. Decades of welfarism have undermined the family as a central social institution, while dysfunctional influences, such as high unemployment and alcohol abuse, which result in high levels of family violence, foetal alcohol syndrome, and associated problems, have diminished community solidarity and the ability of existing social and cultural institutions to counter these influences through methods of informal social control. This situation is compounded by demographics. Aboriginal populations have higher birth rates than non-Aboriginal ones, which means that communities have a hugely disproportionate number of children and youth. In these circumstances the degree to which they can continue to function as healthy *communities* is open to question. This is a crucial question for restorative justice, insofar as it is intimately linked to, and dependent upon, community. It is now well known that more effective justice programs occur where there is a homogeneous community with a sense of social responsibility and some common and identifiable community goals. Even where there are diverse views and opinions among the members of a community (as is the case except in the most closed societies), an ability to accommodate this diversity indicates internal strength and cohesiveness. For purposes of understanding local justice projects, an important question about many Aboriginal communities – particularly those that are smaller – is whether they are truly a 'community,' or simply a collection of groups, families, and/or individuals with separate agendas and little accountability to, or connection with, broader community goals (La Prairie, 1997). A community lacking in cohesion may face almost insurmountable impediments to developing, implementing, and sustaining a successful community justice project.

The prevalence of significant risk factors and high levels of crime and victimization, which as we have seen, are predominately intraracial, raise important questions about the capacity of social, cultural, and local justice institutions to counter them. The role of local justice may be particularly problematic when 'alternatives' such as sentencing circles, panels, and family group conferences are more artifacts of the judiciary and government than of local institutions or local people. Sustaining justice projects may be as much a matter of community will and interest as of resources. While proponents of new alternatives such as sentencing circles readily define the success of these approaches, the issue of what constitutes success and what it would look like given the interrelatedness of problems in communities, as well as who should define it, have rarely been the subject of evaluation. It is ironic that proponents continually argue the success of these programs in the absence of data to confirm these arguments and despite the limited appearance of improvement within Aboriginal communities. The question then becomes, given what we know about what works – and perhaps more importantly, what does not work – in community justice, where do we go from here in our efforts to support communities to realize justice?

CHAPTER 9

Forward Thinking, Looking Back: Where Do We Go from Here in Community Restorative Justice?

The difficulty ... is that comparatively little is known about the specific characteristics and relations of contemporary communities which are assumed to lie at the heart of legitimate, authoritative, appropriate and effective popular justice methods. Indeed, empirical descriptions of communities often give way to a set of nostalgic ideas about communities as bastions of truly human qualities insulated from the dehumanizing effects of legalizing, institutionalising and formalizing the justice system. However, these ideas do not easily translate into the whole range of variation and change in Canadian communities, both Aboriginal and non-Aboriginal.

(Depew, 1996: 28)

References to ancient methods of conflict resolution feature prominently in writing about restorative justice, but in proponents' nostalgic and selective accounts of history nearly every form of informal justice becomes a fine example of restorative justice, while cruel and severe forms of punishment exist solely as the creation of the modern state ... but the history of informal justice contains innumerable examples of how, even with the best of intentions, communities can become as violent and oppressive as the misconduct they seek to control.

(Roche, 2003: 227)

Discussion to this point indicates clearly that the task of improving the administration of justice to Aboriginal communities through the mobilization of community behind restorative justice principles and processes is far more challenging than much state and academic rhetoric would have us believe. Communities, distanced from traditional processes by time and colonial processes, and suffering from a range of social and political problems and economic marginalization, are at once in most need of such processes and, in many cases, least capable of mobilizing them. And while local elites, outside governments, and influential outsiders pressure communities to embrace restorative justice, too often those efforts do not appear to be informed by a realistic appreciation of the magnitude of obstacles facing communities, nor are they accompanied by a commitment to the provision of adequate and sustainable resourcing of the projects or the personnel who are to administer them. In such a situation, restorative justice looks less like self-government and more like offloading by outside governments of functions which they have proven incapable of performing satisfactorily and are happy to devolve onto communities in the guise of empowerment and institutional development. Of course, in the absence of adequate human and other resources, restorative justice in Aboriginal communities is unlikely to achieve either of these ends.

As noted at the outset of this book, the lack of resources and unrealistic expectations behind the restorative justice rhetoric are unacceptable. Aboriginal communities are threatened once again with being forced to serve as a social laboratory for testing an ungrounded theory which, in its practical application to non-Aboriginal communities, is quite different in tone and intent. Restorative processes in non-Aboriginal settings focus largely on youth and minor crimes against property; when applied in Aboriginal contexts, however, restorative projects not only handle these matters, they also take on cases involving serious repeat offenders and serious crimes against the person. Thus while Aboriginal community justice is promoted as assisting communities to take control over conflict and disorder, and thereby remove their people from a two-tiered criminal justice system that offers one form of justice to Aboriginal people and a quite different form to non-Aboriginal people, the unfortunate outcome of these efforts may well be to remove Aboriginal victims and offenders into a third tier which simply replicates in a community setting the unequal and inadequate justice they receive in the dominant system.

What does one do in such a situation? Can the community do a better job than the criminal justice system for Aboriginal people and communities? The danger is that, instead of making things better, restorative justice may well simply exchange one set of unacceptable outcomes for another. We have tried to demonstrate this danger throughout this book, and in so doing to assist communities and those who work with them to avert it. Our ability to provide real assistance, however, is hampered by our lack of knowledge about what works, and by the sheer magnitude of unanswered questions whose resolution might go a fair distance to improving the quality of justice in all our lives, Aboriginal and non-Aboriginal alike. Thus, in these final chapters, we will look briefly to the insights we might gain into our own situation from considering how community justice programs have fared in indigenous contexts internationally. We will look primarily to the experiences of Australia and New Zealand, in a discussion focusing on three issues: (i) efforts to reduce Aboriginal incarceration; (ii) Aboriginal community justice alternatives; and (iii) the 'success' of Aboriginal restorative/community-based justice initiatives. Following this investigation, we will outline what we believe to be the most pressing research questions and priorities in Aboriginal community justice for the near future.

(i) Reducing Aboriginal Incarceration

Despite some variation in over-representation levels among the three countries, the disproportionate representation of indigenous people in institutions of criminal justice remains a significant and compelling problem, differing only by degree among Canada, New Zealand, and Australia. It is a problem that occupies governments and indigenous organizations and community members alike. As Doone (2000) notes about the New Zealand situation, Maori are considerably more likely than non-Maori to be apprehended, convicted, and sentenced to imprisonment, which makes finding a solution to the over-representation problem all the more urgent. Added to this are the findings of Fergusson (2003), who uncovered a small but potentially important bias in the criminal justice system's handling of Maori youth, reinforcing perceptions that over-representation is the result of a complex interplay of factors implicating systems, structures, and society as a whole.

All three countries have challenged the problem of the over-representation of their indigenous populations in correctional institutions in similar ways. Numerous conferences, reports, and royal commissions have been conducted, written, and convened with over-representation as the overriding focus. Despite these activities, and the considerable human and financial resources expended, the problem in each of the three countries has shown little change. What *has* changed is the direction of reform, as all countries have seized upon the belief that restorative/community-based justice will provide the answer. The last decade has seen a significant move in this direction by government and communities alike in all three countries.

Two main strategies for reducing Aboriginal over-representation dominate the literature. The first wave of change was initiated in Canada early in the 1970s, with the implementation of the Native Courtworker Program, which focuses on making changes to the criminal justice processing of Aboriginal offenders. This initiative came about in response to the finding – in Canada, Australia, and New Zealand – that Aboriginal people are over-represented as offenders at every stage of criminal justice system processing, from charging to prosecution to the use of imprisonment (CCJS, 2000b; New Zealand Parliamentary Library, 2000; Carach and Conroy, 1999). As indicated in chapter 3 of this work, the main strategies for reducing this representation have been to increase the number of Aboriginal police officers (either as part of stand-alone Aboriginal forces or attached to existing non-Aboriginal forces), probation and correctional officers, lawyers, and judges, and to provide cultural sensitivity training for criminal justice system personnel. In addition, criminal justice systems in all three countries have implemented special programs such as courtworker and cultural programs in prisons. Despite these initiatives, there is little evidence that the over-representation problem is decreasing. The Update on the Criminal Justice Sector on 3 October 2002, in New Zealand sums up the situation quite succinctly: 'It should be noted that despite the varied and numerous projects aimed at enhancing relationships with Maori, there is little evidence that any of them, either singly or collectively, have greatly reduced Maori rates of offending, re-offending and victimization. Nor do they appear to have significantly reduced the negative views Maori hold to the Police as an institution' (MMD, 2002).

It has generally been accepted in all three countries that Aboriginal input into the policies and interventions developed by criminal justice agencies is essential for reducing Aboriginal over-representation. The need for consultation, and the lack thereof, have been cited as a major problem (Williams, 2001; MMD, 2002). However, the value of consultation and input has not been critically examined, nor have possible differences in need among Aboriginal and non-Aboriginal offenders been appreciated and explored. The assumption has always been that Aboriginal offenders have different needs than non-Aboriginal offenders, and that these needs can be adequately understood and responded to only by Aboriginal people and Aboriginal service providers. The degree to which this is true has generally remained untested and unexplored. Also absent is a critical analysis of Aboriginal input into criminal justice policy making and the impact of this input, where it exists. Initiatives to improve relationships between the various criminal justice agencies and the Maori population in New Zealand have involved systematic evaluation (Doone, 2000), but often generate conflicting information (Williams, 2001: 71). For example, Doone found that while Maori attitudes towards police improved somewhat over the two-year period from 1997 to 1999, there was no such reduction in the level of negativity towards the criminal justice system more generally (2000: 9). This may be due at least in part to perceptions that over-representation continues, and yet one of the key problems facing the judiciary in seeking alternative sentences for Maori offenders is the lack of information about the impact of rehabilitative and alternative programs (Williams, 2001: 72).[1]

Why so little progress in reducing over-representation has been made with the implementation of these process changes is unclear. However, the failure does raise some questions, including those impelled by the lack of evidence of the impact of initiatives to enhance Aboriginal relationships with criminal justice system agents. We still have no evidence to indicate whether the initiatives that have been implemented are effective in reducing over-representation, nor can we be certain that the etiology of over-representation is sufficiently understood to respond positively to the kinds of initiatives implemented. It is also important to consider whose interests are served by the existing initiatives, and whether those initiatives have been promoted by the individuals and groups who are most directly and negatively affected by over-representation. Until we have full answers to these questions, obtained through methodologically sound and systematic research and evaluation, it is unlikely that any significant inroads will be made combatting over-representation in any of these three countries.

As disenchantment with institutional reforms grew – largely as a function of their impotence in ameliorating the problems – and governments and researchers began to look elsewhere for alternative approaches to justice reform, the second wave of reform emerged. Here, as we have seen, the approach to reducing over-representation centres upon empowering local communities to increase their justice responsibilities and activities. Given the magnitude and persistence of the over-representation problem, the turn to community as a possible solution is understandable – but as we have shown, the degree to which this approach is realistic or capable of bringing about a positive outcome is unclear.

The central assumption behind the move to community is that the mainstream system is too culturally insensitive, too rigid, too discriminatory and, generally, too limited to respond in appropriate ways to Aboriginal offenders and offending. By turning justice decision making over to Aboriginal communities and Aboriginal decision makers, we are told, these problems will be overcome and fewer Aboriginal offenders will go to jail. Aboriginal communities, automatically assumed to be culturally homogeneous and devoid of discrimination, will offer a better, 'restorative' justice to their people, and thereby restore offenders and their families as well as the community itself. As we have shown, there is significant research to indicate that some Aboriginal communities may not be equipped to take on such functions, nor are they necessarily the best contexts for restorativeness, which assumes that 'offenders and victims are interested in repairing the harm, and when they are brought together in a restorative process, they will know how to act and what to say. To the contrary, there is little in popular culture or day-to-day understandings of justice processes that prepares victims, offenders, and their supporters for restorative ways of thinking and acting' (Daly and Hayes, 2001: 6).

This 'assumption of restorativeness,' also termed by Daly the 'nirvana story,' suggests that resolution, reparation, and forgiveness are things that can and should happen all of the time, whereas the research suggests these things can only occur in most contexts some of the time. Daly cautions that it may take a very long time for people to become familiar with new justice scripts and social relations in responding to crime (2002: 18). We may have to wait an equally long time to determine whether the new methods are working.

The difficulty is that, where Aboriginal communities are concerned, waiting is problematic. These communities need better justice now, and we need to know sooner rather than later whether restorative measures are 'working,' and if so, how and why. This requires not only considerable research on communities to permit a fuller understanding of the challenges and contexts affecting and informing restorative justice initiatives, but also a willingness to ask some very hard questions about the human and other forms of agency within these communities. We need to know what is in place to support new justice initiatives, what must be developed before those initiatives can be undertaken, and what that development entails. If waiting is inevitable, then it should come before the project is in place; that is, communities may have to wait while people are trained, projects are planned, implementation is phased, and the project brought to the point where it can handle the full range of problems facing the community. As things currently transpire, communities, impelled by outside and self-government concerns, leap to implementation with little planning and limited training, with the result that people wait while more training is done, or while administration is revamped, or because funding may not come forward. This seems a much more problematic type of waiting. Time taken to ensure that a good project is in place will reduce waiting over the long term, and when evaluation does eventually occur, reports may well be better.

When we look at the experiences of implementing and sustaining local justice projects in Aboriginal communities in Canada, we become quickly aware of the many pressures and challenges facing these communities. Not only are communities often vastly different, with widely varying infrastructures, there is also the problem of the interpersonal nature of much of the conflict, and the difficulty in addressing it where the parties involved are often related or well-known to each other. Because of its seemingly rehabilitative and inclusive aspects, restorative justice has been heralded as the most logical and useful way for addressing variation in communities and interpersonal conflict. However, as we have demonstrated, there have been relatively few formal evaluations of restorative justice programs in Canada (Corrections Research and Development [CRD], 2002) and most of the evaluations that have been conducted elsewhere (i.e., Australia and New Zealand) have involved young offenders rather than adults

(Cunneen, 2002). Given that Aboriginal community restorative justice programs appear to involve a significant number of adults, and that research involving youth may not be generalizable in its findings to older program participants, these evaluations are not terribly helpful to Canadian communities or researchers.

In attempting to reduce Aboriginal incarceration, one of the real dilemmas is the victimization of Aboriginal women. Incarceration as a sentencing option is increasingly used in cases of domestic violence. This was not the preferred sentencing approach for many years, or even viewed as an effective means of domestic abuse intervention (batterers were not viewed as criminals), but legislators, judges, and society now consider spousal violence a serious crime for which the full range of sentencing options should be available (Jenkins and Menton, 2003). The disproportionate number of Aboriginal victims of this type of violence presents serious complications for policy makers concerned about reducing Aboriginal over-representation. The situation is similar in Canada, New Zealand, and Australia (CCJS, 2001; MMD 2002); the move to restorative justice for spousal and other kinds of family violence generally poses serious practical and ethical considerations for all offenders and victims. The move to the use of imprisonment for the kinds of offences which Aboriginals disproportionately commit (i.e., spousal violence) may come in direct conflict with the urgent desire on the part of government and Aboriginal groups to reduce Aboriginal imprisonment. This conflict has already been played out to some extent in Canada with the *Gladue* decision, even though it is generally not acknowledged by policy makers and those promoting different sentencing approaches for Aboriginal offenders. These and similar realities must be subjected to serious thought and scrutiny if we are to work effectively and ethically with communities to develop relevant and workable restorative justice projects.

(ii) Aboriginal Community Justice Alternatives

As discussed in chapter 7, in New Zealand the 1980s saw the emergence of potentially positive government policy responses to rising Maori crime statistics, and the 1990s a more liberal, non-retributive criminal justice approach with an emphasis on restorative justice, reparation, rehabilitation, alternate dispute resolution, and crime prevention (Williams, 2001: 33). Inconsistent and generally lukewarm government and public responses to the policy considerations of the early era led to less acceptance and support for the approach of the 1990s, but family group conferences, criminal justice advisory committees, and other community-based initiatives to reduce Maori offending and imprisonment have nonetheless emerged. As noted in chapter 7, these have reflected, in part, an awareness of the need to reflect and adopt Maori values in justice, and to share criminal justice power/authority and resources. Another of the thrusts towards reducing Maori involvement in the criminal justice system has been to improve relationships between the various criminal justice agencies, such as police and corrections, and the Maori population. Improved relationships include a greater responsiveness to Maori culture and values, and the development and implementation of community-based programs that include responding to crime and crime prevention initiatives.

Continuing their efforts to craft responses to the issue of over-representation, the Ministry of Maori Development, in an October 2002 briefing on criminal justice, outlined a new criminal justice project. The project involves a critical commentary on the degree to which the key criminal justice agencies enable Maori and other indigenous groups to obtain input into the development of policies that form the basis of strategies and interventions affecting their communities. This project follows previous suggestions in New Zealand, and practices well established elsewhere, to promote the involvement of indigenous people as criminal justice service deliverers (MMD, 2002: 11).

Community justice in New Zealand is now permanently associated with the rise of family group conferencing and, more broadly, with the restorative justice movement. As an integral part of this movement, Family Group or Community Accountability Conferencing is described as based on Maori cultural models. The Maori themselves, however, may be hard pressed to recognize it as such, and may resent what they see as 'unacknowledged cultural borrowing' (Williams, 2001: 66). Daly takes the point even further when she writes: 'The claim that conferences reflect or are based on indigenous practices (or on pre-modern forms of justice) is ubiquitous. Efforts to write histories of restorative justice, where a pre-modern past is romantically (and selectively) invoked to justify a current justice practice, are not only in error, but also unwittingly re-inscribe an ethnocentrism they wish to avoid' (2001b: 65).

Daly's point is well-taken, and applies equally well to a majority of restorative initiatives undertaken in Canada. Here again, we see a clear need for additional thought. Aboriginal people may need different things in a justice process, but the assumption that those things are necessarily linked with traditional culture is open to question. Our recent focus on culture and tradition as the problems underlying the myriad community and criminal justice problems of Aboriginal communities has meant that we have conspicuously neglected the search for other explanations. 'Acculturation' has taken a serious and, for many communities, debilitating toll, but at this point in time, we may need to look to more than culture to explain the problems and devise solutions. Culture, thus far, has not been revealed as the route to change that many of us had hoped it would be. Insofar as the risk and need profiles of Aboriginal and non-Aboriginal offenders do not diverge as much as cultural explanations suggest they should, there is a distinct possibility that we may learn important things from consulting and combining research focusing on these groups, and in so doing, come to new proposals for resolving shared problems.

Stepping back somewhat from a focus on culture does not necessarily mean we should step back from community-based possibilities. We should not, and for a range of both practical and philosophical reasons. For example, like Canada, western Australia also shows an increase in the use of community-based orders – compared with 1999 figures, the total number of community-based orders issued to offenders in 2000 rose by nearly 11 per cent. A large proportion of the work and development orders were served by Aboriginal people (68 per cent) (Crime Research Centre [CRC], 2002: 4). Thus it appears that community-based orders, and programs to support them, will continue to grow and expand. If so, we will see an expanded need for community programs to support these orders. While the move towards 'community corrections' may well have less to do with a genuine belief in community agency than with the financial gains for government in offloading services to programs fuelled largely by volunteers, and run at much lower cost than traditional criminal justice processes and corrections, it is clear that communities are going to have to work with governments to develop and implement programs for community-sentenced offenders. However, if these programs – and those processed through them – are to survive, we need to have a better understanding of the levels of agency and ability in the community. To reiterate, we need to know what is possible, how we can make it possible, and what this will require in terms of resources.

As discussed in previous chapters, Canada has instituted number of indigenized and stand-alone policing, court, and correctional initiatives, as well as a number and variety of Aboriginal community-based, restorative justice alternatives, designed, in large measure, to address the over-representation problem. However, like Australia and New Zealand, data to describe their effect in reducing over-representation are limited. In Canada, despite the considerable amounts of money expended to support major program initiatives like the federal Department of Justice's Aboriginal Justice Strategy and the Aboriginal Learning Network, little is known about their impact on crime, stability in communities, and/or on over-representation. Even legislative initiatives like the 1996 *Sentencing Reform Act*, which contain specific provisions for reducing Aboriginal over-representation, have not been systematically monitored or evaluated to determine if these objectives have been met, and if they have not, why this should be so.

Other legislation, such as the Saskatchewan *Victim of Domestic Violence Act* (1999), has undergone some process evaluation, and it was discovered that

Emergency Intervention orders are being used more often on reserves in Saskatchewan (Prairie Research Associates, 1999). However, this evaluation did not address the impact of the legislation on levels of over-representation, or on victim/offender and community relations, even though other research in Saskatchewan and elsewhere reveals that the victims of family violence and sexual assault are most often Aboriginal women and children. Aboriginal resource officer positions and Aboriginal family violence programs have been established in urban and rural communities, and victim services have been expanded in Saskatchewan, but there is no information about their impact on Aboriginal over-representation levels or any of the other problems that plague victims, offenders, and communities. One of the most serious gaps in knowledge about these issues relates to First Nation Police Forces, which are now established on many reserves and settlements in Canada. Given that 'indigenization' generally does not seem to have been of much success in reducing over-representation, the continued indigenization of policing through Aboriginal policing policies suggests that, like far too much justice programming in regard to Aboriginal people, we are caught in a cycle in which ideas and policies are adopted, tried, adapted, and tried again, with limited success and in the absence of any serious evaluation. It would thus seem that, in Aboriginal justice policy in particular, we must be prepared to be open to radical departures from old policies. As researchers, we will need to change the psyche with which we approach the problem before we can act effectively to shift the thus-far unproductive cycle of reform.

(iii) The 'Success' of Aboriginal Restorative/Community-Based Justice Initiatives

While there is little information on the majority of Aboriginal-focused projects, a few have undergone process and/or outcome evaluations. For example, monitoring of Maori Safety Community Councils relations in New Zealand reported more effective working relations between Safer Community Councils and local Iwi (communities), and the creation of models for shared responsibility and leadership. Similarly, an outcome evaluation in 1999 indicated progress in building cooperation between Maori-led councils and the wider local community. A number of pilot projects in New Zealand, such as the community panel adult diversion program, have also indicated some success; less well known is their 'transferability' to other communities, and whether continued government funding will be forthcoming to ensure their implementation and operation (Williams, 2001: 7).

Evaluation of the conferencing approach in both Australia and New Zealand has shown that offenders are more likely to respond to their justice experience positively when they perceive it to be fair, and the available evidence suggests that conferencing programs give rise to favourable perceptions on the part of offenders (Strang, 2000b). While they also reduce the victim's anger and fear, offenders, as we have seen, are more likely than victims to be satisfied with the way the case was handled. But there are also limits. As Daly notes, offenders' interests to repair harm are not always strong nor are victims easily encouraged to see offenders in a positive light (2000a: 5). Her research on the South Australian juvenile conferencing project uncovered the further, intriguing finding that *perceptions of fairness do not necessarily translate into 'restorativeness' for victim and offender*, or by extension, for offenders and/or victims and communities. She suggests that restorativeness may be more difficult to accomplish than procedural justice in the conference process; that is, the assumed linkages between procedural fairness and restorative impacts simply may not hold. If this finding is accurate and replicated in other contexts, the implications for programs such as sentencing circles, which rely almost entirely on the alleged fairness of the sentencing process to 'rebuild communities,' may be profound. This should not come as too much of a surprise, insofar as the restoration of communities is a much larger and more complicated task than is sentencing, which may be far more piecemeal and distanced from questions of community agency and resources than the proponents of sentencing circles have previously assumed.

In terms of the impact of restorative justice on recidivism, Cunneen notes that results are mixed, but on balance either show little difference or are favourably inclined towards restorative justice – a finding that in Canada has led to the suggestion that restorative justice should be pursued as a policy direction (CRD, 2002). In reviewing a report on restorative justice and recidivism research in Australia and New Zealand, Cunneen reported that:

> In Victoria there was no significant difference in re-offending when compared with a matched probation group. In South Australia and New Zealand both evaluations found lower rates of recidivism when the young person showed remorse and agreed with the conference outcome. The RISE evaluation in Canberra found a range of results for different types of offenders – very little difference for young property offenders, a six percent increase for drink driving adults, and a 38 percent decrease for young violent offenders ... research in New South Wales found that the young people appearing before youth justice conferences for property and violent crime had a lower re-offending rate than similar young people appearing before the courts. The difference was between 24 and 28 percent (CRD, 2002: 2)

A difficulty in understanding and eliciting information about Aboriginal projects is that untested assumptions made at the time of their development remain unchallenged in evaluation work, possibly because these assessments predominantly involve self-evaluation. A striking example is found in the Saskatchewan Justice framework, which was designed to determine the impact of the federal Aboriginal Justice Strategy (AJS) on policies, programs, and services in Saskatchewan. Two of the recommendations made by the evaluator about the Saskatchewan component of the AJS were to 'continue using the 1993 Aboriginal Justice Strategy as the framework to initiate and implement successful Aboriginal justice reform' and to 'develop a 20-year plan that consists of four five-year cycles based on the vision of Aboriginal justice reform outlined in the Aboriginal Justice Strategy' (Samuelson, 2000: 2). These suggestions are curious, given that the AJS itself had not undergone sufficient outcome evaluation to justify such recommendations, despite having been in place for several years. Even more striking, in an evaluation of the Aboriginal Justice Strategy undertaken in 2000, it was concluded that, in spite of the strategy, 'Aboriginal people continue to be over-represented among admissions to adult correctional facilities relative to their numbers in the general population, [and] it appears this condition is worsening' (Canada, 2000: 3). It was also determined that '[r]esearch strongly supports the need to find more appropriate means by which Aboriginal communities can work to address their socio-economic problems and apply culturally appropriate remedies with potential for long-term sustainable impact' (Canada, 2000:3) – ends that would seem well outside the narrow parameters of justice policy. What is clear in even these most recent evaluations is that we continue to implement essentially similar policies and approaches, all of which seem to maintain the same, remarkably unspectacular outcomes, and we continue to fail to address the underlying assumptions upon which those policies rest. As long as we continue to stand firm in our current direction, without looking closely at what we are standing upon, very little is likely to change in regard to Aboriginal people and justice, community or otherwise.

Although evaluations that explore the impact of alternative/restorative processing on offenders and victims who are members of a wider community, and upon the community itself, are virtually non-existent, some of the findings from evaluations taken outside such contexts are informative. One of the most important of these is the relative ease of achieving *fairness* over *restorativeness* in these processes (Daly, 2002). Daly suggests that 'whereas fairness is established in the relationship between the professionals and participants, restorativeness emerges in the relationship between victim, offender, and their supporters' (2002: 17). While her research centred on young offenders in South Australia, and it is apparent that restorativeness 'requires a degree of emphatic concern and perspective-taking' (Daly, 2002: 17) – qualities which are more frequently evinced for adults than adolescents – research on sentencing circles in Canada, which are used almost exclusively for adults, suggests some of the limitations of restorativeness even within the family circle. The Saskatchewan research on sentencing circles, which revealed that family and friends of victims were much less likely to attend than those of offenders, is suggestive. And even though the majority of victims and offenders were related, only 40 per cent of the victims attended the circles (Saskatchewan Justice, 2003). This is a much lower rate than found in New Zealand and Australia for family group conferences.

The importance of this finding about sentencing circles is twofold. First, if offences mainly involve family members, yet the majority of victims do not attend the circles, how is restorativeness achieved within the family? Second, how does the circle translate into a transformative process for the community when it is mainly offender supporters who attend, and when relations between people may be readily strained with perceptions of one-sidedness or unfairness? As detailed in chapter 5, the impact of the circle process on the wider community has been a cornerstone of the philosophy of circles, yet it is difficult to see how this transformation occurs in the absence of wider community and victim participation. Indeed, one might even say that the limited community and victim participation has the potential to strain relations in communities even further. This strain may be exacerbated by the finding that, of the offenders in Saskatchewan who had participated in a sentencing circle from 1993 to 2000, fully 54 per cent had reoffended. One of the issues that distresses Aboriginal communities most about the mainstream criminal justice is the high rate of reoffending (La Prairie, 1992; 1997). It is difficult to see how sentencing circles, with their apparently broken promise of lower recidivism, can promote more united and cohesive communities.

Information emanating from evaluations of Aboriginal projects is primarily of a process nature. However, even where projects such as the Northern Cree Circuit Court in Saskatchewan, or the Native Courtworker Program (both of which are focused on reducing the impact of the criminal justice process on offenders) are evaluated in this manner, little emphasis is placed on understanding the impact of the program on the broader community. But the impact on that community – especially in the Aboriginal context – is fundamental to the 'success' of restorative justice. We need to be able to ask and, more importantly, *answer*, the questions focusing on the nature of the parameters for understanding the impact of restorative justice in communities in general, and in Aboriginal communities in particular.

Kurki and Pranis (2000) provide some direction for identifying the community parameters. In a paper titled 'Restorative Justice as Direct Democracy and Community Building,' the authors suggest that, despite the failure to estimate the long-term effects of restorative justice on offenders or communities, restorative justice can still provide a context for direct democracy and community development. They outline a number of ways they believe this can occur. They claim, for instance, that restorative justice can produce collective effects, such as the building of social capital, by allowing communities to take responsibility for social conditions linked to crime. As well, when communities offer emotional and even material support to victims, or do favours or create networks of friendships that influence, understand, and monitor community norms and values, positive community development can occur. While this certainly rings true, in many communities asymmetrical power relations and dysfunctional networks would have to be overcome to implement restorative practices and see the type of results Kurki and Pranis believe to be possible. Such a task is not small when, as is the case with many communities, the development of the restorative project requires community workers and outside agencies to work with, and thereby implicitly validate, a political elite and structure that contribute to the asymmetry characterizing communities. It is made worse when, as is sometimes the case, some of these same elite secure important positions in the project. This is not to say that the project cannot prevail, but claims of restorative outcomes from projects must be informed by, and clearly linked with, the realities of relationships and power structures within a given community. Failure to do this results in unrealistic and probably unrealizable goals being ascribed to projects and devolved onto workers and communities, a situation which is unfair to all concerned and unlikely to enhance community perceptions of the legitimacy or credibility of restorative processes.

While the impact of restorative justice on recidivism is commonly the focus of evaluation, Kurki and Pranis (2000) argue that this focus is much too narrow. The effects of restorative justice on victims and communities should be measured first, and offender recidivism, second. Victim effects are operationalized as restitution or compensation received; reduced fear of crime; benefits of involvement in process; and ability to move forward beyond the incident. They want to know if offenders are more likely to attend and finish school, get and hold jobs, participate in community activities, form stable relationships, and not reoffend. Community effects are more difficult to measure, but, following some of the work done by Sampson et al. (1997) in Chicago neighbourhoods, Kurki and Pranis claim that levels of socialization and assistance among neighbours and satisfaction with the neighbourhood are good indicators of social capital and informal social control. If these researchers are correct, then assessments of these factors ought probably to inform the pre-project development work that should be an important part of any community restorative justice initiative. Evaluations from non-Aboriginal programs can also offer insights, although when the focus is shifted to Aboriginal programs, it is important to consider whether there are offender, victim, and community characteristics that are unique to Aboriginal communities, and if so, whether these should be targeted – or at least integrated – in evaluations of restorative justice.

In chapters 1 and 2, we pointed out some of the characteristics of Aboriginal communities that distinguish them from non-Aboriginal communities, and even from small-town Canada. Geographic, cultural, social, and economic factors have shaped Aboriginal communities, and some of the circumstances they endure have the potential to compromise and hinder the most well-intentioned initiatives. Geographic isolation; social problems in the form of unemployment, alcohol and drug dependency, and family violence; local governance where power is often in the hands of a few individuals or families; and disproportionate youth populations with few recreational and employment outlets create daunting challenges for initiatives like restorative justice.

Experience in communities and with restorative justice program implementation and assessment have made clear that, in order for community justice initiatives to be established and to be successful, a number of factors must be in place. At base, there must be a functional, healthy group of people willing to support community justice initiatives. Projects are fuelled largely by volunteers, and their volunteerism must be sustained and consistent. As well, as far as possible, these should be persons who are uncontroversial within the community. They need not be paragons of virtue, or to have remained entirely out of politics. In most Aboriginal communities, the ubiquity of politics is such that total avoidance is impossible, and no one is entirely without enemies or friends. But those involved in the programs should, as far as practicable, be insulated from the larger controversies such that, whatever their shortcomings, there is a reasonably consistent community opinion that this person is fair and ethical. Similarly, this should not be taken as a criteria that would automatically eliminate anyone who has experienced conflict with the law, or who has been a victim or offender; as long as they are clearly healed and whole, such experiences may grant these individuals important insights into 'justice' and restorative processes.

Within the preceding group, or at least working in cooperation with it, there must be a group of individuals who possess a good understanding of the workings of the criminal justice system. This is simply a practical requirement, as most restorative processes will, of necessity, have to interact with the larger system. The lack of any persons in the community who know that system, and how it functions, can create a significant handicap for the project. It is important for community members to bear in mind that knowing the system does not automatically imply accepting the values and outcomes of that system. But knowledge is power, and this type of knowledge is central to empowering community members to assume control over local justice matters.

More difficult to overcome are those key ingredients to a successful project that speak to local power relations. While historically there may have been little separation between law and politics in Aboriginal communities, in the modern era, where traditional political structures are either absent or warped by time and colonial pressures, the ability of the local justice process to function free from interference and pressure by local elites or power groups is crucial. As discussed above, the entry of fear or favour into the process undermines its capacity to function and destroys its credibility. In a similar light, those who administer the process and participate in decision making or the construction of resolutions must be capable of maintaining their dedication to victim needs even where these conflict with family and community power relations. Failure to do so will unseat the balance of the process and eliminate any restorative potential for parties to it, their families, and the community.

Finally, there must be a range of options in place for responding to offender and victim needs. Here we encounter the sticky issue of community resources and agency, and the difficult realities of state funding. An important part of the pre-project development process must be a community resource assessment to reveal in realistic terms precisely what sorts of programs and personnel are available to support the types of sentences or resolutions that emerge from the restorative process. For example, if in the process it is determined that much of an offender's problem is rooted in substance abuse, it is likely that any resolution or agreement will require this person to address his or her substance abuse problem. If the community has nothing in place to assist the offender in this regard he or she is unlikely to be able to keep many of the promises or undertakings made in the process. In similar fashion, if a family agrees in a sentencing circle to take on supervision of an offender and oversee the completion of the terms of his or her sentence, what community supports are in place to assist the family in this role? As discussed in chapter 5, in the *Moses* case, the offender was affected with Foetal Alcohol Syndrome – and yet no provision was made in the sentence, nor did there appear to be any structures in the community, to assist the family to meet the needs created by this very difficult condition. Serious attention must be given to what the community can realistically provide to support the work that goes on in the community justice project; it is doubtful that any project can stand alone and function successfully. Where a community lacks options and supports, these need to be developed in tandem with the community justice project. This may make realization of a community justice project more difficult, but it will also improve its chances of success and survival. It may also make important contributions to the overall institutional development of the community, with concomitant consequences for community empowerment and, possibly, increased self-government.

Communities must also look closely at themselves while they are in the process of developing a justice project. Here we are concerned not with institutional considerations, but with what is actually happening on the ground in the community. Hard questions must be asked about the nature of the issues that a project may unearth, and the community must be prepared to deal with those issues. For example, communities must be prepared to confront difficult issues of sexual and other forms of abuse which may have been whispered about in the past, but now will be thrown into relief for all to examine. The possibility of resistance from individuals in the community who have participated in abusive situations should be understood. By implication, then, the community needs to be aware that aspects of their collective identity which were unknown or ignored may well surface. More than one community restorative justice program has been undermined or delayed in its implementation owing to entrenched positions on issues which have long been apparent, but have been ignored and left to fester, or which vested interests in the community have determined to control themselves. If communities wish to take ownership of their conflicts, and of the processes and structures to deal with them, they may also have to accept ownership of larger, more intransigent issues, the resolution of which is a prerequisite to both restorative and community justice.

One such issue that may prove to be a significant stumbling block for many communities in their development of a justice project is that of the project's jurisdiction. It must be determined in advance who will have access to the program, whether as a client, volunteer, or employee, and this may give rise (as it has in some communities in Canada) to discussions about membership and 'who belongs.' In our experience, this issue is a dangerous one – communities seeking control over justice must avoid being seduced into equating access with 'Indianness,' and dividing communities further with debates over blood, membership, and rights. While the appropriate reach of a project will have to be determined, it sets a troubling precedent for a 'justice project' if one of its first tasks is an assessment of who should have access to justice as a function of blood and belonging.

None of these are easy matters to handle, but the failure to engage them seriously will undermine any community restorative justice initiative. Communities must be encouraged to ensure that the positive requirements are in place before a project is developed and implemented; they must also ensure that, even if all of the negative issues and obstacles cannot be removed, their presence – or the possibility of their presence – is acknowledged. Projects and those who develop them must talk to their communities – there must be strong lines of communication to facilitate community ownership, education, and access to the project.

Ownership, however, must be accompanied by accountability. Too often, accountability seems to be viewed as implicit in community development and implementation; that is, a community project is accountable to the community. And yet the majority of projects are silent on the particulars of this accountability or who or what constitutes the 'community' for purposes of securing accountability and making it real. It is on this point that restorative justice receives some of its most compelling criticisms. Given the power that community justice projects place in the hands of communities – whether Aboriginal or non-Aboriginal – it is not unreasonable to ask that some manner of checks and balances be in place to ensure that this power is used appropriately and well. This would seem to be a basic moral requirement, but there may also be considerable practical benefits to accountability, given that 'when decision-makers are required to explain their actions – or proposed actions – they are more likely to make better decisions, and their eventual decisions are more likely to be regarded as fair and legitimate' (Roche, 2003: 228).

And yet the process of 'responsibilization' seems conspicuously absent in the larger move to develop responsible communities through restorative justice. The reluctance to evaluate programs comprehensively and thoroughly is one part of that absence, as is the failure of most projects to impose a structure of accountability beyond the rather nebulous claim equating community ownership with community accountability. Although these respective gaps are probably rooted in a similar reluctance to rain on the parade of restorative justice, especially in Aboriginal communities, the failure to hold projects accountable places both parties and communities at risk. As noted by Roche, 'restorative justice utilizes programmes designed around the hope that people will be compassionate, when from a humanitarian perspective, they should be designed around the fear that they will not be ... There is a real risk that participants in restorative justice meetings may have unfettered discretion to bully, hector, harass and traumatize one another' (2003: 228). Classic accountability, then, is in some respects inconsistent with the theme of trust and empowerment in the restorative justice movement; at the same time, if it is imposed from outside the community, perhaps by government or funding agencies, accountability may also be challenged as inconsistent with self-government and disrespectful of communities. It may also be very difficult to achieve, as the discussions or content of many restorative processes are confidential, to the point where parties are asked to determine at the outset the degree of confidentiality they require in order to participate fully and freely in the restorative process, and facilitators' notes are destroyed following a session. To the degree that parties are constrained from public disclosure of the discussions held in 'the circle,' or the rationale behind resolution agreements or restorative outcomes, the opportunity for accountability seems limited.

Roche asserts that, while many restorative processes appear to be character-ized by an absence of formal accountability, this lack is less problematic than critics of restorative justice would believe. In his view, since most restorative processes centre upon a gathering of parties who then engage in a facilitated discussion of a conflict event with the goal of determining how best to resolve that conflict and encourage healing and recovery from it, 'there is a type of accountability inherent in the deliberative process ... a type of mutual account-ability is built into meetings where participants provide verbal accounts which are scrutinized and assessed by other participants, whose own accounts are in turn scrutinized' (Roche, 2003: 79–80).

As we observed earlier, the degree to which the free-flow of information implicit in this description of the 'deliberative process,' or the trust which would seem a prerequisite to it, characterizes Aboriginal restorative justice approaches is open to question. In order to be scrutinized effectively, an account must first be given, and there is no imperative in place requiring participants to provide one – although Roche appears to suggest that such an imperative is implicit in attending a circle or similar process in which all participants have agreed, at least in principle, to offer accounts. This agreement, it is argued, results in a de facto enforcement of the shared obligation to disclose, and the competition of disclo-sures seems to be regarded as a form of 'account quality control': 'meetings rely on participants to informally enforce against each other the requirement to give accounts. A participant's concern about what other participants think of him or her makes him or her accountable to them. In other words, participants' ability to grant or withhold approval and censure is an immediate enforcement mecha-nism of deliberative accountability' (Roche, 2003: 81). The question, as Roche frames it, is whether approval matters – he claims it does and it should, and he is probably right. The problem is, of course, that approval may not be linked with the sort of pro-social communication and account giving Roche seems to suggest it is. There seems to be an explicit assumption that approval is linked with telling the truth, but what happens to deliberative accountability if approval is linked with *not* telling the truth, or with a very selective form of truth-telling? As we have seen, much of the work of community justice processes in Aboriginal communities involves violent crimes against the person, usually directed at women and children; at the same time, significant pressures in communities against disclosing abuse often render the costs of full account-giving much greater than the benefits. If a victim's extended family, or that of the offender, would prefer some aspects of the account to be left out, the sort of approval implicit in adhering to their request may be more attractive to a victim than the uncertain approval promised by the deliberative accountability claimed to char-acterize the circle. This is especially so where community programs are insufficiently developed to ensure that parties other than the victim are subjected to accountability once the circle is closed. While the possibility of deliberative accountability is undoubtedly present in some justice projects, in many others it is not. More troubling, the accountability that flows between parties in a circle or forum may not only be unidirectional, it may also be of a variety quite apart from that anticipated by Roche. Thus we come again to the same issue – if the restorative process cannot escape the asymmetrical power relations and dysfunction present in the larger community and families which form the context for the justice project, deliberative accountability is likely to be either absent or warped in ways that Roche could not possibly have intended.

Roche asserts that for deliberative accountability to work, those implementing restorative processes must 'give careful attention to the identity of participants and the conditions of deliberations' (2003: 80); domination of a party or parties by others in the process must be prevented. Yet even where these factors are carefully attended to, such attention may mitigate not one whit the tensions described above. Domination can only be dealt with if it is visible, and it is not always so; the conditions for deliberations may appear favourable, while they are not. Trust may be more apparent than real. In response to such concerns, Roche asserts that informal modes of accountability must be accompanied by such formal modes of accountability as judicial review (2003: 80). Formal accountability would seem to be in place in sentencing circles in theory, insofar as participants may always appeal sentence, if they have the means and agency to do so. This restorative process may more closely approximate the type of process envisaged when Roche speaks of deliberative accountability. He also asserts that there must be accountability in the circle for the decisions made; that is, outcomes must be public, follow-up must be in place, and there must be a clear chain of accountability. This chain should take the form of iterative accountability: those to whom the project is accountable must, in turn, be accountable themselves. For example, a given circle or forum would be required to account for process and outcome to a justice committee, which is accountable to the band council, which is accountable to the community members who participated in the circle or forum. While this form of 'recursive accountability' has potential, it may be hindered by established power relations in communities and the general ambivalence that characterizes follow-up in too many contexts. The commitment of outside governments to participate in accountability, whether through funding arrangements or a greater commitment to evaluation, offers additional potential, but this would require a radical remobilization of the state on such issues, something which seems unlikely given current political and economic exigencies.

And yet, accountability needs to occur at a range of locations in restorative processes – there should be accountability for those determining which cases should proceed, and for their movement through the process in a timely and efficient manner; there should be some form of accountability for restorative outcomes, insofar as agreements for resolution or restitution should be accompanied by some explanation of their contents, made public, and subject to follow-up. If agreements are never fulfilled, some accountability mechanism must be in place to catch this, answer for it, and ensure compliance. Roche asserts that whatever form these accountability measures assume, they must be characterized by simplicity and follow promptly from the conclusion of the process; they must deter those who would participate in a restorative process for the wrong reasons, or who abuse their right to participate once the process is underway. Accountability must transpire in a public context and it must be inclusive – the more people who must be answered to, the more careful those responsible for a process are likely to be about their decisions. The form and process of accountability would undoubtedly vary across communities and projects, and ensuring it is a workable and central part of those projects is crucial to their legitimacy, both within and outside of communities. Accountability, if properly articulated and implemented, could go a long way towards enhancing the fairness of restorative processes and, in doing so, enhance the viability of the resolutions they create.

Finally, to fully support communities, there must be a commitment to full and realistic appraisal of what can work and what is required to make those things work. This implies a full commitment to sustainable funding, realistic and informed policy, and full, systematic, and methodologically sound evaluation. If we are not prepared to do this for and with communities, we can hardly ask communities to fulfil their roles in restorative justice. We have failed Aboriginal people and communities before; it is important that we not fail them now. Restorative justice has made strong promises to communities; it is our hope that this book will contribute positively to ensuring that this promise is one which we keep.

CHAPTER 10

Some Concluding Comments and Thoughts

Nearly four years ago, we attended a conference on justice held by the Grand Council of the Crees of James Bay, entitled 'Taking Responsibility.' The conference was held in the last Cree settlement on the eastern shores of James Bay, located just steps away from its intersection with Hudson Bay and the onset of Inuit country. It was January, and it was cold. Caught up in the compelling debates about justice among representatives of nine Cree communities, we later found ourselves standing in a hallway of the visitors' lodgings, discussing at length the emergent pressure on Aboriginal communities to 'take responsibility' for the conflict gripping so many of them and the difficulties they experienced when trying to resolve it. Despite years of intervening initiatives, the conference had a déjà vu flavour for us: we had heard the same concerns expressed when we first started working in the Cree communities a decade earlier. As our own discussions continued – late into the night and undoubtedly to the consternation of other lodgers trying to sleep – we realized that our respective experiences as researchers in Aboriginal justice had brought us to a number of common ideas and concerns. We shared a similar trepidation regarding the current drive by the state and local elites to have Aboriginal communities articulate their 'responsibleness' through the adoption or development of largely externally defined and developed restorative justice programs and structures, whether or not these were relevant to their specific situations, needs, and capacities. 'Taking responsibility' was presented both at this conference, as in many others we had attended over the years, as a kind of magic bullet that would empower communities and solve their problems. This conversation and our shared concern about the rush to adopt and impose restorative justice as the solution for Aboriginal communities was the genesis of this book. The themes we have explored are rooted in ideas we shared in that rather cold hallway.

We were then, and remain, concerned about the assumptions which appear to inform Aboriginal community and restorative justice. Many involve a concept of community that is too often inadequately investigated and considered. As we demonstrated, Aboriginal communities are as complex, challenging, and mutable as other communities – and in some ways, more so. While this observation may seem unremarkable, outdated ideas and stereotypes of Aboriginal communities continue to animate the popular consciousness and, perhaps more importantly, approaches to understanding and assisting communities to develop positive responses to the many challenges they face. Aboriginal communities are too often viewed as the romanticized last bastions of 'noble savages,' or as deeply impoverished, highly dysfunctional entities in desperate need of the benevolent aid of outsiders. These extremes distort and deny reality, for inasmuch as too many Aboriginal communities are characterized by poverty, asymmetrical power relations, and blocked opportunities, they remain 'home' and, notwithstanding how difficult life can be there, where the heart is for many First Nations people. Probably all communities require the assistance of experts and outsiders to develop adequate responses to shared social problems. But even the most disadvantaged Aboriginal communities will tend to manifest a small but crucial core of individuals who have the agency and ability to initiate change, if adequately supported and resourced. The challenge is to locate these individuals and ensure that their abilities are respected and enlisted in navigating the change, and that their agency is not eroded under the demands and pressures of leading the way. It is important to remember, too, that insofar as non-Aboriginal policies and practices have long fed into and encouraged the poverty and dysfunction that now affects too many Aboriginal lives, it is hardly fair to expect communities to walk the path to a better place alone. The state and its experts were long willing to push Aboriginal communities into their current locations, and it is our moral and – given current articulations of Aboriginal and treaty rights – legal obligation to assist them to shift course.

While maintaining that Aboriginal communities are far more complex and varied than most popular assumptions would suggest, we also challenged the romanticized view of Aboriginal communities implicit in descriptions promoted by such authors as Ross (1992, 1996). These depictions of Aboriginal communities as impeded in their development and interaction with the outside world owing to the persistence and robustness of traditional culture are arguably little less problematic than the unidimensional stereotype of Aboriginal communities discussed above. This is not to say that tradition and traditional culture do not remain important and influential aspects of many Aboriginal communities, or that these somehow become less legitimate with time and change. Rather, the issue here is that the elevation of culture per se and the selective reification of certain aspects of tradition are too often a means for resisting change, or a justification for moving in a particular, too often unclear, direction.

Let us look first to the question of culture. It was not our place or intention to query whether and to what degree Aboriginal culture remains true to its historical roots (Hobsbawm and Ranger [1983] demonstrated the irrelevance of such exercises long ago). Rather, our consideration of culture focused on two levels, first, as the root of an argument that culture is the key to understanding Aboriginal conflict with the law, most notably as this is articulated in over-representation of Aboriginal people at almost every level of the system. Our second focus was a logical extension of the first, whereby the 'problem of culture' is seen as implicating it as the solution as well – a view which has dominated most policy attempts to reduce over-representation. Thus we have seen attempts to render policing, courts, and corrections more culturally aware and appropriate through indigenization, cross-cultural training, and culturally-focused programs, and by fostering a greater sensitivity to the implications of cultural difference for Aboriginal people when they interact with the law and the system that administers it. We have appointed Aboriginal justices of the peace and judges, recruited Aboriginal police and pressed for band policing, and we have created 'healing lodges' to replace prisons – and nearly three decades later we still have not managed to reduce over-representation. Providing for Aboriginal people to be arrested by Aboriginal cops, defended by Aboriginal lawyers before Aboriginal judges, and sent to places of healing rather than correction did not reduce the sheer numbers of them in the system, or improve their risk factors for recidivism; if anything, the numbers continue to climb. If the justice system was made more 'appropriate' or less foreign, it was also made much more 'effective' by these changes, as more Aboriginal people were drawn into it. As noted in Part II, if this sort of effectiveness equates with success in justice reform, then the architects of such policies are to be congratulated. If, on the other hand, we were aiming for reduced rates of incarceration and recidivism, clearly some rethinking is required.

Despite the fact that our policy choices do not appear to be achieving the ends to which they were directed, we have clung with surprising tenacity to 'culture' as both the cause and the cure of over-representation. When indigenization and cultural sensitivity did not fix the problem, instead of reassessing our preferred solution and the particular construction of the problem it entailed, we simply pressed the solution harder – hence the changes to the Criminal Code contained in section 718, by which all judges were now required to actively consider Aboriginal background and its implications when imposing sentence. Despite the fact that sentences result from a complex balancing of a range of elements relevant to the offence, and ample available evidence to indicate that a remarkable number of judges already included assessments of culture and disadvantage in that mix, the sentencing reforms were seized upon by many as the coup d'état in combatting over-representation. After all, if judges send people to prison, ensuring that they only do so for the 'right' reasons should result in a reduction in over-representation of Aboriginal people. The difficulty, of course, is to determine precisely which of the reasons are the right ones to send offenders to prison. Yes, too many Aboriginal people are in prisons, but the substantial majority of them are repeat offenders serving time for violent crimes perpetrated predominantly against Aboriginal women and children. Since judges are required to consider the nature and gravity of the offence, prior offence histories, and risk/need levels, the gravity of these factors may in some cases outweigh the influences on sentence of Aboriginality or any disadvantages associated with this. While we do not suggest abandoning this criteria, we stress that it needs to be approached with caution. As noted, most of the Aboriginal offenders to whom the sentencing reforms are applied have Aboriginal victims, and there is no less imperative to consider their interests and ensure they are treated fairly. If we must respect Aboriginal offenders by keeping them out of prison, why do we not equally respect Aboriginal victims and their communities by keeping violent, repetitive offenders away? Assuming that victims and communities may not desire the return of their most problematic citizens, we need to be cautious in our implementation of the sentencing reforms, and mindful of the possibility that, in some cases at least, by focusing on Aboriginal offenders, we may harm Aboriginal communities.

Once again, then, we come back to the challenge of community. When we undertake to return Aboriginal offenders to their communities – a practice which has emerged as the logical extension of sentencing reforms in particular – we have an obligation to ensure not only that the community is willing to accept them, but that they are able to do so. We must be sensitive to the needs and interests of the victims, and to the fact that in some communities obtaining the victim's views on the offence, the offender, and what should be done with him or her may prove difficult. As we indicated in Part II, far too many of the community restorative justice initiatives intended to facilitate the sentencing process (sentencing circles in particular) or provide the context and programming in which the sentence is served (such as the CHCH), rely upon a level of functionality and freedom that may not always be present. As Crnkovich (1995), Ryan and Calliou (2002), and others have documented, such forums assume that victims will be supported and able to speak freely in community justice projects, and that their interests will be considered at least as equal to those of the offender. In far too many cases, this support and ability are absent, and victims who recognize this and reject local processes do so at considerable risk. Those who damn the context and speak freely in the circle or conference may face the condemnation of relatives or peers who are uncomfortable with such levels of disclosure and the negative attention it may attract. Those who, mindful of the risks, refuse to participate at all, may be criticized for undermining local justice, and therefore self-government, while those who participate in them are forced to censor their input and accept the program's output as the 'will of the community.' In all cases, there is a problematic degree of revictimization.

The pressure placed on victims to accept and participate in community restorative justice projects is directly related to the pressures exerted on First Nations to develop these programs and make them work. Community justice is presented as an important part of self-government, or at least a key indication that communities are moving in that direction by taking control over, and care of, their most troubled members. In many communities, however, the presence of the very problems which have encouraged high levels of conflict with the law and over-representation will undermine a restorative justice project. Hence the fundamental flaw in restorative justice: to succeed in community justice requires successful, healthy communities. Far too many Aboriginal communities are a long way from healthy; they are riven by asymmetrical power relations, dysfunctional families, poverty and unemployment, boredom and the substance abuse that offers a fleeting escape from all these things. This bleak reality poses two fundamental challenges to the positive futures promised by restorative justice to Aboriginal communities. First, definitions of community justice must expand far beyond the confines of restorative justice projects to include a much larger social justice component. Social justice requires meaningful employment for Aboriginal people within their own territories, the construction of a positive lived environment in communities, and the support of families, social services, and education. In other words, we must work with Aboriginal people to develop communities before developing community justice projects. The absence of social justice in First Nations is the leading cause of over-representation, and yet we continue to ignore this, preferring instead to cling to culture as the way out of the morass. Perhaps this is because ignoring socio-economic conditions in the majority of communities in favour of culture enables us to turn a blind eye to the costs of colonialism to First Nations, and assert instead that the problems are caused by our failure to address those aspects of Aboriginal cultures and tradition which have survived colonialism. In one fell swoop, we are able to diminish the impacts of the acts of our ancestors by focusing on those aspects of culture which endure, while at the same time assuaging our collective conscience by focusing on those aspects in policy and programs. While working towards better understanding between cultures is not necessarily a bad thing, in the realm of justice policy in Aboriginal communities, it is a pretty safe route for the system and the larger Canadian society. It does not require us to shift our priorities and resources to social justice considerations; all we have to do is know and understand Aboriginal peoples and cultures. This is arguably a much less expensive and, for the majority of Canadians, less disruptive approach. Politically, it is also easier and less disruptive than challenging Aboriginal politicians and leaders to promote social justice in communities.

The absence of social justice on reserves especially has led to the second of what we feel are the most compelling challenges facing Aboriginal justice: the increasing migration of First Nations peoples from reserves into the urban centres. The conditions on far too many reserves for far too many people are such that over 70 per cent of Aboriginal people have left them for the cities, a trend which, if we fail to work diligently with communities to improve conditions, is unlikely to change. But the urban environment presents special challenges for restorative justice. In the city, the role of culture as the cause and cure of over-representation takes on a whole new dimension, and the complexities of this context have left policy makers floundering in a quagmire of uncertainty.

Much of this confusion is generated by the nature of the urban environment. We are most familiar with restorative justice in relation to the setting we know best for Aboriginal people – reserves, which are historically and geographically bounded and where we feel most comfortable in our understanding of culture. In earlier chapters we explored some of the urban and over-representation issues; we now reiterate briefly to illustrate what we believe are the outstanding challenges for restorative justice in the urban environment.

The first dilemma we face is how to operationalize restorative justice outside the context of the Aboriginal-specific reserve environment. So much of the discourse about restorative justice and Aboriginal communities revolves around the closeness and familiarity of people, and the use of shame and public pressure to generate conformity to restorative justice outcomes. Victims are usually in close physical (if not emotional) proximity to offenders and, in theory, 'healing' can occur in such a way that promotes well-being for victims, offenders, and community members. In cities, victims and offenders may be strangers, and the 'community' has to be artificially constructed through a search for people who are Aboriginal, rather than for people who are meaningful to the offender and victim. While some urban agencies have set up 'restorative' diversion programs for Aboriginal offenders (which look little different from those for non-Aboriginal offenders), the results have been ambiguous at best. Clearly, the whole issue of designing and implementing restorative justice for Aboriginal offenders and victims in the urban environment requires much more consideration and research.

A second dilemma also confronts reserve communities but, for purposes of criminal justice, it has particular resonance for the urban environment. Research findings reveal that a majority of Aboriginal people serving sentences in Canadian correctional institutions committed the offences for which they are incarcerated in cities. This raises an important question about where the emphasis and resources to address over-representation should be placed. Should these be focused on how to operationalize and make restorative justice 'work better' in cities, or should they address the factors that most disadvantage Aboriginal people living in cities? While we believe that all realistic and reasonable avenues for keeping people out of prison should be explored, we are also convinced that the larger social and economic factors that make people most vulnerable to involvement in the criminal justice and correctional systems are urgent and must be addressed.

Recent research about Aboriginal over-representation supports this view. Weatherburn et al. (2004) and La Prairie and Stenning (2003) note that the relationship between socio-economic disadvantage and involvement in the criminal justice system is not confined to Aboriginal people. For Aboriginal and non-Aboriginal people alike, the most disadvantaged are disproportionately represented as offenders in the criminal justice system. Canadian Aboriginal people, increasingly concentrated in urban centres and more particularly in the inner cores of metropolitan areas, generate both the highest crime rates and the highest criminal justice over-representation of the Aboriginal and non-Aboriginal disadvantaged. But some Canadian researchers (Stenning and Roberts, 2001; La Prairie, 2002) also argue that in order to understand Aboriginal over-representation in the criminal justice system, we must recognize the significant regional variations in the disadvantages faced by Aboriginal people, and that one way to do this is to analyse city-by-city differences. Population concentrations, demographics, and the socio-economic circumstances of Aboriginal populations in the Prairie cities are very different from those in cities elsewhere in the country. The cities with the largest proportions of Aboriginal people living in extremely poor neighbourhoods are Winnipeg, Saskatoon, and Regina; the cities with the smallest are Toronto, Vancouver, and Edmonton. If one is Aboriginal and living in a city, the degree of advantage or disadvantage experienced relates to the geographic location of that city. But living on- or off-reserve is not necessarily the real issue. In Nova Scotia and New Brunswick, for example, more people live on- than off- reserve, but those provinces also have some of the lowest levels of Aboriginal involvement in the criminal justice system. What these provinces do *not* have is a concentration of poor, single-parent, and poorly educated Aboriginal people in the inner core of their large cities.

Sampson and Raudenbush's findings from Chicago neighbourhoods (2001), and Hagan and McCarthy's work on social capital (1998), suggest that social and economic organization and related structures of advantage or disadvantage profoundly affect people's lives and dictate crime and disorder, both on reserve and in city neighbourhoods. These dictate, as well, who stays and who leaves reserves, and who succeeds and who fails in cities. In the eastern cities similar proportions of Aboriginal and non-Aboriginal people live in poor neighbourhoods, but in Prairie cities the proportion of Aboriginal people living in these circumstances is three or four times that of non-Aboriginal people. In Vancouver and Edmonton, the number is twice as high. These findings correspond closely to regional levels of Aboriginal over-representation (Richards, 2001).

Unfortunately, regional variations in over-representation have never been seriously explored by any of the commissions established in Canada to examine the issue of Aboriginal involvement in the criminal justice and correctional systems. Nor has serious attention been given to factors such as geographic location of reserves, proximity to urban centres, reserve/urban links, on- and off-reserve migratory patterns, social, cultural, and political organization of reserves, reserve social structure, and the nature of reserve life. We have generally neglected to study band governance, Aboriginal social structure and organization in inner cites, levels of Aboriginal services in inner cites, and/or characteristics of urban centres. These gaps in knowledge prevent us from fully understanding or explaining social and economic disparities within Aboriginal or between Aboriginal and non-Aboriginal urban populations, and the impact of these disparities on involvement in the criminal justice system.

How can disadvantage be addressed? One way might be to look at social capital theory, discussed earlier in this book, which suggests people acquire at birth and throughout their lives, unequal shares of capital which affect their life chances. Social capital can be enhanced for individuals through such initiatives as improved education attainment, extended periods of employment, and other measures that improve one's life chances. But social capital can accumulate within communities as well and may affect the distribution of crime. Research in Chicago, which tested the assumption that social and physical disorder in neighbourhoods can escalate to serious crime, showed that although related, disorder did not directly promote crime. More important is the absence of 'collective efficacy,' defined as cohesion among neighbourhood residents, combined with shared expectations for informal control of public space, which was shown to be a significant factor in explaining levels of crime and disorder. In neighbourhoods where collective efficacy was strong, rates of violence were low regardless of socio-demographic composition. The researchers concluded that increasing collective efficacy, rather than reducing disorder, may be the most promising means for preventing crime. Thus policies that rely solely on tough law enforcement tactics are misdirected. Mobilizing community residents to create and strengthen social ties, and increasing awareness of commitment to neighbourhood and to maintaining public order where residents and not police are responsible, are essential to reducing crime (Sampson and Raudenbush, 2001).

Community and family capital can be enhanced through the provision of services and resources, increasing options and opportunities. The criminal justice system may not be in a position to address structural issues, but it can influence crime prevention, and other related initiatives, to implement strategies that are known to work. There is a growing body of 'what works' literature in criminal justice for policy makers and planners in the most disadvantaged and vulnerable communities to draw upon and emulate (Sherman et al., 1998). For the criminal justice system, a greater awareness of the regional distribution of 'within group' Aboriginal as well as Aboriginal/non-Aboriginal advantage and disadvantage might also direct governments in how and where to target resources to support the most disadvantaged people and communities.[1] At the same time, while the system and state must become better informed and more strategic in their policies, they must resist the tendency to develop 'solutions' to problems in inner cities independently and externally, imposing them on those neighbourhoods from outside and above (Sommers, 2001). 'Outsiders' can help, but the community efficacy findings reinforce the need for communities themselves to begin the process of building capacity to deal with their own problems and to influence the governmental social and economic policies that affect them.

The importance of working with the urban Aboriginal community to enhance levels of efficacy and agency is echoed in the rural, reserve community context. Throughout this book we have reinforced the point that effective community justice requires effective communities, and that it cannot be 'parachuted in,' as many programs and reforms have been in the past. Communities must have support and resources to develop their agency and potential from within; they must be built – or rebuilt – into the solid foundations necessary to counteract forces favouring dysfunction and conflict which threaten all our communities. Once this foundation is in place, the sort of positive symbiosis between community and community programs that fosters healthy lived environments can arise and persist. If, however, larger community issues are neglected in favour of criminal justice issues, little more will be done than ensure that any restorative justice programs implemented in communities will face robust and entrenched caseloads and challenges, few of which they have the resources to resolve.

In sum, there is little question that the over-representation of Aboriginal people in the Canadian criminal justice system is deeply troubling, as is the more general absence of social justice in the lives of First Nations people. We hope that this book will contribute in some small way to finding a sustainable, meaningful solution to these problems, and in closing we would like to state once again the views with which we began: we believe in the possibilities and potential of Aboriginal community restorative justice, and we hold this belief in large measure because, despite their problems and the challenges they face, we believe profoundly in the strength and resilience of communities. It is imperative that those who would work with them to achieve positive change share this belief, and remember always that, notwithstanding those challenges, Aboriginal people are seeking nothing more than what the rest of us expect: peaceful communities, just application of the laws, and fairness in the process. We must also remember that, despite the focus on Aboriginal offending rates and over-incarceration, the majority of Aboriginal people do not commit crimes. As observed by Weatherburn et al. in Australia, if we wish to work with First Nations to address high crime rates, we need to do so in the same manner that we approach this end in non-Aboriginal communities; that is, 'we need to understand what it is that distinguishes Aboriginal people who frequently come into conflict with the law from those who do not' (2003: 13). While limited information is available in this regard, what evidence does exist indicates that what separates Aboriginal people who experience conflict with the law from those who do not are factors such as family dissolution, poor school performance, unemployment, and substance abuse (Weatherburn et al., 2003: 13) – the same sorts of factors that encourage non-Aboriginal people into high rates of conflict with the law. This would seem to suggest at least a couple of things we might do differently in responding to over-representation. Insofar as the factors facilitating over-representation seem to have social policy roots rather than criminal justice ones, here we have further argument to suggest that the way to keep people out of conflict with the law is to give them healthy, prosperous communities to live in. Once again, the answer to our criminal justice problems would seem to lie in the realm of a greater commitment to social justice, and this must be recognized by governments and Aboriginal communities alike.

Finally, in direct contradiction to previous policy approaches to ameliorating Aboriginal over-involvement in the criminal justice system, which have focused on culture and reducing the implications of difference, perhaps it would be more helpful to focus on our similarities. If the research is correct, and the factors that lead Aboriginal people to prison are the same sort of things that result in non-Aboriginal people going to prison, we might want to start thinking about our shared responsibilities to those who are most affected by unemployment, poverty, and family breakdown, and work diligently to ensure that all our communities are characterized by social justice. Success in this approach would go a great distance towards restoring communities, empowering and healing their members, thereby rendering the need for restorative justice obsolete.

Notes

Introduction

1 Robert Depew aptly summarizes this tendency to equate Aboriginal justice with popular or restorative justice structures, and criticizes it as based upon 'questionable cultural and linguistic models' as well as tending to overlook a range of important issues, including erosion of relevant cultural systems and varying degrees of efficacy and agency in communities (1996: 49).

2 Barry Stuart, one of the most vocal proponents of sentencing circles (discussed later in this work), argues that, as one form of restorative justice, these circles have the power to 'engender moral growth, foster positive attitudes, empower individuals, resolve differences, generate enduring solutions, remove the causes of crime, build a sense of community and to create safe communities' (1996: 45).

1 Deconstructing Community: The Theory and Reality of Communities in Aboriginal Restorative Justice

1 That this comprehensive canvass of community as a theoretical construct and an object of study fails to consider Aboriginal communities as one manifestation of community in Canada would seem to confirm our concerns that the Aboriginal community has been neglected as an important focus of study.

2 An interesting example of this is found in the controversies surrounding the federal government's new governance legislation proposed in Bill C-7. This legislation, which has been vehemently opposed by the majority of elected band councils as well as the Assembly of First Nations which represents them, seems less controversial among many at the grass roots of communities. Yet as the media and the corridors of state power are filled primarily with one type of voice from one category of leader, it is impossible to gain a real sense of what it is that communities feel about

the proposed legislation. This is obviously a problematic situation, and one which is that much more compelling for those who have spent time in communities, and understand the complex layers of politics and the differing definitions and manifestations of 'leadership' therein.

3 In its decision in R. v. Powley in 2003, the Supreme Court of Canada added a new definition to the term 'Métis.' In this case the court held that '[t]he term "Métis" in s. 35 of the Constitution Act, 1982 does not encompass all individuals with mixed Indian and European heritage; rather, it refers to distinctive peoples who, in addition to their mixed ancestry, developed their own customs, and recognizable group identity separate from their Indian or Inuit and European forebears. A Métis community is a group of Métis with a distinctive collective identity, living together in the same geographical area and sharing a common way of life.' While there is little doubt that a definition which emerges from such an authority as the Supreme Court of Canada may be defined as very much 'top-down,' like other 'legal definitions' applied to Aboriginal peoples, the Powley definition may be expected to carry implications for the Métis which are quite disproportionate to the degree of ownership that Métis may have for this meaning, given its imposition on them from above.

4 Many Aboriginal people today find the term 'Indian' outdated and offensive, and prefer the term 'First Nation' or, simply, Aboriginal people. However, insofar as 'Indian' is a legal term, when discussing what are essentially legal definitions of First Nations and Aboriginal peoples, use of the word 'Indian' is essentially unavoidable.

5 Personal communication with Professor David Elliott, Law Department, Carleton University, Ottawa, September 2002.

6 Ibid.

7 However, in terms of actual numbers in the population it should be noted that seventy-seven reserves refused to participate in the census in both 1991 and 1996.

8 As compared to 4.6 per cent in Alberta, 3.8 per cent in British Columbia, 1.3 per cent in Ontario, 1.6 per cent in the Atlantic provinces, and 1.0 per cent in Quebec.

9 One encouraging sign of this happening is that in the ten-year period from 1988 to 1998, the percentage of the population aged four to eighteen enrolled in schools on-reserve increased by 37 per cent.

10 Statistics Canada defines Low Income Cut-Off (LICO) as a set of income cut-offs below which people may be said to live in straitened circumstances. Most people who use the LICO data treat the cut-offs as poverty lines.

11 If the Aboriginal identity group was sub-categorized by North American Indian and Métis, the income and LICO differences might change again.

12 In 1982 over 5 per cent of the Registered Indian population lived in remote areas but this was reduced to 1.7 per cent by 1998.

13 For a fuller discussion of the cultural erosion/culture clash arguments see Alberta Justice, 1999; Hazelhurst, 1990, 1995.

2 Communities and Conflict: Offending Patterns and Over-Representation

1 The reality that 'the Aboriginal population is not uniform in its class orientation, and that broad generalizations concerning the Aboriginal population are not appropriate' has been stressed by Jeremy Hull (2001: 58). Hull also informs that, in Manitoba at least, 'non-participants in the labour force represent a minority of the Aboriginal population,' and that a majority of the Aboriginal population in this province participate in the labour market, albeit with varying degrees of success, and for a rate of remuneration which is, for most, 'heavily weighted toward the lowest income groups' (2001: 55). Variations across the Aboriginal population were influenced by whether an individual was male or female, registered or not, and whether residence was on- or off-reserve.

2 However, given what is known about the similarities in social and economic conditions and characteristics of indigenous populations in Australia, New Zealand, and Canada, it would be surprising if the same findings that relate to over-representation would not apply in Canada.

3 The research methodology was the same in the four cities. Interviews were conducted with approximately 150 inner city Aboriginal people in the cities about various aspects of their childhoods, their life in the city and their involvement with the criminal justice system. The data are all self-report (La Prairie, 1994).

4 One exception to this, however, is the Atlantic provinces where, surprisingly, non-Aboriginal have less education than Aboriginal offenders (CCJS, 2000b: 210).

5 A 1996 one-day snapshot of inmates in all correctional facilities across the country revealed that more Aboriginal than non-Aboriginal inmates were incarcerated for assault, were considered higher risk to reoffend, and had higher needs. This research revealed that in provincial/territorial facilities 57 per cent of Aboriginal inmates were classified as high risk compared to 44 per cent of non-Aboriginal. In federal facilities, 69 per cent of Aboriginal inmates were classified as high risk, compared to 57 per cent of the non-Aboriginal group. Aboriginal inmates were also classified as having higher needs than non-Aboriginal on most dimensions (Finn et al., 1999). Interestingly, more non-Aboriginal than Aboriginal offenders in Newfoundland were classified high risk, and, in New Brunswick, it was the non-Aboriginal offenders who had the more extensive criminal histories.

6 The recent evaluation of the Aboriginal Legal Services of Toronto found that the factors most related to post-program convictions were disrupted childhoods, substance abuse problems, and the involvement of alcohol and/or drugs in the diverted offences. Surprisingly, receiving additional help from the program was also related to post-program convictions but this may simply reflect a high-risk group who required more intensive involvement (Campbell Research Associates, 2000).

7 Given these intragroup differences among Aboriginal offenders, it may be that on- and off-reserve risk factors may vary in some parts of the country, and that risk

predictors should be formulated specifically for reserves. It also suggests that general risk prediction scales are appropriate for the general Aboriginal group (La Prairie, 1994; Bonta, 1997; Trevethan, 1991).

8 Interestingly, the discriminatory use of remand in Ontario was found to affect the Black population, whom Kellough and Wortley (2002) found were denied bail significantly more often than were non-Black.

9 See also Hamilton and Sinclair (1991); Linn (1992); Cawsey (1991). None of these inquiries, except, to a limited extent the Manitoba Inquiry, conducted the kind of systematic participant observation and / or file data research that would have allowed for a better understanding of the contribution of decision making at various stages of criminal justice processing to the over-representation of Aboriginal people in correctional institutions.

3 Severing the Gordian Knot: Efforts at Institutional and the Rise of Restorative Approaches

1 A brief word on the samples and study design: 'Data were collected from six separate courses of the programme in a time period spanning April–December 1994. A total of 62 participants across the six courses participated in the evaluation. this included 39 women, and 23 men. The mean age of the total sample was 41.90 years (SD=12.10). Ages ranged from 22 to 70 years. There was no significant difference in age between women and men. Thirty-one of the 62 participants returned the longitudinal questionnaire for a return rate of 50 per cent. Mean age of this sample was 41.26 years old (SD=21.19). The returned sample consisted of 18 women and 12 men. There was, again, no significant difference in the age of men and women. The study design was a quasi-experimental pre-post design, with a second post test conducted 3 months after completing the programme' (Hill and Augoustinos, 2001: 250).

2 The term is Hill and Augoustinos's, not ours, despite its suitability to the discussion. The researchers not only set out to assess 'modern racism' and 'old-fashioned redneck racism' - the difference between the concepts is largely one of degree, it would seem. The former tends to be rather more sophisticated and may involve both positive and negative stereotypes, while the latter appears to reflect the crude, open displays of ignorance focusing only upon negative stereotyping of the target group.

3 While the new agreements recently struck with the Cree of James Bay may alter the nature of some justice programs as they existed under the original James Bay and Northern Quebec Agreement, the entrenchment of current policing bodies and models in most James Bay communities renders radical alterations to present approaches unlikely.

4 It is important to note that within this category of questions, 48 per cent of respondents expressed a belief that poor treatment was a result of the behaviour of the

native person towards the police, and a further 21 per cent felt poor treatment was a consequence of the actions and attitudes of individual officers. This suggests, first, a sense of shared responsibility for the problems between inner city Aboriginal people and police, and second, that again, we must not focus on cultural differences at the expense of understanding and working to ameliorate other factors which are potentially just as, or more, important in distancing Aboriginal people and the police.

5   This research is discussed extensively in chapter 2, at 43–7.

4 Restorative Justice in Aboriginal Communities: Origins and Early Development

1   When criminal matters are involved, restorative justice processes are applied to offenders who have plead guilty to an offence (Daly, 2001; Ferguson, 2001).

2   Daly and Hayes (2001) note that there was intense debate in the 1990's about the merits of police versus non-police run conferencing with the result that there is now country-by-country variation in the adoption of the approaches used.

3   Family violence is often cited as a significant problem in Aboriginal communities and is the focus of the Family Group Decision-Making project in Newfoundland and Labrador, patterned on the Family Group or Community Accountability Conferencing model (Pennell and Burford, 1994).

5 Providing a Context for the Challenge of Community Justice: Exploring the Implications for Restorative Initiatives in Disordered Environments

1   We include Aboriginal victimization here because the extremely disproportionate levels suggest an important window for better understanding over-representation and for examining the feasibility of community-based alternatives such as those employing the principles and practices of restorative justice.

2   Moyer (2000) notes that few Canadian jurisdictions permit pre-trial diversion of persons accused of domestic violence. In fact, in most jurisdictions, there is a policy that diversion cannot be considered in family violence cases. In the Northwest Territories, pre-charge diversion can occur in exceptional circumstances only if the RCMP, the local justice committee, and Justice Canada agree. Similarly, in British Columbia, the Crown policy manual states that while diversion is generally inappropriate, it may be considered in exceptional circumstances.

6 Testing the 'Magic': Sentencing Circles in Aboriginal Community Restorative Justice

1   In a sentencing circle observed by Dickson-Gilmore, some evidence was discovered to suggest a clear absence of such illusions. During a break in a circle which had

appeared to involve quite compelling exchanges of stories of the event, descriptions of its impacts, and an exchange of apologies and gifts, the offenders were encountered in conversation with their counsel discussing whether the circle 'bought it' and whether the judge would go along with a sentence that would keep the perpetrators of the crime (assault) out of jail. Admittedly, these offenders would appear to be among those which Stuart and others assert could be ruled out of a circle process through good pre-circle preparation, as individuals who do not come to the circle with the proper motivations or intentions. However, it is interesting that, in this case which appeared to have reasonable pre-circle preparation, a supportive community and court, and an established justice project with a reasonable degree of resources available to support circle participants, these offenders easily adopted a conciliatory and 'restorative' role in the circle while apparently motivated by an adversarial intention. They did not go to jail, but one party was quick to recidivate.

7 'Taking Responsibility': Conferencing and Forums in Canadian Aboriginal Communities

1 The description of the conduct of the FGC contained on page 201 of the brief report does not indicate at any point that the plan of action determined by the family group separately from the rest of the conference participants was returned to the larger group for discussion. This seems a rather problematic omission which, when added to the reluctance of victims, police, and lawyers to participate, may well have influenced the willingness of the court to accept the sentencing recommendations made by the FGC. See Longclaws et al., 200–2.

2 Lane et al. cite Hodgson et al. (1998), in support of their view that institutional treatment programs not only show very limited success, but are not cost-effective when compared with community-based treatment approaches (Lane et al., 2002: 25).

3 The Community Holistic Circle Healing Program is 'a progeny of the original Wanipigow Resource Team, [and] serves the needs of the four communities of the area, sometimes referred to as MASH (Manigotagan, Ahbaming, Seymourville, and Hollow Water First Nation, where the program is based). These four communities, located approximately 150 miles northeast of Winnipeg, Manitoba, constitute what is commonly referred to as 'Hollow Water' (Couture et al., 2001: 10).

4 The Seven Sacred Teachings consist of *courage* (to face responsibility for one's actions; to seek forgiveness and make apology); spiritual *knowledge*; *respect* for others, the earth, and for oneself; *honesty*; *humility*; *love*; and *truth* (Couture et al., 2001: 28).

5 The Cleansing Ceremony most commonly assumes the form of a community feast.

8 The Bottom Line: What Do We Know, and How Do We Know It?

1 While the perceptions of external agencies that have been documented are generally positive, there are some exceptions. Police linked with the Sandy Lake and Attawapiscat projects and, originally, at least, to the Youth Justice Committee in Alberta, were less supportive of these programs and their efforts.

9 Forward Thinking, Looking Back: Where Do We Go from Here in Community Restorative Justice?

1 The recommendations of a 2001 New South Wales workshop focusing on diversion of Aboriginal adults from the justice system go some way to filling existing knowledge gaps. The workshop identified the need for a diversionary framework to encourage greater diversion from police and courts, particularly to local Aboriginal communities. This framework included a legislative basis for adult diversion; pooled and coordinated funding of diversion programs; the development of diversionary program principles and evaluation standards; and local police, court, and community coordination. The attorney general of New South Wales, in a speech to the same workshop participants, stated that his department was in the process of developing a broad framework to divert Aboriginal offenders and that what was produced in the workshop would be invaluable. Whether it actually built on and implemented those recommendations is unknown.

10 Some Concluding Comments and Thoughts

1 Targeting those people most in need might reduce the likelihood that general 'Aboriginal' policies to enhance opportunities are used most often by those who are already advantaged.

References

Aboriginal Justice Implementation Commission (AJIC). 1999. *The Justice System and Aboriginal People*. November. Online at: http://www.ajic.mb.ca/volume1/toc.html

Alberta Justice. 1999. Treaty 8 Submission to the Alberta Summit on Justice, Alberta Summit on Justice.

Alder, Christine, and Joy Wundersitz, eds. 1994. *Family Conferencing and Juvenile Justice: The Way Forward or Misplaced Optimism?* Canberra: Australian Institute of Criminology. Online at: http://www.aic.gov.au/publications/lcj/family/

Anderson, Chris. 1998. Governing Aboriginal Justice in Canada: Constructing Responsible Individuals and Communities Through 'Tradition.' *Crime, Law, and Social Change* 31 (4): 303–26.

Andrews, D.A., and James Bonta. 1994. *The Psychology of Criminal Conduct*. Cincinnati, OH: Anderson Publishing.

Arnot, David. 1994. Sentencing Circles Permit Community Healing. *National* (Canadian Bar Association).

Auger, D., A. Doob, and P. Driben. 1992. Crime and Control in Three Nishnawbe-Aski Communities: An Exploratory Investigation. *Canadian Journal of Criminology* 34 (3–4): 317–38.

Australian Institute of Criminology (AIC). 1999. *Restorative Justice in Australia*. Canberra: Australian Institute of Criminology.

Bayley, David. 2001. Security and Justice for All. In *Restorative Justice and Civil Society*, ed. Heather Strang and John Braithwaite, 9–15. Cambridge: Cambridge University Press.

Bazemore, Gordon, and Mara Schiff. 1996. Community Justice/Restorative Justice: Prospects for a New Social Ecology for Community Corrections. *International Journal of Comparative and Applied Criminal Justice* 20 (2): 301–35.

Bazemore, Gordon, and Mark Umbreit. 1999. *Conferences, Circles, Boards, and Mediations: Restorative Justice and Citizen Involvement in the Response to Youth Crime*. St Paul, MN: Balanced and Restorative Justice Project.

B.C. Institute Against Family Violence [B.C. IAFV]. 2001. *Family Violence and Aboriginal People* 8 (2) (Summer/Autumn).

B.C. Resources Community Project. 1998. Geography Department, University of Northern British Columbia, Prince George, B.C.

Birkenmeyer, A.C. and S. Jolly. 1981. *The Native Inmate in Ontario.* Toronto: Ministry of Correctional Services and the Ontario Native Council on Justice.

Bittle, Steve, Nathalie Quann, and Tina Hattem. 2000. *One-Day Snapshot of Aboriginal Youth in Custody Across Canada.* Ottawa: Department of Justice.

Blagg, H. 1996. *A Just Measure of Shame? Aboriginal Youth and Conferencing in Australia.* Perth: University of Western Australia.

Boe, Roger. 2000. Aboriginal Inmates: Demographic Trends and Projections. *Forum* 12 (1) (January): 7–9. Online at: http://www.csc-scc.gc.ca/text/pblct/forum/v12n1/v12n1a3e.pdf

Bonta, James, Carol La Prairie, and Suzanne Wallace-Capretta. 1997. Risk Prediction and Re-Offending: Aboriginal and Non-Aboriginal Offenders. *Canadian Journal of Criminology* 39 (2) (April): 127–44.

Bopp, M., and J. Bopp. 1997. *Aboriginal Sex Offending in Canada.* Ottawa: Aboriginal Healing Foundation.

Bracken, Dennis. 1994. *An Evaluation of the Dakota-Ojibway Probation Service (D.O.P.S.).* Ottawa: Ministry of the Solicitor General.

Braithwaite, John. 1989. *Crime, Shame, and Reintegration.* Cambridge: Cambridge University Press.

Braithwaite, John, and S. Mugford. 1994. Conditions of Successful Reintergration Ceremonies. *British Journal of Criminology* 34 (2) 39–169.

British Columbia Resource Communities Project. 1998. Community Participation in the New Forest Economy, Discussion Paper on Concepts: 'Community.' Online at: http://quarles.unbc.ca/frbc/bkgrd1.htm

Brodeur, Jean-Paul, and Yves Leguerrier. 1991. *Justice for the Cree: Policing and Alternative Dispute Resolution.* Quebec: Grand Council of the Cree.

Brody, Maggie. 1993. Giving Away the Grog: An Ethnography of Aboriginal Drinkers who Quit Without Help. *Drug and Alcohol Review* 11 (12) 401–11.

Bursik, Robert. 1988. Social Disorganization and Theories of Crime and Delinquency: Problems and Prospects. *Criminology* 26 (4) 519–51.

Burrows, John, and Leonard Rotman. 1998. *Aboriginal Legal Issues: Cases, Materials & Commentary.* Toronto: Butterworths.

Campbell Research Associates. 1994. *Evaluation of the Nishnawbe-Aski Legal Services Corporation.* Ottawa: Department of Justice.

– 1995. *Evaluation of the Justice Development Worker Program.* Ottawa: Aboriginal Justice Directorate.

– 1999. *A Framework for Community Justice in the Western Arctic.* Yellowknife: Government of the NWT, Department of Justice.

– 2000a. *Evaluation of the Aboriginal Legal Services of Toronto, Community Council Program.* Report prepared for the ALST Community Council Program Evaluation Committee.

– 2000b. *Evaluation of the Thunder Bay Indian Friendship Centre Aboriginal Community Council Program.* Submitted to the Tripartite Evaluation Committee.

Canada. Canadian Sentencing Commission. 1987. *Report on Sentencing Reform: A Canadian Approach.* Ottawa: Minister of Supply and Services Canada.

Canada. Department of Justice. 2000. *Final Evaluation: Aboriginal Justice Strategy.* Evaluation Division, Policy Integration and Coordination Section (Technical Report), October.

Canada. House of Commons, Standing Committee on Justice and Solicitor General. 1988a. *Report: Taking Responsibility.* Ottawa: Queen's Printer.

Canada. Royal Commission on Aboriginal Peoples. 1996. *Bridging the Cultural Divide: A Report on Aboriginal People and Criminal Justice in Canada.* Ottawa: Ministry of Supply and Services.

Canada. Solicitor General. 1988b. *Task Force on Aboriginal People in Federal Corrections: Final Report.* Ottawa: Ministry of the Solicitor General.

– 1998. *Towards a Just, Peaceful, and Safe Society: The Corrections and Conditional Release Act Five Years Later.* Ottawa: Ministry of the Solicitor General.

Canadian Centre for Justice Statistics [CCJS]. 2000a. *Police-Reported Aboriginal Crime in Saskatchewan.* Ottawa: Statistics Canada.

– 2000b. *The Over-Representation of Aboriginal People in the Justice System.* Ottawa: Statistics Canada.

– 2001. *A Profile of Criminal Victimization: Results of the 1999 General Social Survey.* Ottawa: Statistics Canada.

Carach, C., A. Grant, and R. Conroy. 1999. Australian Corrections: The Imprisonment of Indigenous People. *Trends & Issues* 137:1–6.

Carter, L., and L.J. Parker. 1991. Intrafamilial Sexual Abuse in American Indian Families. In *Family Sexual Abuse*, ed. Patio Quinn, 106–17. Newbury Park: Sage Publications.

Cawsey, Robert. 1991. *Report of the Task Force on the Criminal Justice System and its Impact on the Indian and Metis People of Alberta.* Edmonton: Solicitor General. Online at: http://www4.gov.ab.ca/just/pub/publ_result.cfm?p_id=2495

Center for Restorative Justice and Mediation [CRJM]. 1996. *Restorative Justice: For Victims, Communities, and Offenders.* St Paul: University of Minnesota Press.

Christie, Nils. 1997. Conflict as Property. *British Journal of Criminology* 17 (1): 1–14.

– 1993. *Crime Control as Industry.* New York: Routledge.

Church Council on Justice and Corrections [CCJC]. 1996. *Satisfying Justice: Safe Community Options that Attempt to Repair Harm from Crime and Reduce the Use or Length of Imprisonment.* Ottawa: Church Council on Justice and Corrections.

Clairmont, Don. 1994. *Alternative Justice Issues for Aboriginal Justice.* Paper prepared for the Aboriginal Justice Directorate. Ottawa: Department of Justice.

- 1994b. *Community Assessment of Crime, Justice, and Diversion*. Halifax: Tripartite Forum on Native Justice.
- 1996. Alternative Justice Issues for Aboriginal Justice. *Journal of Legal Pluralism* 36: 125–57.

Clark, S. 1989. *The Mi'kmaq and Criminal Justice in Nova Scotia*. Halifax: Government Printer.

Comack, Elizabeth. 1993. *Women Offender's Experiences with Physical and Sexual Abuse*. Winnipeg: University of Manitoba.

Corrections Research and Development [CRD]. 2002. Restorative Justice: Promising Beginnings. *Research Summary* 7 (5): 1–2.

Couture, J., T. Parker, R. Couture, P. Laboucane, and Native Counselling Services of Alberta (NCSA). 2001. *A Cost-Benefit Analysis of Hollow Water's Community Holistic Circle Healing Process*. Ottawa: Ministry of the Solicitor General.

Cove, John. 1997. New Zealand Family Group Conferences and Restorative Justice. Paper prepared for the Research and Statistics Division, Department of Justice, Canada, 17 January.

Cove, John. 2001. Containing Maori Justice: Youth Justice and Restorative Justice in New Zealand. Unpublished paper.

Crawford, Adam. 1997. *The Local Governance of Crime: Appeals to Community and Partnership*. Oxford: Clarendon Press.

Crime Research Centre [CRC]. 2002. *Executive Summary: Crime and Justice Statistics for WA*. Perth: University of Western Australia.

Crnkovich, Mary. 1995. The Role of the Victim in the Criminal Justice System: Circle Sentencing in Inuit Communities. Paper prepared for the Canadian Institute for the Administration of Justice Conference, Banff, Alberta, 11–14 October.
- 1996. A Sentencing Circle. *Journal of Legal Pluralism* 36: 159–81.

Cunneen, C. 2002. Restorative Justice: Emerging Views. *The Drawing Board: An Australian Review of Public Affairs, 2000–2003*. Sydney: University of Sydney, School of Economics and Political Science.

Daly, Kathleen. 1996. *Gender, Crime, and Punishment*. Yale: Yale University Press.
- 2000a. Restorative Justice in Diverse and Unequal Societies. *Law in Context – Special Issue on Criminal Justice in Diverse Communities* 17 (special issue):
- 2000b. Restorative Justice: The Real Story. Paper (revised) presented to the Scottish Criminology Conference, Edinburgh, 21–2 September.
- 2000c. Making Variation a Virtue: Elevating the Potential and Limits of Restorative Justice. Revision of paper presented to the Fourth International Conference on Restorative Justice for Juveniles, 1–4 October.
- 2001. Conferencing in Australia and New Zealand: Variations, Research Findings and Prospects. In *Justice for Juveniles: Conferencing, Mediation and Circles*, ed. Allison Morris and Gabrielle Maxwell, 59–84. Oxford: Oxford University Press.

– 2002. Mind the Gap: Restorative Justice in Theory and Practice. In *Restorative Justice and Criminal Justice: Competing or Reconcilable Paradigms*, ed. A. von Hirsch, et al., 231–6. Oxford: Hart Publishing.

Daly, Kathleen, and H. Hayes. 2001. Restorative Justice and Conferencing in Australia. *Trends and Issues* 186: 221–36.

Daly, Kathleen, and Jan Kitcher. 1999. The R(evolution) of Restorative Justice Through Researcher-Practitioner Partnerships. *Ethics and Justice* 2 (1): 1–11. Online at: www.gu.edu.au/school/ccj/kdaly_docs/kdpaper3.pdf

Dasgupta, Satadal. 1996. *The Community in Canada: Rural and Urban*. Lanham, MD: University Press of America.

Department of Indian Affairs and Northern Development [DIAND]. 2001. *Registered Indian Population by CMA, 1996*. Ottawa: First Nations and Northern Statistics Section, Corporate Information Management Directorate.

Depew, Robert. 1994. *Popular Justice and Aboriginal Communities: Some Preliminary Considerations*. Paper prepared for the Aboriginal Justice Directorate, Department of Justice.

– 1996. Popular Justice and Aboriginal Communities. *Journal of Legal Pluralism* 36: 21–67.

Dickason, Olive. 2002. *Canada's First Nations: A History of Founding Peoples from Earliest Times*. 3rd ed. Don Mills, ON: Oxford University Press.

Dickson-Gilmore, Jane. 1992. Resurrecting the Peace: Traditionalist Approaches to Separate Justice in the Kahnawake Mohawk Nation. In *Aboriginal Peoples and Canadian Criminal Justice*, ed. R.A. Silverman and M.O. Nielsen, 261–70. Toronto: Butterworths.

Donlevy, Bonnie. 1994. *Sentencing Circles and the Search for Aboriginal Law*. Saskatoon: University of Saskatchewan, Indian and Aboriginal Law.

Doob, Anthony, Michelle Grossman, and Raymond Auger. 1994. Aboriginal Homicides in Ontario. *Canadian Journal of Criminology* 36 (1) (January): 29–62.

Doone, Peter. 2000. *Report on Combating and Preventing Maori Crime* (HEI WHAKARURUTANGA MO TE AO). Wellington: Department of the Prime Minister and Cabinet. Online at: http://www.justice.govt.nz/cpu/publications/2000/doone_rpt/

Drost, Helmar. 2001. Labour Market Relations and Income Distribution of Aboriginal Residents in Canada's Metropolitan Areas. Presentation at the Policy Conference on Options for Aboriginal People in Canada's Cities, Regina Saskatchewan, 2 May.

Evans, J.R., R. Hann, and J. Nuffield. 1998. *Crime and Corrections in the Northwest Territories*. Yellowknife: Department of Justice.

Ferguson, Gerald. 2001. Community Participation in Jury Trials and Restorative Justice Programs. Paper prepared for the Law Commission of Canada, First Draft, July.

Fergusson, David M., L. John Horwood, and Nicola Swain-Campbell. 2003. Ethnicity and Criminal Convictions: Results of a 21-year Longitudinal Study. *Australian and New Zealand Journal of Criminology* 6 (3): 354–67.

Finn, A.S. Shelley Trevethan, Gisèle Carrière, and Melanie Kowalski. 1999. Female Inmates, Aboriginal Inmates, and Inmates Serving Life Sentences: A One Day Snapshot. *Juristat* 19 (5).

Foden, B. 1996. Sentencing Circles Gaining Acceptance from Lawyers. *Lawyers Weekly.* 13 December, 14.

Galway, Bert, and Joe Hudson. 1996. *Restorative Justice: International Perspectives.* Monsey: Criminal Justice Press.

Garland, David. 1996. The Limits of the Sovereign State. *British Journal of Criminology* 36 (4): 445–71.

Gerber, Linda. 1979. The Development of Canadian Indian Communities: A Two-Dimensional Typology Reflecting Strategies of Adaptation to the Modern World. *Canadian Review of Sociology and Anthropology* 16 (4): 404–24.

Grant, Brian, and Frank Porporino. 1992. Are Native Offenders Treated Differently in the Granting of Temporary Absences from Federal Correctional Institutions? *Canadian Journal of Criminology* 34 (3) (July): 525–32.

Green, Ross Gordon. 1995. Aboriginal Sentencing and Mediation Initiatives: The Sentencing Circle and other Community Participation Models in Six Aboriginal Communities. LL.M. thesis, University of Manitoba.

– 1998. *Justice in Aboriginal Communities: Sentencing Alternatives.* Saskatoon: Purich Publishing.

Greenfeld, Lawrence, and Steven Smith. 1999. *American Indians and Crime.* Washington, DC: Department of Justice, February. Online at: http://www.ojp.usdoj.gov/bjs/pub/pdf/aic.pdf

Griffiths, C.T. 1996. Sanctioning and Healing: Restorative Justice in Canadian Aboriginal Communities. *International Journal of Comparative and Applied Criminal Justice* 20 (2) 195–208.

Griffiths, C.T., and R. Hamilton. 1996. Spiritual Renewal, Community Revitalization and Healing: Experience in Traditional Aboriginal Justice in Canada. *International Journal of Comparative and Applied Criminal Justice* 20 (2): 289–311.

Griffiths, C.T., E. Zellerer, D.S. Wood, and G. Saville. 1995. *Crime, Law and Justice Among the Inuit in the Baffin Region, N.W.T. Canada.* Vancouver: Criminology Research Center, Simon Fraser University.

Grobsmith, Elizabeth. 1989. The Relationship Between Substance Abuse and Crime Among Native American Inmates in the Nebraska Department of Corrections. *Human Organization* 48 (4): 283–98.

Hagan, John. 1975. Law, Order, and Sentencing: A Study of Attitude in Action. *Sociometry* 38 (2) 375–84.

Hagan, John, and Bill McCarthy. 1998. *Mean Streets: Youth Crime and Homelessness.* Cambridge: Cambridge University Press.

Hallendy, Norman. 1994. The Last Known Traditional Inuit Trial on Southwest Baffin Island in the Canadian Arctic. Paper presented at the World Archeological Congress.

Hamilton, Alvin, and C.M. Sinclair. 1991. *Report of the Aboriginal Justice Inquiry of Manitoba, Volume 1: The Justice System and Aboriginal People.* Winnipeg: Queen's Printer.

Hann, Robert, and William Harman. 1992. *Predicting General Release Risk for Canadian Penitentiary Inmates.* Ottawa: Ministry of the Solicitor General.

Hanselmann, Calvin. 2003. Ensuring the Urban Dream: Shared Responsibility and Effective Urban Aboriginal Voices. In *Not Strangers in These Parts: Urban Aboriginal People,* ed. David Newhouse and Evelyn Peters, 167–77. Canada: Policy Research Initiative.

Harding, Jim. 1992. Policing and Aboriginal Justice. In *Understanding Policing,* ed. Kevin McCormick and Livy Visano, 625–46. Toronto: Canadian Scholars' Press.

Harding, R., R. Broadhurst, A. Ferrante, and N. Loh. 1995. *Aboriginal Contact with the Criminal Justice System and the Impact of the Royal Commission into Aboriginal Deaths in Custody.* Perth: University of Western Australia, Hawkins Press.

Hassall, Ian. 1996. Origins and Development of Family Group Conferences. In *Family Group Conferences: Perspectives on Policy and Practice,* ed. Joe Hudson et al., 17–36. New York: Willow Tree Press.

Hazelhurst, Kayleen M. 1990. *Crime Prevention for Aboriginal Communities.* Crime Prevention Series. Canberra: Australian Institute of Criminology.

– 1995. *Legal Pluralism and the Colonial Legacy: Indigenous Experiences in Canada, Australia and New Zealand.* Aldershot: Avebury.

Hill, Miriam, and Martha Augoustinos. 2001. Stereotype Change and Prejudice Reduction: Short- and Long-term Evaluation of a Cross-cultural Awareness Programme. *Journal of Community and Applied Social Psychology* 11: 243.

Hobsbawn, Eric, and Terence Ranger, eds. 1983. *The Invention of Tradition.* Cambridge: Cambridge University Press.

Hull, Jeremy. 2001. *Aboriginal People and Social Class in Manitoba.* Winnipeg: Canadian Centre for Policy Alternatives. Online at: http://www.policyalternatives.ca/ manitoba/aboriginal-class.pdf

Immarigeon, Russ. 1996. Family Group Conferences in Canada and the United States: An Overview. In *Family Group Conferences: Perspectives on Policy and Practice,* ed. Joe Hudson et al., 167–79. New York: Willow Tree Press.

Ingstrup, Ole. 1998. Keynote Address to the National Elder and Native Liaison Conference, Chilliwack, B.C., 24 March. Online at: http://www.csc-scc.gc.ca/text/ speeches/commish/mar2498e.shtml

Irvine, M.J. *The Native Inmate in Ontario.* 1978. Toronto: Ministry of Correctional Services and the Ontario Native Council on Justice.

Jenkins, J.A., and C. Menton. 2003. The Relationship Between Incarcerated Batterers'

Cognitive Characteristics and the Effectiveness of Behavioural Treatment. *Corrections Compendium* 28 (3): 6–8.

Johnson, Joseph. 1997. *Aboriginal Offender Survey: Case Files and Interview Sample.* Ottawa: Correctional Services Canada.

Kaufman, Thomas, and Associates. 2000. *Report on Metis and Off-Reserve Aboriginal Issues.* Ottawa: Aboriginal Justice Implementation Commission.

Kellough, Gail, and Scot Wortley. 2002. Remand for Plea: Bail Decisions and Plea Bargains as Commensurate Decisions. *British Journal of Criminology* 42 (1) (Winter): 186–210.

Kurki, L., and Kay Pranis. 2000. *Restorative Justice as Direct Democracy and Community Building.* St Paul: Minnesota Department of Corrections, Community and Juvenile Services Division.

Lajeunesse, Therese. 1996. *Evaluation of the Hollow Water Community Holistic Circle Healing Project,* Ottawa: Solicitor General Canada.

Lane, Phil, Michael Bopp, Judie Bopp, and Julian Norris. 2002. *Mapping the Healing Journey: The Final Report of a First Nations Research Project on Healing in Canadian Aboriginal Communities.* Ottawa: Ministry of the Solicitor General.

La Prairie, Carol. 1990. The Role of Sentencing in the Over-Representation of Aboriginal People in Correctional Institutions. *Canadian Journal of Criminology* 39 (3): 429–40.

– 1992. *Exploring the Boundaries of Justice: Aboriginal Justice in the Yukon.* Whitehorse: Yukon Territorial Government, Department of Justice.

– 1994. *Seen But Not Heard: Native People in the Inner City.* Ottawa: Department of Justice, 1994.

– 1995. Altering Course: New Directions in Criminal Justice – Sentencing Circles and Family Group Conferences. *Australian and New Zealand Journal of Criminology – Special Issue: Crime, Criminology, and Public Policy.* (December): 79–99.

– 1996. *Examining Aboriginal Corrections in Canada.* Ottawa: Ministry of the Solicitor General. Online at: http://www.sgc.gc.ca/publications/abor_corrections/199614_e.pdf

– 1997. *Seeking Change: Justice Development in Laloche.* Saskatoon: Saskatchewan Justice.

– 1998. The 'New' Justice: Some Implications for Aboriginal Communities. *Canadian Journal of Criminology* 20 (1): 61–80.

– 1999. The Impact of Aboriginal Research on Policy: A Marginal Past and an Even More Uncertain Future. *Canadian Journal of Criminology* 42 (2) (April): 249–60.

– 2002. Aboriginal Over-Representation in the Criminal Justice System: A Tale of Nine Cities. *Canadian Journal of Criminology* 44 (2): 209–32.

La Prairie, Carol, and C. Koegl. 1998. *The Use of Conditional Sentences: An Overview of Early Trends.* Unpublished. Ottawa: Department of Justice.

La Prairie, Carol, and Yves Leguerrier. 1991. *Justice for the Cree: Communities, Conflict, and Order.* Quebec: Grand Council of the Crees.

La Prairie, Carol, and Philip Stenning. 2003. Exile on Main Street: Some Thoughts on Aboriginal Over-representation in the Criminal Justice System. In *Not Strangers in these Parts: Urban Aboriginal People*, ed. David Newhouse and Evelyn Peters, 178–94. Ottawa: Policy Research Initiative.

Latimer, J., C. Dowden, and D. Muisse. 2001. *The Effectiveness of Restorative Justice Practices: A Meta-Analysis*. Ottawa: Department of Justice.

Law Reform Commission of Canada [LRCC]. 1974. *The Principles of Sentencing and Disposition*. Working Paper 3. Ottawa: LRCC.

Lee, Gloria. 1996. Defining Traditional Healing. *Justice as Healing* 1 (4) (Winter): 1–5. Online at: http://www.usask.ca/nativelaw/publications/jah/lee.html

Lee, Nella. 1997. Culture, Conflict and Crime in Alaskan Native Villages. *Journal of Criminal Justice* 23 (2): 177–89.

Levrant, Sharon, Francis T. Cullen, Betsey Fulton, and John F. Wozniak. 1999. Reconsidering Restorative Justice: The Corruption of Benevolence Revisited? *Crime and Delinquency* 45 (1): 3–27.

Lilles, Heino. 2002. Circle Sentencing: Part of the Restorative Justice Continuum. Paper presented to *Dreaming of a New Reality*, the Third International Conference on Conferencing, Circles, and other Restorative Practices, Minneapolis, Minnesota, 8–10 August. Online at: http://www.iirp.org/library/mn02/mn02_lilles.html

Linden, R. n.d. The Role of Strategic Planning, Policy Implementation and Evaluation in Crime Prevention. Winnipeg: University of Manitoba, Criminology Research Center, unpublished.

Linn, Patricia. 1992. *Report of the Saskatchewan Indian Justice Review Committee*. Regina: Saskatchewan Justice.

Llewellyn, Jennifer, and Robert Howse. 1999. *Restorative Justice: A Conceptual Framework*. Ottawa: Law Commission of Canada.

Longclaws, Lyle, Burt Galaway, and Lawrence Barkwell. 1996. Piloting Family Group Conferences for Young Aboriginal Offenders in Winnipeg, Canada. In *Family Group Conferences: Perspectives on Policy and Practice*, ed. Joe Hudson et al., 195–205. New York: Willow Tree Press.

Marshall, William. 1990. Treatment of Sexual Offenders: Current Approaches with Non-Aboriginals and Their Relevance for Aboriginal Offenders. In *Handbook of Sexual Assault: Issues, Theories and Treatment of the Offender*, ed. William Marshall, D.R. Laws, and H.E. Barbaree, 257–75. New York: Plenum Press.

Maxwell, Gabrielle, and Allison Morris. 1994. The New Zealand Family Model of Family Group Conferences. In *Family Conferencing and Juvenile Justice: The Way Forward or Misplaced Optimism?* ed. Christine Alder and Joy Wundersitz, 15–44. Canberra: Australian Institute of Criminology. Online at: http://www.aic.gov.au/publications/lcj/family/

McCaskill, Don. 1976. *A Study of Needs and Resources Related to Offenders of Native Origin in Manitoba: A Longitudinal Analysis*. Ottawa: Ministry of the Solicitor General.

McCold, Paul. 1995. Restorative Justice: The Role of the Community. Boston: Paper presented to the Academy of Criminal Justice Sciences Annual Conference. Online at: http://www.realjustice.org/Pages/community3.html

– 1996. Restorative Justice and the Role of the Community. In *Restorative Justice: International Perspectives*, ed. Burt Galaway and Joe Hudson, 85–101. Monsey: Criminal Justice Press.

McDonnell, Roger. 1992. *Justice for the Cree: Customary Beliefs and Practice*. Quebec: Grand Council of the Cree.

– 1995. Prospects for Accountability in Canadian Aboriginal Justice Systems. In *Accountability for Criminal Justice: Selected Essays*, ed. P.C. Stenning, 449–77. Toronto: University of Toronto Press.

McGillivray, A., and B. Comaskey. 1999. *Black Eyes All of the Time*. Toronto: University of Toronto Press.

McMahon, Maeve. 1992. *Persistent Prison?: Rethinking Decarceration and Penal Reform*. Toronto: University of Toronto Press.

McNamara, Luke. 2000. Appellate Court Scrutiny of Circle Sentencing. *Manitoba Law Journal* 27: 209–40.

Messmer, Heinz, and Hans-Uwe Otto, eds. 1992. *Restorative Justice on Trial*. Dordrecht: Kluwer Academic Publishers.

Ministry of Maori Development [MMD]. 2002. *Update Briefing on the Criminal Justice Sector*. Wellington: Minister of Maori Affairs.

Monture, Patricia. 1991. Reflecting on Flint Woman. In *First Nations Issues*, ed. Richard Devlin, 13–26. Canadian Perspectives on Legal Theory Series. Toronto: Edmond Montgomery Publications Limited.

Monture-Okanee, Patricia. 1995. Thinking About Change. *Justice as Healing: A Newsletter on Aboriginal Concepts of Justice*. Saskatoon: Native Law Center.

Moore, David, and Terry O'Connell. 1994. Family Conferencing in Wagga Wagga: A Communitarian Model of Justice. In *Family Conferencing and Juvenile Justice: The Way Forward or Misplaced Optimism?* ed. Christine Alder and Joy Wundersitz, 45–74. Canberra: Australian Institute of Criminology. Online at: http://www.aic.gov.au/publications/lcj/family/

Morris, Allison, and Gabrielle Maxwell. 1998a. Understanding Reoffending. *Criminology* 10: 10–13.

– 1998b. Restorative Justice in New Zealand: Family Group Conferences as a Case Study. *Western Criminology Review* 1: 1. Online at: http://wcr.sonoma.edu/v1n1/morris.html

Moyer, Sharon. 1987. *Homicides Involving Adult Subjects 1962–1984: A Comparison of Natives and Non-Natives*. Ottawa: Ministry of the Solicitor General.

– 1992. *Race, Gender, and Homicide: Comparisons between Aboriginals and Other Canadians*. Ottawa: Ministry of the Solicitor General.

– 2000. Alternatives to Prosecution in Domestic Violence Cases: An Overview of the Research Literature. Paper prepared for the Department of Justice.

Moyer, Sharon, and Lee Axon. 1993. *An Implementation Evaluation of the Native Community Council Project of the Aboriginal Legal Services of Toronto.* Ottawa: Ministry of the Attorney General.

Moyer, Sharon, F. Kopelman, B. Billinaskey, and C. La Prairie. 1987. *Native and Non-Native Admissions to Federal and Provincial Correctional Institutions.* Ottawa: Ministry of the Solicitor General.

Mullen, Paul E. 1990. The Prevalence of Sexual Abuse of Female Children and Adolescents. In *Family Violence: Perspectives on Treatment, Research and Policy*, ed. Ronald Roesch, Donald G. Dutton, and Vincent F. Sacco, 21–37. Vancouver: British Columbia Institute on Family Violence.

Mullen, Paul E., and Jillian Fleming. 1998. Long-term Effects of Child Sexual Abuse. National Child Protection Clearinghouse, Melbourne, Australia, Issue Paper 8. *Issues in Child Abuse Prevention.*

National Crime Prevention Centre [NCPC]. 2000. *Fact Sheet: Aboriginal Canadian – Violence, Victimization, and Prevention.* Ottawa: Department of Justice.

Neilsen, M. 1995. Canadian Native Youth Justice Committees and the Navajo Peacemakers Courts: A Comparison of Developmental Issues and Organizational Structures. Paper presented at the American Society of Criminology Annual Meeting, Boston, 14–18 November.

Newhouse, David, and Evelyn Peters. 2003. Introduction. *Not Strangers in These Parts: Urban Aboriginal People*, ed. David Newhouse and Evelyn Peters, 5–13. Ottawa: Policy Research Initiative.

New Zealand, Parliamentary Library of. 2000. *Crime in New Zealand: A Statistical Profile, Background Note.* Wellington: Information Briefing Service for Member of Parliament.

Norris, Clive, Nigel Fielding, Charles Kemp, and Jane Fielding. 1994. The status of this demeanor: An Analysis of the Influence of Social Status on Being Stopped by the Police. Draft paper prepared for the British Criminology Conference, University of Wales, Cardiff, 28 July–1 August 1993, quoted in Carol La Prairie, *Seen But Not Heard: Native People in the Inner City*, 62. Ottawa: Department of Justice.

Nuffield, Joan. 1997. *Evaluation of the Adult Victim-Offender Program – Saskatoon Community Mediation Services.* Saskatoon: Saskatchewan Justice. Online at: http://web.mala.bc.ca/crim/rj/RJ_Nuffield.doc

O'Malley, Pat. n.d. Tradition and Self-Determination: Crime Prevention in Remote Aboriginal Communities. Unpublished paper.

Obonsawin-Irwin. 1992. *An Evaluation of the Sandy Lake First Nation Justice Pilot Project, An Evaluation of the Attawapiskat First Nation Justice Pilot Project.* Toronto: Ministry of the Attorney General.

Ontario. 1989. Task Force on Race Relations and Policing, *Report of the Task Force on Race Relations on Policing*. Toronto, Ontario.

Opekokew, Delia. 1994. Review of Ethnocentric Bias Facing Indian Witnesses. In *Continuing Poundmaker and Riel's Quest: Presentation Made at a Conference on Aboriginal Peoples and Justice*, ed. Richard Gosse, James Youngblood Henderson, and Roger Carter, 192–205. Saskatoon: Purich Publishing.

Pennell, J., and G. Burford. 1994. Widening the Circle: The Family Group Decision-Making Project. *Journal of Child & Youth Care* 9 (1): 1–12.

Phillips, M.R., and T.S. Inui. 1986. The Interaction of Mental Illness, Criminal Behaviour, and Culture: Native Alaskan Mentally Ill Criminal Offenders. *Culture, Medicine and Psychiatry* 10: 123–49.

Planning Branch, Treasury Board Secretariat. 1975. *The Native Inmate within the Federal Penitentiary System*. Ottawa: Treasury Board.

Polk, Ken. 1994. Family Conferencing: Theoretical and Evaluative Questions. In *Family Conferencing and Juvenile Justice: The Way Forward or Misplaced Optimism?*, ed. Christine Alder and Joy Wundersitz, 123–40. Canberra: Australian Institute of Criminology. Online at: http://www.aic.gov.au/publications/lcj/family/

Prairie Research Associates. 1999. *Evaluations of the Victim of Domestic Violence Act, 1996*. Saskatoon: Saskatchewan Justice, Policy, Planning and Evaluation.

Pranis, Kay. 1998. *Engaging the Community in Restorative Justice*. St Paul, MN: Balanced and Restorative Justice Project.

Presser, Lois, and Elaine Gunnison. 1999. Strange Bedfellows: Is Sex Offender Notification a Form of Community Justice? *Forum* 45 (3) (July): 299–315.

Prince George Urban Aboriginal Justice Society. 2000. *Youth Diversion Program Evaluation*. Prince George.

RCMP. 1998. *Native Spirituality Guide*. Ottawa: RCMP Public Affairs Directorate. Online at: http://www.rcmp.ca/pdfs/spiritgde.pdf

Reid, Angus. 1994a. *Canadians and Aboriginal Peoples*. Ottawa: Angus Reid Group.

– 1994b. Canadian Views on the Criminal Justice System. *The Reid Report* 9 (7):

Richards, John. 2001. *Neighbours Matter: Poor Neighbourhoods and Urban Aboriginal Policy*. Toronto: C.D. Howe Commentary, No.156, November.

Roach, Kent, and Jonathan Rudin. 2000. Gladue: The Judicial and Political Reception of a Promising Decision. *Canadian Journal of Criminology* 42 (3) (July): 355–88.

Roberts, Julian, and Anthony N. Doob. 1994. Race, Crime, and Criminal Justice in Canada. Background paper prepared for: Conference on Race, Ethnicity, and Criminal Justice. All Souls College, Oxford University, England, 24–6 September.

Roberts, Julian, and Carol La Prairie. 1996. Sentencing Circles: Some Unanswered Questions. *Criminal Law Quarterly* 39: 69–83.

Robertson, Jeremy. 1996. Research on Family Group Conferences in Child Welfare in

New Zealand. In *Family Group Conferences: Perspectives on Policy and Practice*, ed. Joe Hudson et al., 49–64. New York: Willow Tree Press.

Roche, Declan. 2003. *Accountability in Restorative Justice*. Oxford: Clarendon Series in Criminology, Oxford University Press.

Rose, Elizabeth M. 2002. *Are Sentencing Circles a Viable Alternative for Aboriginal Offenders*. Ottawa: Carleton University Press.

Ross, Rupert. 1992. *Dancing with a Ghost: Exploring Indian Reality*. Toronto: Octopus.

– 1996. *Returning to the Teachings: Exploring Aboriginal Justice* Toronto: Penguin Books.

– 2001. Victims and Criminal Justice: Exploring the Disconnect? Paper prepared for the 27th Annual Conference of the National Organization for Victim Assistance, Edmonton, 22 August.

Ryan, Joan, and Brian Calliou. 2002. Aboriginal Restorative Justice Alternatives: Two Case Studies. Paper prepared for the Law Commission of Canada, January.

Sampson, R.J., and W.J. William. 1991. Toward a Theory of Race, Crime, and Inequality. Paper presented at the 50th Annual Meeting of the American Society of Criminology.

Sampson, Robert, S. Raudenbush, and F. Earls. 1997. Neighbourhoods and Violent Crime: A Multilevel Study of Collective Efficacy. *Science* 277: 918–24.

Sampson, Robert, and Stephen Raudenbush. 2001. Disorder in Urban Neighbourhoods – Does it Lead to Crime? *Research In Brief*. Washington: National Institute of Justice. Online at: http://www.ncjrs.org/pdffiles1/nij/186049.pdf

Samuelson, L. 2000. *The Origins, Rationale, and Implementation Process: An Evaluation Report*. Regina: Saskatchewan Justice, Research Summary, No. 5.

Saskatchewan Justice (SJ). 2003. *Sentencing Circle Review*. Saskatoon: Saskatchewan Justice Aboriginal Strategy: Policy, Planning and Evaluation.

Satzewich, Vic, and Terry Wotherspoon. 1993. Aboriginal People and Economic Relations: Underclass or Class Fractions. In *First Nations: Race, Class, and Gender Relations*, 43–74. Scarborough, ON: Nelson Canada.

Shaw, Margaret. 1991. *Survey of Federally Sentenced Women: Report to the Task Force on Federally Sentenced Women on the Prison Survey*. Ottawa: Solicitor General Canada.

– 1994. *Ontario Women in Conflict with the Law*. Toronto: Ministry of Correctional Services.

Sherman, Lawrence W., Denise C. Gottfredson, Doris L. MacKenzie, John Eck, Peter Reuter, and Shawn D. Bushway. 1998. *Preventing Crime: What Works, What Doesn't, What's Promising*. U.S. Department of Justice, Office of Justice Programs. Washington, DC: National Institute of Justice.

Sherman, Lawrence, and Heather Strang. 1997. The Right Kind of Shame for Crime Prevention. *RISE Working Papers: Paper No. 1*. Canberra: Australian Institute of Criminology.

Siggner, Andrew. 2001. Demographic, Social & Economic Profile of Aboriginal Peoples in Selected Western Cities. Presentation at the Policy Conference on Options for Aboriginal People in Canada's Cities, Regina, Saskatchewan, 2 May.

– 2003. Urban Aborignal Populations: An Update Using the 2001 Census Results. In *Not Strangers in These Parts: Urban Aboriginal People*, ed. David Newhouse and Evelyn Peters, 15–21. Ottawa: Policy Research Initiative.

Silverman, R., and L. Kennedy. 1993. Canadian Indian Involvement in Murder. In *Deadly Deeds: Murder in Canada*, ed. R. Silverman and L. Kennedy, 211–30. Toronto: Nelson Canada.

Sinclair, Murray. 1994. Cross Cultural Dialogue Between Governments. In *Continuing Poundmaker and Riel's Quest: Presentation Made at a Conference on Aboriginal Peoples and Justice*, ed. Richard Gosse, James Youngblood Henderson, and Roger Carter, 171–3. Saskatoon: Purich Publishing.

Smandych, Russell. 1997. The Exclusionary Effect of Colonial Law: Indigenous Peoples and English Law in the Canadian West to 1860. Paper presented at the Studies in History of Law and Society in the Canadian North-West Territories and Prairie Provinces, 1670–1990, Conference, Lethbridge, Alberta, 2–5 April.

Sommers, Jeffrey D. 2001. The Place of the Poor: Poverty, Space and the Politics of Representation in Downtown Vancouver, 1950–1977. PhD dissertation, Simon Fraser University.

Spiteri, Melanie. 2000. Sentencing Circles for Aboriginal Offenders in Canada: Furthering the Idea of Aboriginal Justice within a Western Justice Framework. Paper presented to the IIRP Conference, 9 August. Online at: http://www.plumesociety.com/karonta/melanie.html

Statistics Canada (Statscan). 1999a. *Census of Population*. Ottawa: Census Operations Division.

– 1999b. *Profile of the Urban Aboriginal Population, Canada, 1996*. Ottawa: Housing, Family and Social Statistics Division.

– 2000. Adult Correctional Services in Canada, 1989–99. *Juristat* 22: 10.

– 2003. *Aboriginal Peoples of Canada: A Demographic Profile, 2001 Census Analysis Series*. Ottawa: Census Operations Division.

Steinbachs, John. 1999. Offender Discredits Sentencing Circle. *Whitehorse Star*, 8 April.

Stenning, Philip. 2003. Policing the Cultural Kaleidoscope: Recent Canadian Experience. *Police & Society* 7 (April): 12-47.

Stenning, Philip, and Julian Roberts. 2001. Empty Promises: Parliament, The Supreme Court, and the Sentencing of Aboriginal Offenders. *Saskatchewan Law Review* 64 (1) 137–68.

Stevens, Sam. 1997. Native Self-Determination and Justice. In *Justice for Natives: Searching for Common Ground*, ed. Andrea P. Morrison and Irwin Cotler, 28–33. Montreal: McGill-Queen's University Press.

Stoneall, Linda. 1983. *Country Life, City Life: Five Theories of Community*. New York: Praegar.

Strang, Heather. 2000a. The Lived Experience of Victims: How Restorative Justice Worked in Canberra. Chapter 6 of Ph.D. dissertation, Australian National University.

– 2000b. The Future of Restorative Justice. In *Crime and the Criminal Justice System in Australia: 2000 and Beyond*, ed. D. Chappell and P. Wilson, 22–33. Sydney: Butterworths.

Strang, Heather. 2001. *Restorative Justice Programs in Australia: A Report to the Criminology Research Council*. Australia: Criminology Research Council.

Strang, Heather, and John Braithwaite, eds. 2001. Introduction. In *Restorative Justice and Civil Society*, 1–23. Cambridge: Cambridge University Press.

Stuart, Barry. 1995. Circles into Square Systems: Can Community Processes be Partnered with the Formal Justice System? Unpublished paper.

– 1997. *Sentencing Circles: Making 'Real' Differences*. In *Rethinking Disputes: The Mediation Alternative*, ed. Julie MacFarlane, 201–32. Toronto: Edmond Montgomery Publications.

Surgeon General. 2001. *Youth Violence: Report of the Surgeon General*. Washington, DC: Public Health Service.

Tatz, C. 1990. Aboriginal Violence: A Return to Pessimism. *Australian Journal of Social Issues* 25 (4): 245–60.

Tauri, Juan Marcellus. 1999. Family Group Conferencing: The Myth of Indigenous Enmpowerment in New Zealand. *Justice as Healing* 4 (1): Online at: http://www.usask.ca/nativelaw/publications/jah/tauri.html

Tomaszewski, A. 1995. Rethinking Crime and Criminal Justice in Nunavut. Unpublished research paper.

Tonry, Michael. 1994. Racial Disproportionality in US Prisons. *British Journal of Criminology* 34 (special issue): 97–115.

Trevethan, S. 1991. *Police-Reported Aboriginal Crime in Calgary, Regina, and Saskatoon*. Ottawa: Canadian Centre for Justice Statistics.

Turpel, Mary-Ellen. 1991. Aboriginal Peoples and the Canadian Charter: Interpretive Differences, Cultural Monopolies. In *First Nations Issues*, ed. Richard Devlin, 40–62. Canadian Perspectives on Legal Theory Series. Toronto: Edmond Montgomery Publications.

Van Ness, Daniel, and Karen Heetderks Strong. 1996. *Restoring Justice*. Cincinnati, OH: Anderson Publishing.

Waldram, John. 1992. Cultural Profiling and the Forensic Treatment of Aboriginal Offenders in Canada. Presentation to the American Society of Criminology Meetings, New Orleans, November.

Waters, Andrew Grant. 1993. The Wagga Wagga Effective Cautioning Program: Reintegrative or Degrading? Working paper, Department of Criminology, University of Melbourne. Wagga Wagga, N.S.W.

Weatherburn, Don, Jackie Fitzgerald, and Jiuzhao Hua. 2004. Reducing Aboriginal Over-Represenation in Prison. *Australian Journal of Public Administration* 62(3): 65–73.

Weitekamp, Elmar. 1993. Towards a Victim Oriented System.' *European Journal on Criminal Policy and Research* 1(1): 70–93.

Williams, C. 2001. *The Too-Hard Basket: Maori and the Criminal Justice System Since 1980.* Wellington: University Victoria of Wellington.

Wilson, Bertha. 1990. Will Women Judges Make a Difference? The Fourth Annual Barbara Betcherman Memorial Lecture. Toronto: Osgoode Hall Law School, 8 February.

York, Peter. 1995. *The Aboriginal Federal Offender: A Comparative Analysis Between Aboriginal and Non-Aboriginal Offenders.* Ottawa: Correctional Services Canada.

Zellerer, Evelyn. 1999. Restorative Justice in Indigenous Communities: Critical Issues in Confronting Violence Against Women. *International Review of Victimology* 6: 1–13.

Cases and Statutes

Reference re the Term 'Indians,' [1939] S.C.R. 104.

R. v. Gladue, [1999] 1 S.C.R. 688.

R. v. Joseyounen, [1995] 6 W.W.R. 438.

R. v. Moses, [1992] Y.J. No. 50 DRS 93-00327; also reported at 11 C.R. (4th) 357.

R. v. Powley, [2003] S.C.R. 43.

R. v. Sparrow, [1990] 1 S.C.R. 1075.

R. v. Wells, (2000) S.C.C. 10.

Canadian Criminal Code, R.S.C. 1985, c. C-46.

Indian Act, R.S.C. 1985, c. I-5.

Index